Lawson Traphagen Hill is founder of the
Lawson Hill Leather and Shoe Company—which was
the largest company selling shoes by mail at the
time he sold it—and the British Isles Collection,
a mail-order company that attained the highest
sales per catalog in the gift and clothing fields.
He is currently a consultant in mail order and a
regular contributor to *Catalog Age* magazine.

PRENTICE-HALL, INC., Englewood Cliffs, New Jersey 07632

How to build a
MULTI-MILLION DOLLAR CATALOG MAIL-ORDER BUSINESS
by someone who did

Lawson Traphagen Hill

Library of Congress Cataloging in Publication Data

Hill, Lawson Traphagen.
  How to build a multi-million dollar catalog mail-order business by someone who did.

  "A Spectrum Book."
  Bibliography: p.
  Includes index.
  1. Mail-order business.   I. Title.
HF5466.H56   1984   658.8'72   83-24674
ISBN 0-13-396565-1
ISBN 0-13-396557-0 (pbk.)

10 9 8 7 6 5 4 3 2 1

ISBN 0-13-396565-1

ISBN 0-13-396557-0 {PBK.}

Editorial/production supervision by Norma G. Ledbetter
Cover design by Hal Siegel
Manufacturing buyer: Pat Mahoney

This book is available at a special discount when ordered in
bulk quantities. Contact Prentice-Hall, Inc., General
Publishing Division, Special Sales, Englewood Cliffs, N.J. 07632.

PRENTICE-HALL INTERNATIONAL, INC., *London*
PRENTICE-HALL OF AUSTRALIA PTY. LIMITED, *Sydney*
PRENTICE-HALL CANADA INC., *Toronto*
PRENTICE-HALL OF INDIA PRIVATE LIMITED, *New Delhi*
PRENTICE-HALL OF JAPAN, INC., *Tokyo*
PRENTICE-HALL OF SOUTHEAST ASIA PTE. LTD., *Singapore*
WHITEHALL BOOKS LIMITED, *Wellington, New Zealand*
EDITORA PRENTICE-HALL DO BRASIL LTDA., *Rio de Janeiro*

*This book is dedicated
to my wife,
Marcia Hill,
to my children and their mates,
Brenda and John Forde, and
Lawson Bruce and Cynthia Hill,
and to my parents,
Florence Emilie Hoffman Hill
and Lawson Traphagen Hill, Sr.*

contents

**The Dynamics
of Catalog
Mail Order**

Opportunities

preface

This book tells how you can build a catalog mail-order business. It avoids trivia and that which can easily be learned elsewhere and concentrates instead on the essentials for success. What you will learn are the secrets of mail-order success that I learned from having founded and built two multi-million dollar catalog mail-order companies of my own: Lawson Hill Leather and Shoe Co., which was the largest company selling shoes by mail at the time I sold it, and British Isles Collection, whose start was marked by some of the highest results from the use of rental lists in the mail-order industry. These secrets are collectively the dynamics and the basics of the catalog mail-order business. This book explains how to build strong dynamics and gain mastery of the basics. If you have an understanding of this book, you will have the knowledge with which to build your own *catalog* mail-order company.

The emphasis is on the word *catalog*. Many authors have written books about mail order. The mail order about which they have written is mostly the placing of ads in magazines and newspapers to solicit orders. Little space in these books is devoted to catalogs—sometimes as much as a chapter but often less. Only one of these authors that I know of ever published a catalog himself. Yet almost all successful mail-order businesses, sooner or later, end up with a catalog. A catalog is the natural consequence of a successful mail-order ad program. Indeed, a catalog is often the only medium that will successfully sell some products by mail order. The person wishing to enter mail order must, therefore, understand catalog mail order and what makes it successful. This is the objective of this book and what distinguishes it from all others. It concentrates on catalog mail order.

This book is written for both the beginner and the experienced mail marketer. It shows the beginner the strategies for starting a catalog mail-order business. Then all the areas of knowledge required for its successful operation are covered in depth and in easy-to-understand language. When terms are out of the ordinary, the book provides you with a glossary that defines and explains such terms. Finally, so that you can see how all the pieces of mail-order knowledge explained in the book interrelate, Chapter 25, "Catalog Mail Order Step by Step," gives the steps for starting and operating a catalog mail-order business.

The experienced mail marketer, on the other hand, will benefit because the book treats each aspect of catalog mail order in a depth intended to give the experienced person new insight and to be thought-provoking. For example, judging from the catalogs one receives in the mail, many mail marketers are unaware of the importance of good eye flow or choosing the right background color for their photographs. Whole chapters are devoted to the explanation of these sophisticated concepts.

Whether you are a novice or an experienced mail marketer, you must concentrate most of your efforts on the dynamics of your business. The dynamics are the forces that drive the catalog in the marketplace. The foundation upon which strong dynamics are built is the concept of the business. Without a well-thought-out concept of the business, your business is doomed to mediocrity or even failure. This, therefore, is the first subject this book addresses in Part One. Then, because your mail-order company will not go far without strong dynamics, the next five chapters are devoted to what they are and what makes them strong.

However, strong dynamics can be undermined by poor graphics. A survey of other books on mail order reveals little or nothing written about layout, the economics and principles of catalog design, photography, color separation, and printing, to say nothing of background colors and eye flow. Yet you must spend much time on these considerations. Part Two of this book, "Build Strong Dynamics Through Better Graphics," shows you how you can make your graphics more effective.

Dynamics and their graphic presentation are only half of mail order. The other half is the basics. The basics are not called basics because anyone who has been in mail order knows them. In fact, most mail marketers are weak in at least one and possibly more of them. The basics are called *basic* because they are basic to building a strong mail-order business. These are presented to you in Part Three, "The Basics of Catalog Mail Order."

The explanation of the basics starts with the most fundamental consideration: how you should view your profit and loss statement. It then proceeds to describe how you should measure the most significant components of your profit and loss statement: the cost of your catalog mailings and ads and the sales produced by them.

The format for presenting the costs and sales results of your mailings and ads is a unique feature of this book, for the results are presented in such a manner that they lock directly into the profit and loss statement. You can see instantly how and to what degree each ad or mailing affects profit and loss.

Another unique feature in the presentation of the basics is the illustration, in the form of a case study of the Mayflower Gift Company, of how to budget and draw up a three-year plan. Although the Mayflower Gift Company itself is fictitious, the case study is realistic because the steps for budgeting and planning closely parallel the ones that were actually taken to launch the British Isles Collection.

In addition to these basics, the book shows you how to mail to obtain the most sales per catalog, how to control inventory so that you do not become financially overextended or refund too many orders, how to set up a manual operating system, what an operating system should do for you, and what a computer should do for you.

Part Four "Opportunities," concludes the book with opportunities for the mail marketer that do not fall within the scope of the preceding parts. Chapter 21 shows you opportunities to increase your sales through customized computer letters. Chapter 22 explains how solo mailings will increase your sales from your house list without subtracting sales from your catalog mailings, and Chapter 23, "Mail-Order Synergism," shows how you can add one new element—a retail store, a new catalog, or a new product line under your old brand—and produce a result that far exceeds the money and time you put into it.

How to Build a Multi-Million Dollar Catalog Mail-Order Business by Someone Who Did is written for both the beginner and the experienced mail marketer. If you are a beginner, it provides the knowledge you need to start and sustain a catalog mail-order business and, if you are an experienced mail marketer, it provides this knowledge in a depth that you will find stimulating and thought-provoking. This knowledge is embodied in the dynamics and basics of catalog mail-order. Strong dynamics and mastery of the basics will put you well on your way to successfully building a multi-million dollar catalog mail-order business.

acknowledgments

I wish to thank those who helped to make this book possible.

Louis Leber of Concord Mail-Order Company, Concord, Massachusetts, is a consultant who taught me the basics of mail order and whose instruction contributed greatly to the development of my first mail-order company, Lawson Hill Leather and Shoe Co. His constant encouragement, advice, and support have sustained me throughout much of my mail-order career.

Louis Cheskin, a pioneer of market research and the director of the Color Research Institute until his death in 1981, taught me all I know about color, light, eye flow, and the psychology of the marketplace. To him I owe a debt that I shall not be able to repay.

Cabell Brand, president of Stuart McGuire Co. in Salem, Virginia, is my oldest and closest business associate. He has long been an inspiration, an example, a mentor, and a friend whom I shall forever appreciate. To him, I owe thanks for the opportunity to develop the British Isles Collection.

I thank Don Cody for the years he spent helping me build Lawson Hill Leather and Shoe Co. I also thank him for reading the chapter on mailing effectiveness and his many excellent suggestions for its improvement.

I thank Jim Melancon for reading and evaluating the chapter on computer output; Aaron Yundt, the chapter on color separating; Louis Leber, the chapters on photography and starting a mail-order business; and Vivian Cheskin and Davis and Bonnie Masten of Louis Cheskin Associates, for reading the chapter on eye flow and the sections of Chapter 1 on logotypes and symbolism.

I thank Alicia Hawkes, who through her cryptoanalytic skills broke the cipher of my handwriting and successfully typed the manuscript.

Above all I owe a debt to my wife, Marcia. For it was she who suggested that I try selling shoes by mail, and it was she who made Lawson Hill Leather and Shoe Co. possible by selecting with her innate wisdom the women's shoe styles that made it a success. She was the one who bore with me the adversity that is inevitably associated with a business and was constantly at my side.

challenge and opportunity

I shall never forget the thrill that day in spring 1968 when my secretary lifted up a bunch of perhaps 20 envelopes and then let them flutter down to the table. "People are sending for our catalog!" she cried. Three weeks later I was even more excited when the people to whom we had sent catalogs started sending in orders. My wife, Marcia, had suggested to me a few months before that we try selling by mail order the shoes we were offering in hard-to-find sizes in our retail stores. Without contemplating the difficulties that might be in store for me, I plunged into the idea with enthusiasm, printing a tiny catalog and running ads in *The New York Times Magazine, Yankee* magazine, and *House & Gardens.*

I made many mistakes but did a few things right. There was not much competition in the mail-order shoe business in those days, and so despite my mistakes our business grew.

Other mail-order companies were growing as well. There were real old-timers such as L. L. Bean, Orvis, and Carroll Reed. Then there were those that had started not long after the end of World War II—Johnny Appleseed, Hitchcock Shoes, and Old Pueblo Traders. Brookstone, Stitch and Knit, and Horchow started at about the same time we did. As I look back, we all were unsophisticated in mail-order techniques, but we grew anyway. Mail order was easy then.

During the 1970s, many people, recognizing the marketing potential of catalogs, entered with their own. At the end of the decade there were more than half a dozen new shoe companies. It seemed as though everyone who had a gift shop was publishing a catalog. Catalogs that catered to a multitude of interests sprang up.

In addition, all mail-order companies, having learned how to mail their catalogs more effectively, were mailing many more catalogs. Mailing lists grew, and so more names became available to rent. And they were rented. Some companies, such as L. L. Bean, Talbots, and Eddie Bauer, grew to enormous proportions. It was a small company that mailed only a

1

million catalogs a year. My own company, Lawson Hill Leather and Shoe Co., which had started with printing 5,000 catalogs, was mailing well over 10,000,000 a year when I sold it in 1977. Printers catering to the catalog trade, such as Spencer Press of Hingham, Massachusetts, prospered, bought new and bigger presses, and then built new printing plants. For a while there were so many people printing catalogs that there was even a paper shortage, and those who dragged out paying their bills didn't get their catalog printed.

In the euphoria of growth and success, many felt at the close of the decade that their upper limits were nowhere in sight. I heard more than one person assert that mail order had just reached the threshold of its development.

But sometime in the early 1980s, something happened. A new expression was coined—"mailbox glut." Consumers began complaining about ten catalogs a day arriving in their mailboxes. Catalog response was down for many companies. Rumors grew that some of the gift and gadget companies were in trouble, especially those offering lower-priced gifts. Then a granddaddy of gifts and gadgets closed its doors. And in the fall of 1982 I was saddened to learn that a dear friend was forced to shut down the mail-order company that he had built up with great toil and much hope. For others, the same thing happened.

What occurred was not the demise of the mail-order industry or even its peaking out. What happened was that in easy times the mail-order industry had overexpanded, and the forces of natural selection were eliminating the weak and inefficient. Just as years ago the American auto industry was reduced from hundreds to three major companies and one minor and yet grew to tremendous size, so too are mail-order companies now being challenged to prove their worth to continue as the industry expands. While some mail-order companies have faltered, others are pushing ahead.

Why do I foresee that the mail-order industry will continue to grow? Because mail order offers certain marketing advantages over retail stores which are still largely unexploited. As these advantages are exploited, the industry will continue to develop.

One of these advantages is the power of words to explain the product. Retail stores are largely mute. Merchandise sits silently on shelves, while clerks, often unavailable or even more often uninformed, give little explanation of the products that the customer might buy. Furthermore, the opportunity exists in mail order not only to explain the product through the copy but also to sell the concept and theme of the business, something which is underdone or poorly done in most catalogs.

Mail order has the advantage of concentration of inventory in one location rather than in many retail outlets. This allows the mail marketer to increase selection and at the same time increase turnover. This, in fact, was the reason for the growth of Lawson Hill Leather and Shoe Co.—we offered five to ten times as many combinations of styles, sizes, and widths as any ordinary retail shoe store, yet we turned our inventory faster.

Because mail-order companies can concentrate business from all over the country, they have the opportunity to specialize and to be leaders in serving the interests to which they cater.

Mail order saves time. Busy men and women, occupied with full-time jobs, have little time to shop and so often leave their shopping undone. Mail order fills the void; they can avoid tramping from store to store, consuming precious hours, and buy directly from the catalogs that arrive at their homes.

But even if the consumer has the time to shop, mail order often has the advantage of getting to the customer before the customer gets to a retail store. And, the customer, seeing something he wants in a catalog and not knowing if it is available in a local retail store, buys from the catalog. Mail order creates an awareness in the consumer of the variety of merchandise that is available, an awareness that would be otherwise quite dim for the person who must work and has little time to visit stores.

To the advantage of shopping at home must be added the convenience of not being confined to normal store hours. Most mail-order companies have 24-hour shopping with either people or recording machines answering the phones.

To these advantages that the mail marketer enjoys must be added the promise of the changing buying habits of the American people. When L. L. Bean pioneered the Maine hunting shoe, few people bought by mail. As recently as the 1960s, the majority of Americans would not buy anything that they could not see or feel. But as more women have taken jobs, fewer of them have had the time to shop. Women have increasingly resorted to catalogs. As catalogs have proliferated, often glutting the mailboxes, they have nevertheless made new converts to the idea of buying by mail order.

So if mail-order companies have been challenged, they also have opportunities—opportunities to take advantage of the marketing strengths of catalog mail order and to share in its continued growth. The companies that successfully meet the challenge and seize the opportunities will have strong dynamics and command of the basics. How to develop strong dynamics and what the basics are will unfold in the chapters that follow.

Part

one

The Dynamics of
Catalog Mail Order

1

the foundation: the concept and theme of the business

The challenge that faces the mail marketer is the competing catalogs that crowd mailboxes. It is a challenge that first must be met by strong mail-order dynamics.

What are mail-order dynamics? They are all the forces that drive a catalog in the marketplace. Strong dynamics cause a consumer to pick up a catalog when he receives it, look beyond its covers and buy, and discard catalogs with weaker dynamics. In short, dynamics are the order-getting powers of a catalog.

Mail-order dynamics involve such things as the concept of the business, theme, merchandise, pricing, mood conveying in the catalog, means for creating customer confidence, and methods of presenting them. Layout, photography, copy, and other graphics all influence dynamics, as do average order and some devices such as sales, discount coupons, and sweepstakes. To have strong dynamics, however, a catalog must have leadership.

Leadership

Why does a consumer study one catalog and buy from it but give scant consideration to another? To learn the answer, one must first understand the concept of leadership that is implicit in the question.

Leadership exists for a company when a customer with a specific desire or interest will turn to that company for satisfaction preferring it to all other companies. For that customer, the company is a leader. When a plurality of customers in the market served by the company prefer it to others, then the company enjoys market leadership. The key word in the concept is *preferring;* the customer buys from the company not merely because its products are available, but also because of some reason he prefers the company or its merchandise.

For the mail marketer this means that, if he has leadership, business will flow to his catalog from other catalogs. Benjamin Franklin said it well enough over two centuries ago: "Build a better mousetrap and the world will beat a path to your door." Implied, but not said, is that the world will cease going to the doors of other mousetrap makers. In other words, the leader gets the most business at, as we shall see, a lower marketing cost.

An example of a better mousetrap maker in mail order is Touch of Class. Fred and Carla Bell, owners of the firm, pioneered the selling of bed linens, down comforters, and other items for the bedroom and the bathroom. Recently, several firms, seeing how well Touch of Class was doing, entered the field. But a comparison of the Touch of Class catalog with the competing ones reveals that there is no comparison at all. Touch of Class surpasses all others in its dazzling selection, the attractiveness of its merchandise, and the appeal of its presentation. It is clearly the leader of those who cater to the desire for goods for the bedroom and bathroom. While they are larger because they were first to see the opportunity to satisfy this consumer desire and interest, they obviously will remain that way unless the competition improves; even then they will have a momentum that the competition will find hard to overcome.

This tendency for business to flow to the leader more than to others means that for the leader marketing expense [1] as a percentage of sales is lower. The leader, therefore, should earn a profit. Furthermore, the competition will be only marginally profitable. As Peter Drucker explains,[2] economic results, that is, profits, are earned only by leadership and not mere competence. Companies that do not lead in some way become marginal and are forced out in a recession. That they exist at all is because of prior momentum, because consumers are slow to change and tolerate the company, because the leader does not fully cover the market, or because the company has great financial resources upon which it can draw. If your marketing costs are too high and your profits too low, the problem may well be that your firm lacks leadership.

Leadership, however, is not necessarily characterized by large size. Large size may be the result of a company attempting to satisfy many customer interests, yet in any one customer interest, there are other companies that satisfy it better. Or, the large size may occur because the company has "bought" a large market share by mailing many catalogs at an unprofitable marketing cost (publicity); that is not leadership because customer preference did not produce the large size and a profit did not result.[3]

Leadership may come in any form for which a customer is willing to pay: a unique product (leadership by default), the best selection, the best quality, the best service, the best price in acceptable quality, or the best presentation of the product.

Few companies can be leaders in all things; at best they can be leaders in a few areas. DuPont is a leader in chemistry, but only in certain aspects of it. Dow Chemical is a leader in others. Touch of Class is the leader in products for the bedroom and bathroom, but not in gourmet supplies, where Williams-Sonoma is the leader. To have leadership, the mail marketer must first define the area in which the catalog will excel. This definition is the concept of the business.

---

[1] In mail order and later in this book, marketing expense is usually called "publicity expense."

[2] Peter F. Drucker, *Managing for Results,* (New York: Harper & Row, 1964), p. 6.

[3] However, buying a share of the market may be a sound strategy provided customer preference and leadership exist or will follow.

The starting point in building a mail-order business is defining the concept of the business. This definition sets the limits of the area within which the company intends to lead. These questions must be asked: "What are the desires and interests of my customers that I should seek to satisfy?" and "What are the desires and interests to which I am actually catering?" Answering these questions determines the breadth of the company's intended area of leadership. Robinson's Wallcoverings, a consulting client of mine, illustrates how the answers define the concept of the business.

For years Robinson's had a steadily growing business selling attractively-priced wallpaper to people who ordered by mail from a catalog of swatches. They had always thought of themselves as satisfying their customers' needs for wallpaper and giving them good value. To be sure, they had leadership because most of their customers could not buy such good wallpaper for so little money, an opportunity that Robinson's buying strength made possible. But I suggested to them a broader concept. Were not their customers really interested in decorating their homes? Were they not painting the trim of a room as well as papering the walls, and might they want paint to coordinate perfectly with their paper? Would they be interested in changing their drapes and possibly the slipcovers of their furniture to match their wallpaper? If the answers to these questions were "Yes," then Robinson's was actually catering to a broader interest and the concept of their business had been too narrowly defined. They should have thought of their business as satisfying their customers' *decorating* needs at low cost. This broader concept would permit Robinson's to better satisfy the desires and interests of their customers and thereby sell more products. A woman who can buy slipcovers to coordinate with her wallpaper is more likely to buy the wallpaper itself. Thus Robinson's would sell not only slipcovers but more wallpaper as well.

In another case, I failed to consider the concept of the business and wasted a considerable amount of money for my company, Lawson Hill Leather and Shoe Co. Our business was to supply shoes to women with hard-to-find sizes, but while I was in Italy looking for shoe styles, I became enchanted with and then put into our catalog the beautiful leather goods made in Florence—wallets, handbags, key cases, and the like. Our customers bought few of them. Leather goods were not our business; as nice as they were, they did not satisfy the interest which had originally attracted our customers to our catalog.

Not content to make a mistake once, I did it again. I started a catalog of men's shoes made in Britain in hard-to-find sizes. I also put four pages of men's shoes in the women's catalog and four pages of women's shoes in the men's catalog. None of the alien pages in each catalog earned their keep. Once again, we would have been better off to use those four pages to better present the merchandise that fulfilled the concept of the business of each catalog—that is, women's shoes in hard-to-find sizes in one and men's shoes in hard-to-find sizes in the other.

I attribute much of the success of the British Isles Collection to the fact that we thought through and defined the concept of the business from the very beginning. What we needed to decide upon was the customer interest and desire that we should seek to satisfy. British-made men's shoes, we felt, were too narrow in scope. Men's shoes from Britain, Italy, the U.S.A., and other countries had no common denominator, except shoes, which would make us little different from an ordinary shoe store and deprive us of the British theme. We liked a theme based upon British-made goods because we felt there was a broad group of people who liked and respected them. However, while a catalog of British-made men's shoes, clothing, crystal, bone china, and foods provided us with the theme that British-made products are superior, it lacked specialization. Furthermore, the customer for Loake English shoes was not likely to be a customer for bone china. He was likely, however, to buy a Harris Tweed sports jacket, a camel's hair sweater, or a pair of cashmere socks. What we needed for a concept of the business was something that would give us an image of specialization, have a theme, and appeal to a single concern, yet have a breadth of products so that the customer would have more reasons to buy and come back repeatedly.

We decided that the concept of the business should be fine-quality shoes and clothing from the British Isles. By specializing in shoes and clothing from the British Isles, we concentrated our merchandise into one category, thus giving ourselves the best selection and leadership within that category. Our theme was that things made in the British Isles are superior. The single concern to which we addressed the catalog was the customer's interest in dressing himself. Yet we retained a breadth of products because when he buys shoes he is dressing himself and so could be interested in clothing as well as shoes. By deciding to sell goods from the British Isles and not just the United Kingdom, we were able to include Irish woolens without creating a confusing image.

We went through a similar thought process in defining the concept of the business when I founded Lawson Hill Leather and Shoe Co.[4] in 1968. At the time, Shoe Craft on Fifth Avenue in New York City was the leading company selling women's shoes in unusual sizes. They specialized in shoes for women with long feet. In Boston, Cinderella sold shoes to women with short feet. In New York City, Mooney & Gilbert carried shoes for women with narrow feet, and in Philadelphia, Syd Kushner catered to women with wide feet. For mail order, we decided that each of these specializations was too narrow and that it was likely that our ad would be read in a magazine or our catalog would be received through list rental in proportion to the density of each group of women in the country's population. We decided, therefore, that the concept of our business would be to provide women with shoes in hard-to-find sizes, whether they were long, short, narrow, or wide, and in common sizes as well. The theme became "We have your size," which was reinforced in the copy by featuring my wife, Marcia Hill, who wears size 11AAAA, a very difficult-to-find size. Thus we had a broader market, yet for each class of women customers we were specialists.

The concept of the business must, therefore, be neither too narrow nor too broad, and it must satisfy strongly felt desires of the customers. Narrowness concentrates money and effort on doing a few things well. It provides an image of specialization and, therefore, conveys a feeling of leadership. But too narrow a concept may make it unprofitable to mail a catalog and may mean that one does not fully satisfy a customer's needs, as I felt occurred with Robinson's Wallcoverings, where they could expect to sell more wallpaper if they offered a complete decorating package.

Too broad a concept of the business, however, squanders resources on the irrelevant, conveys a confusing image of the business, and detracts from the look of leadership that comes from specialization.

As I wrote earlier, defining the concept of the business is the first block in building leadership and thus strong dynamics; for once a mail

---

[4] After I sold the company in 1977, the new owners changed the name to Lawson Hill Shoe Co.

marketer has defined the concept of his business, he knows what he must do well. It provides the guiding principles for the theme of the business and for making future decisions.

The Theme of the Business

The theme of the business is the expression of the concept of the business in the catalog. It goes beyond the concept, however, because it gives its principles and rationale. It tells the customer why he should buy from the company, as in: "Why British clothing?" "Because it is of enduring quality."

For many mail-order companies, the concept of the business is only a vague notion with no theme at all. Products are added in a random manner, so that often products are not consistent with one another; copy and graphics reinforce no theme; and the name itself suggests nothing about the company. These mail-order businesses are built like a house constructed with no plans; they are a hodgepodge. And because the would-be customer cannot tell what the business stands for, he sees no reason to look through its catalog.

Other companies have a theme but express it through the look of their catalog and their merchandise. Sometimes they express it in the copy on the inside front cover. Occasionally they put it in a headline on the front cover as Norm Thompson puts "ESCAPE from the ordinary." At British Isles Collection we thought the theme was so important that we started out by saying it in so many words right on the cover. We began with a headline reading "Fine Shoes and Clothing from England, Scotland, Wales and Ireland," which told the customer what products to expect inside. Our credo followed:

Our Credo

Our central theme in this catalog is that natural materials worked by crafts-men in the British Isles result in a product of enduring quality, long to be appreciated. We believe it is better to have fewer things of fine quality, to wear and enjoy them often, than to have something which is not as nice and of which one tires quickly and discards.

Smith & Hawken, vendors of garden tools, write in their catalog: ". . . Our reasoning here is that if a tool is really useful it will be used a lot. And if used intensively, it must be made of quality material and crafted with skill, lest it be just another throwaway object in a culture that is already too cluttered." When I read this, I was convinced that they had the best garden tools. If I were interested in gardening, I would buy from them.

The concept of the business is the master plan. The theme is a statement of that plan and of the company's principles and rationale; it appeals to the customer's interest and desires that the business is designed to satisfy. It tells the customer what he can expect: what he can buy, and whether or not the company's values are the same as his. It gives the reasons why the customer should buy from the company and forces management to adhere to the concept of the business. The theme sells the catalog and all it contains. For this reason, it is one of the most important elements of a catalog; it should, therefore, be first expressed in the front where the customer will see it at once.

Supporting the Theme

The theme, however, should not appear just in the text. Rather, it should be expressed many times and in many ways. Because it sells the whole catalog, it unifies the catalog and should run throughout. It should be expressed and supported by every element of the catalog: merchandise, institutional copy, individual product copy, photography, company name and logotype, symbols, and mood. Each of these must state and restate the theme in its own way.

The copy

Of these elements, copy, because it is the most direct, can be the most powerful. Because of its importance, I am only outlining its function in expressing the theme; I cover it in greater depth in Chapter 3.

The theme can be stated in an introductory letter by the management or succinctly in a credo. But it should be expanded upon in the institutional section, usually occupying pages two and three. At British Isles Collection we stated the theme in a credo on the cover. We then explained the reason for the catalog in a letter on the inside front cover. We had institutional copy under the headings "Why we like things from the British Isles," "About our Loake and other British shoes," and "We love natural materials." These all served to reinforce our theme that shoes and clothing made in the British Isles were of enduring quality.

If it is important to state and amplify the theme in the institutional section frequently found in the beginning of a catalog, it is even more important to do so in the copy that describes the individual products—after all, this is the copy that is read most often. Yet rarely do I find copy describing products that also reinforces the theme and sells the whole catalog. The British Isles Collection catalog copy describing the Wicklow jacket, a handknit brushed wool jacket with Irish fisherman motifs, is typical of how we reinforced our theme, thus selling the whole catalog and the product at the same time:

> We love handmade things, and in Ireland, as nowhere else in Europe that we have seen, can one obtain so many lovely things made by hand. The Wicklow jacket is an outstanding example of Irish artistry for no machine exists which can knit the fisherman stitches and then shift to the nubby brushed wool yarns and draw them through their needles all the while knitting the changing design and pockets.

In saying that "nowhere else in Europe as in Ireland could one obtain so many lovely things made by hand," we sold all the other Irish handcrafts in the catalog.

Usually a single sentence or clause will suffice to reinforce the theme. This sentence preceded our description of the Loake zipper boot: "We never cease to be impressed by the quality of Loake shoes." And before the copy describing the Loake Classic Brogues we wrote: "When it comes to classic brogues nobody makes them better than the British." By salting sentences like these throughout the catalog, we kept reinforcing the British image of quality, thus selling everything.

The merchandise

Nothing other than the copy can express the theme better than the merchandise itself; yet it is often the merchandise that is inconsistent with the theme. Is the theme "quality clothing"? Then one should not carry acrylic sweaters. Is the theme "We have your size," as it was for the catalog of women's shoes in hard-to-find sizes at Lawson Hill Leather and Shoe Co.? Then one should not, as I mistakenly did, carry Italian leather goods, no matter how beautiful they might be.

But it is not enough for merchandise to be consistent; it must, as much as possible, express the theme. This can often be designed into the merchandise. At British Isles Collection, our theme was that shoes and clothing from the British Isles were of enduring quality. How does one prove the quality of shoes on a printed page where they cannot actually be seen or touched? We did it by building quality features into our Loake shoes about which we could talk: leather linings, leather insoles and soles, calfskin leathers, guaranteed lifetime heels, and unbreakable laces. These were all earmarks that proved our quality.

Sometimes the character of the merchandise is such that it goes beyond merely representing or illustrating the theme and expresses it in an extraordinary manner. Implicit in our British Isles theme was the idea that the history and tradition of the people of the British Isles enforced the quality of the merchandise we offered. None of our merchandise conveyed this idea better than our authentic Wellington boots. These boots were first made for the Iron Duke to his design sometime after he dealt Napoleon his final defeat at Waterloo. They have been made continuously since that time for different British military units, including the Guards. Pollard & Son, our manufacturer, has been making them since at least as far back as 1857. These boots gave us the opportunity to tell a bit of British history and to tie the product to it. We did the same thing with R.A.F. flight jackets identical to those worn during the Battle of Britain. We were able to tell of the brave defense of Britain by intrepid pilots and how the jacket protected the pilots at cold temperatures. Wilkinson swords, once again, gave us an opportunity to tell some history and link the product to that history.

Vermont common crackers are an item in the Vermont Country Store Catalog that to an extraordinary degree expresses the theme of the catalog. Vermont County Store does not express its theme outright, but it is clear enough because the merchandise and the copy describing the merchandise and the company all appear to say "Old-fashioned country things and old-fashioned methods, as has been done for many years in Vermont, are still the best." Their common crackers are made on an old-fashioned cracker machine that the firm resurrected and is illustrated in the catalog. They sell the crackers, among other ways, in a real wooden barrel. Vermont County Store tells the story of cracker-making and how crackers and the cracker barrel were important parts of rural American life. The Vermont common crackers are just one of many items in a well-merchandised catalog that expresses the catalog's theme.

Every catalog needs some merchandise that expresses the theme of the company in an extraordinary manner. Even if the merchandise is not profitable, the catalog should carry it. My experience is that any merchandise that expresses the theme well is also a best seller.

The name of the company

It almost goes without saying that the name of the company should at least suggest the theme. When a catalog is taken out of the mailbox, the cover is the first thing a customer looks at, and the first or second[5] thing looked at on the cover is the name of the company. Stacks of catalogs arrive daily

---

[5] The second element is the center of interest, discussed in Chapter 5.

in the mailbox of today's mail-order buyer. Few buyers have time to read them all; each must make the decision whether to read through a catalog or discard it. That decision is determined by the front cover and, to a lesser extent, the back cover. In the first short moment that the catalog is looked at, its fate is determined. The customer sees the center of interest (usually an illustration) and the name and logotype of the company. These will evoke either "interesting—look further" or "no interest—discard." The name and logotype combination is one of the two cover elements that determines whether or not a mail-order buyer looks further.

When one reflects on this fact, it is surprising that so few mail-order companies have names that convey anything at all about them. The names *Eddie Bauer, Norm Thompson, Talbots,* and *L. L. Bean* convey nothing about these companies. That they are not consigned to oblivion is due to the enormous momentum they built up when mail order was less competitive. Everybody knows that *Eddie Bauer* means down-filled clothing, sleeping bags and sporting goods; that *Norm Thompson* means unusual things and clothing; and that *Talbots* has clothing for the traditionally-attired American woman. *L. L. Bean* has become virtually synonymous with the state of Maine and its backwoods. How inadequate these names would be, however, if these companies were starting from scratch today. The name *Eddie Bauer* would be much stronger if it were expressed *Eddie Bauer, Outfitter.* They once were outfitters, supplying various Himalayan expeditions. Why aren't they still outfitting expeditions with down clothing and describing it on the front of their catalog?

The names of a few mail-order companies say something about the companies themselves, as do Cable Car Clothiers, The Renovator's Supply, and Smith & Hawken Tool Co. *The Horchow Collection* has connotations that are suggestive of their theme—nice things that are brought together in a collection from which the customer can choose. The most felicitous choice of a name for a mail-order company has to be *French Creek Sheep and Wool Co.* It has an elemental ring to it; it says that their products are made of natural materials, wool, and sheepskins. *French Creek* conveys their rural setting and suggests that their products are handcrafted. One would feel sure from the name that their products are not turned out in high-speed plants in unending, monotonous uniformity. The theme is beautifully orchestrated in many of their catalogs, which show the sheep, the barn, and the people who make their sheepskin coats and sweaters. Their customers must have a feeling of going to the source and of obtaining something that is much better than what they could buy at ordinary retail stores.

Choosing a name is usually a subjective decision, but it should be objective. The name should say what the company is and should have positive psychological associations. A name can contribute positively to the image of a company, it can be neutral, or it can detract. I subjectively feel that *French Creek Sheep and Wool Co.* was a great choice of a name, but to know this with objective certainty, the name would have to be tested in the target market on an unconscious level.

Testing on an unconscious level means that the person being interviewed is unaware of what is really being tested and that his true feelings are revealed (rather than what he would like the interviewer to think about him, something which influences the answer to every direct question). The pioneer of unconscious testing was Louis Cheskin, who did much of it for oil companies, auto companies, and cigarette companies, and who wrote many books on the subject.[6] At Lawson Hill Leather and Shoe Co., we used his firm extensively in settling upon a name for our company and designing a logotype.

The logotype

The logotype is the way of writing the name and its associated design. It is the company's symbol and serves to aid customers in identifying the company. A logotype should be memorable and easily read and have high visibility and favorable associations.

Because a logotype must be memorable, it should always be written in the same way. People think in pictures. To change the design is to depart from the picture that the customer has in mind, making recognition difficult. This sounds elementary enough; yet in more than one instance I have seen companies change the color of a logotype, not realizing that color is a part of the picture that customers visualize. The change in color requires an effort on the part of the customer to equate the logo with the changed color to the one he previously saw.

R.E.I. Coop, a recreational equipment company, makes an even greater blunder. Not only does it not write its name consistently in the same color, but it also changes the manner in which its name is written from catalog to catalog. Thus, the only aid to recognition are the words of the name (and *R.E.I.* is not even a word); no aid to recognition is given by type style, logotype, or color.

The logotype can have favorable or unfavorable psychological associations that are transferred to the company. The logotype and its typeface can give an image of high quality or of low quality, of femininity or masculinity, modernity or traditionalism, and others. In its own way, the logotype can support or detract from the theme of the catalog.

At Lawson Hill Leather and Shoe Co., we used the services of Louis Cheskin Associates to develop our Marcia Hill logotype. The name *Marcia Hill* was predetermined because we wanted to tell in the catalog the real story of a woman who wore a hard-to-find shoe size (size 11AAAA) and inspired the shoe company. We selected a script typeface that Louis Cheskin's research had determined to have high favorable associations with women. It was modified slightly by rounding the pointed tops of the *M* as his research also revealed that women dislike things with sharp points (triangles, for example). *Marcia Hill* was written in white reverse on a magenta (a pinkish color) oval. We knew from his research that the oval is one of the most pleasing shapes to a woman and that magenta has the highest color preference for them. Furthermore, magenta has high visibility and memorability. Finally, we almost always placed the oval in the upper left-hand corner of the cover so that our catalog would gain even further recognition by always having the logo in the same location.

The same attention we paid to the design of our logotype should be paid by the heads of all mail-order companies to their logotypes. The payoff is that a good logotype will support the theme and also build brand recognition. Each time they mail catalogs to list rental names, their logotype, if it has favorable associations, will create a good impression. If the logotype is memorable, that impression will linger on. Then, as catalogs are mailed

[6] Those who wish to have subconscious testing done on the name or other elements of their catalog might want to contact Louis Cheskin's firm: Louis Cheskin Associates, 535 Middlefield Road, Menlo Park, CA 94025.

repeatedly, catalog recognition will grow. As catalog recognition grows, so too will sales. Mail marketers should have a logotype designed that is based upon scientific research; it should be tested on the unconscious level by a firm such as Louis Cheskin Associates.

Changing the name or logotype

Sometimes the name of a company and its logotype are so well-established that management fears to change them. Yet management suspects or has tested and found out that there are problems with it, such as poor memorability and unfavorable associations. These can be improved through a gradual change.

Back in the early 1960s the Ortho-vent Shoe Co., a direct-selling shoe company with a catalog, learned that their name suggested that their shoes were for people with foot problems, not suitable to the company's desired image of up-to-date footwear. They wanted to change their name to Stuart McGuire, a name that they had tested and found to have favorable psychological associations. It was a big change from Ortho-vent to Stuart McGuire, but they achieved it in stages without disrupting their customer base. The first season they had *Ortho-vent Shoe Co.* at the top of their catalog in large type and *Stuart McGuire* at the bottom in small type. The second season they enlarged the type of *Stuart McGuire*. The third season they put *Stuart McGuire* at the top and *Ortho-vent* at the bottom of the catalog. The fourth season they dropped the Ortho-vent name altogether. Thus they built the recognition of the new name, *Stuart McGuire*, before they dropped *Ortho-vent*. The transition was so smooth that no negative effect upon their customer base was observed.

Using symbolism

People almost always think of communication as being verbal. Mail marketers often do not realize that they can communicate with symbolism as well. Copy can have the disadvantage, especially when it is unbelievable, of setting up defense mechanisms within the reader and producing a contrary result. When they read copy, people are conscious that the writer is trying to influence them and they resist. But with symbolism they are unaware that they are being influenced and so there is no defense mechanism to overcome. For this reason, symbolism can be an effective means for conveying the theme of the catalog.

Symbolism can be embodied in the name, logotype, photography, and merchandise. Symbols may express the company and its theme. A symbol can be the crest and Union Jack that we used at British Isles Collection, or the photograph we used of the 13th-century castle of Eilean Donan reflected in the waters of Loch Alsh in Scotland. These symbolize the long British tradition and the quality that flows from it.

In the French Creek Sheep and Wool Co. catalog there is a picture of Eric Flaxenburg, the owner, hugging a lamb in his arms. This not only directly portrays the source of their products, but it also symbolizes his love for them and suggests that their products are warm and soft. There is no caption under the picture; none is needed. It expresses the theme of the catalog eloquently and wordlessly.

Talbots has a red door as a part of their trademark, perhaps not symbolizing their theme, but nevertheless saying "Welcome to our catalog." L. L. Bean uses pictures of hunting scenes and game birds to suggest its down east character and show that it has hunting equipment. These are some of the symbols employed by mail marketers to express their theme;

but, in truth, as I have searched through catalogs to find examples of symbols used to communicate a theme, I find precious few. The fact is that while a good many catalog companies have a concept of their business and a theme, few express their theme, and fewer still express it symbolically. Mail marketers are apparently unaware that symbols can be very effective in expressing the theme—often more effective than words because consumers have no defense mechanisms set up against them.

Symbols take space in a catalog, and this may be another reason why they are not employed more. Every square inch of a catalog has a cost that the mail marketer must recover through sales; most mail marketers know this. Space devoted to symbols can otherwise be used for revenue-producing merchandise. The offset to the cost of the space occupied by symbols, however, is that symbols sell the whole catalog. The sales of each product in the catalog is elevated slightly by a symbol. The sum of the sales increases of all the products, if effective symbols are used, is more than the sales that would be produced if the symbol's space were occupied by merchandise.

It goes without saying that the symbols selected must be effective ones. Symbols can be neutral, conveying nothing, or, worse, can even detract. Symbols are most effective when the concept of the business and the theme are clearly defined. Where symbols occupy very costly space or where they are repeated in many catalogs and long press runs, their effectiveness in communicating the theme of the company should be tested on an unconscious level. Once again, this can be done at Louis Cheskin Associates.

What Confers Leadership?

We have seen in this chapter that the foundation of a mail-order catalog is the definition of the concept of the business. At the outset, the mail marketer must think through carefully and define the concept of the business. The concept of the business must be broad enough to satisfy all the related customer desires and to sell enough product. Yet, although it must be broad, it must also be narrow. It must be narrow enough to permit leadership.

Leadership is the secret of a mail-order catalog's success. Leadership is in the mind of the customer. It is what causes the customer to prefer one catalog over another. While a strongly presented theme supported by well-written copy, powerful symbolism, a good name and logotype, and good graphics will provide a competitive edge, even leadership, leadership must be primarily in merchandise. How does one develop merchandise that confers leadership? That is the subject of the next chapter.

how to achieve
leadership in merchandise

Success follows strong dynamics, and strong dynamics follow leadership. Just as water drains to the lowest well, so, too, business flows to the company that leads in what it sets out to do, leaving dry those firms that did not drill their wells as deep.

Leadership must be primarily in merchandise. Merchandise fulfills the concept of the business—it is, after all, what the customer pays for. Business will gravitate to those companies with the most well-developed selection, the best quality, the best value in an acceptable quality, or unique merchandise.

The merchandise must distinguish the catalog. A better presentation of the merchandise with effective graphics, good photography, and potent copywriting improves the customer's perception of the merchandise and thus redirects the flow of business. However, the customer still buys from the firm that he perceives to have the merchandise that best satisfies his desires. It is folly to rely on graphics to overcome a merchandise weakness.

The merchandiser, therefore, is the supreme person on the mail-marketing organization chart. More than anything else, the success of the catalog is determined by his ability to develop merchandise that establishes leadership and fulfills the concept of the business.

How does a merchandiser insure the success of a catalog? Eddie Bauer provides a good example. The company is preeminent in goose down products: it has the best values in down, the best and largest selection of products filled with down, and the longest history in the business. When few others were selling anything made with down, Eddie Bauer was outfitting Himalayan expeditions with down insulating products and promoting down. Thus, today, when most people receive an Eddie Bauer catalog, they open it knowing that when it comes to down insulating products Eddie Bauer has the best selection and the best values.

This is product leadership. When someone wants a down product, he or she is more likely to buy it from Eddie Bauer than from anyone else.

And having bought from Eddie Bauer once and having been satisfied, that person becomes an Eddie Bauer customer and is likely to buy from the other categories of products offered. Thus, their leadership in down results in their not only selling down products but also all their other products. Without down, Eddie Bauer would be a competently-produced catalog but just another one in a sea of competently-produced catalogs. It is Eddie Bauer's leadership in down insulating products that distinguishes it from all others and confers its success.

The merchandiser distinguishes a company and gives it leadership by the merchandise he develops. Gokey's is supreme in handsewn footwear, led by its incomparable Bottes Sauvage snakeproof boot. Following the Bottes Sauvage are handsewn boots of every height and description, handsewn moccasins, and handsewn shoes. If one wants a snakeproof boot, Gokey's is almost the only place where one can get one. This excellence in handsewn footwear gives Gokey's a loyal following whose interest spreads to the other products that Gokey's sells.

Gokey's illustrates another aspect of what merchandise leadership can be: the development of a product category in depth. By developing a product category in depth, the merchandiser makes the customer feel that the selection is good, that he need look no further, and that a complete choice exists within the merchandiser's catalog. Thus a barrier to buying is removed. All other factors being equal, people shop where the selection is best.

Development in depth is one of the reasons why we were successful at British Isles Collection. Because of my previous experience in selling men's shoes by mail order, we were able to safely offer a broad selection of Loake men's shoes despite the risks normally associated with shoes because of their many stockkeeping units. If we had started cautiously by offering just a few styles, we would not have appeared to really be in the shoe business. We would not only have had fewer styles on which we were selling shoes, we might well have sold fewer pairs on the styles that we did carry. In other words, our customers saw that we had a broad selection, complete enough for them to choose from, and they knew that they needed to look no further.

Similarly, we opened up with the broadest selection of women's kilts available. As a result, kilts became the most important category of women's clothing in our catalog. Conversely, our selection of sheepskin coats contained only a few models. If our catalog arrived in a home the same day as the catalog of the French Creek Sheep and Wool Co., price and style being equal, we would lose the sheepskin coat business to them.

There is a limit, of course, to how broad a selection can profitably be. Each new article within a product category increases choice and so attracts more customers to the catalog. More customers increase the likelihood that products in other categories will be sold as well. But more products within a category take more space, space which must come from other products or by increasing the size of the catalog. And each new product within a category tends to take away sales from other products within the category. The merchandiser must guard against too much overlapping of products and make sure that each appeals to a distinct desire.

It goes without saying that, if one wishes to establish leadership through selection, one does so with an important category. Shoes are an important category because everyone buys several pairs a year and people want a choice when they buy shoes. The other extreme is men's socks—establishing leadership in men's socks will hardly excite many men and build a mail-order business.

How to Develop Products for a Catalog

The secret to successfully developing products for a catalog is to be systematic. Fortunately for the mail marketer, an item that is successful in one issue of a catalog will usually be successful in succeeding catalogs. This permits him or her to build, issue after issue, a steadily stronger base of repeat merchandise. The method, therefore, is initially to test many different items and categories of items. Those items that sell well should be repeated, and those categories that do well should be expanded. Items that do poorly should be dropped or have less space allocated to them, and categories that do poorly should have the number of items and space reduced.

Each season the merchandiser replaces poorly-selling items with new ones, some of which will sell well and be retained for later issues. Steadily, he or she will build a catalog of more winners and fewer losers.

The key is testing. The testing of merchandise must be done not only in the beginning years of a catalog; it must always be done. Testing of merchandise may seem expensive, but it pays. One loser loses the revenue that should have been produced by the space it occupies and must be marked down, but for one season only. One winner discovered, however, will generate profits season after season, paying for many mistakes.

Finding Merchandise That Sells

If there is one secret to finding merchandise that sells, it is plenty of exposure to resources, ideas, other catalogs, retail stores, and magazines, followed up with liberal sampling and backed up with a publicity cost analysis of what previous catalogs have sold (see Chapter 7 for catalog analysis). Then at decision-making time the merchandiser will have a broad assortment of merchandise ideas from which he or she can choose.

There are also some principles of merchandising the merchandiser can use in making the rounds of sample rooms and studying the competition.

Find unusual merchandise. Your chances for a successful catalog are surely greater if you have a high proportion of unusual merchandise. Unusual, or preferably unique, merchandise is by definition leadership: if someone wants the merchandise he or she must buy it from you. On the other hand, if your catalog is filled with merchandise that is readily available in retail stores, then there is little incentive for someone to buy from you.

Find merchandise with ideas. The big advantage that mail order has over the retail store is its capability to express ideas. It is not possible for retail clerks to be thoroughly knowledgeable about all the merchandise, but even if they were, they are often unavailable when a customer needs to have a product explained. But in a catalog the medium is the written word. Products can be explained, diagrams can be drawn, and features can be highlighted.

The successful merchandiser seeks out merchandise with ideas and selling points about which copy can be written. For example, Stuart McGuire had a shoe in their catalog that was unchanged for 20 years. It was called the Soft Shoe. The upper leather was shrunken cowhide shoulders, the softest leather they could find. The box toes and counters were extra soft. There was cushioning in the insole and the tongue under the laces. The full leather linings were as soft as deerskin. The heel was extra soft, and the sole was of the softest leather tannage. The shoe began as an idea of what might be sold on the printed page—a super-soft shoe. Then the shoe was designed and made to fit the idea.

Similarly, the Loake shoes for the British Isles Collection catalog were not shoes off the shelf at the Loake factory. The shoes were designed specifically for the catalog with features that we thought would sell the shoes.

One tool that has helped me immeasurably in developing merchandise is a pocket dictating machine. As I travel from vendor to vendor and show to show, I keep it on my hip in a leather holster. As I get ideas for merchandise, I dictate them into the machine before they escape. Sometimes I dictate actual catalog copy so that when review time comes I know how a certain product might be sold.

Find high-currency items with a unique difference. High-currency items are items for which there is much demand. The problem with them is that they can be bought everywhere; there is no need for the consumer to buy them from you. Here's a good example from British Isles Collection. In our initial test mailing, we offered a Harris Tweed jacket. But it was an ordinary Harris Tweed jacket; there was nothing special about it. Almost any well-dressed man might wear one, yet it sold poorly. But in the following season when we introduced a Harris Tweed jacket with leather trim that coordinated with a leather vest and the same fabric was used in a hat, the jacket sold well. It was the unique difference of the leather trim and coordination that made it sell.

Consider yesterday's national best seller. A phenomenon that often occurs in mail order is that yesterday's national best seller, a product that once was in every retail store in the country, keeps right on selling in mail order. What happens is that after a period of peak popularity, the sales of an item fall off. Retail stores, finding that they are overstocked, dump their merchandise in sales and almost no store continues to sell the item. But although demand may have fallen off, say two-thirds, there remains one-third of the potential customers who still want it.

We had this experience in women's stretch boots at Lawson Hill Leather and Shoe Co. Stretch boots were tremendously popular. Every retailer of women's footwear sold them and we sold our share too. But then demand appeared to die; the dealers' shelves were loaded. They panicked and dumped their boots at distress prices. Manufacturers offered stretch boots to us at a dollar a pair. But all the while, we kept right on selling stretch boots. As fewer and fewer shoe retailers carried them, more and more women turned to us to buy them.

Look for add-ons. Add-on items can boost your average order. Usually they are lower-priced and are not a big buying decision for the customer. Frequently they have an association with the main products being sold. While writing an order, the customer adds them on. For example, we offered hosiery at Lawson Hill Leather and Shoe Co. to go with our women's shoes, and shoe trees with our men's shoes.

Look for order-starters. Order-starters are lower-priced items of broad appeal or lower-priced items that are an outstanding value and still of considerable popular appeal. In either case, the fact that it is lower-priced means that a decision to buy it is not major, and the fact that it has broad appeal or is an outstanding value means that many people will buy it.

Having gotten into buying the order-starter, some of the customers will consider other merchandise and add it to their orders.

I should caution, however, customers who have bought only the order-starter are of lower quality. They are much less likely to follow up well in later mailings than someone who has bought higher-priced items. More about this in a later chapter.

Design your line of merchandise for bigger or more frequent sales. Make sure that you retain the image of specialization and make sure that you do not select merchandise that is incongruous. Yet, within the customer interest to which you cater have as broad a selection as possible. The customer who bought a pair of shoes is dressing himself, and he can think of you as supplying everything he wants to wear. If he buys men's shoes, he can buy sports jackets. Sports jackets satisfy a separate need and don't compete with shoes except for the customer's dollars. So do sweaters, pants, and ties.

Where possible, offer consumable products. A mail-order marketer of bird feeders should sell bird seed (not ordinary bird seed but exclusive mixes). One reason shoes sell well by mail is that they wear out faster than most other articles of clothing and so customers reorder more frequently.

Develop merchandise that sells year-round. This word of advice is to alert the person who is considering entering mail order that there are problems, not insurmountable, that are associated with a one-season business and merchandise that sells in only one season.

In a one-season business, cash flow shuts off at the end of the season. If too much inventory has been bought, then the owner will find himself loaded with inventory, short of cash, and with his trade terms expiring and vendor bills coming due. For six months, he will have no sales coming in to generate the cash needed to pay debts. Furthermore, overhead expenses will continue and employees will have to be laid off at the end of the season.

One-season merchandise can have a similar effect upon what is a two-season business, but the effect is not so devastating. A women's boot sells only in the fall and early winter. A women's sandal sells only in the spring and summer. But a women's walking shoe sells year-round. If it is difficult to control the inventory because of long manufacturer's lead times and many stockkeeping units, as in boots and sandals, then the owner of the business must plan for enough cash to carry the residual inventory and customer refunds if he tries to keep his inventory to a maximum.

There is one other disadvantage to a one-season business: growth is halved. The mail marketer with a one-season business cannot mail catalogs to prospects during his off-season and add more customers to his list. As a result, he must wait a year before he can mail again.

These are all problems that are associated with a one-season business and one-season merchandise. That they can be overcome is well-proven by such successes as Figi Cheese, Harry & David (fruit), and French Creek Sheep and Wool Co.

Recognize the distinction in merchandising for customers and merchandising for prospective customers. People who have not bought from you will respond differently to merchandise than do your regular customers.

Regular customers, because they have bought from you, tend to think of you as their usual resource. For this reason, they will buy their ordinary needs from you. An item that is not out of the ordinary will sell well to regular customers while it will sell poorly to prospective customers. A good example is the boat moccasin, a handsewn moccasin with a white nonskid sole, such as the Sperry Top-Sider and Sebago Docksides®. The boat moccasin is so commonplace that it can be bought in almost any shoe store. A consulting client of mine discovered that it would sell well in catalogs going out to present customers but not in catalogs going out to list rental (prospective) customers. The existing customer bought it from the client because he was accustomed to buying shoes from him. But the prospective customer saw no reason to start out buying the boat moccasin from someone he did not know.

Existing customers need fresh merchandise. Good items have great longevity in mail order but they tend to wear out with customers after repeated mailings. Customers select from the catalog what they want and leave unbought what they don't want. To keep customers interested, new merchandise must be introduced each season.

The degree to which fresh merchandise is required depends upon the product line. High-fashion women's ready-to-wear, as sold by Brownstone Studio or FBS, must be kept very fresh. Figi Cheese and Harry & David (fruit) have favorites that keep selling year after year. L. L. Bean has been selling their Maine hunting shoe since the company's inception. But L. L. Bean still needs new merchandise to interest their existing customers.

Catalogs being mailed to prospective customers do not need fresh merchandise because many prospective customers have not seen the catalog before and those that have seen it haven't seen it frequently. Catalogs that are mailed out to list rental prospects should contain proven winners and must have unusual merchandise.

In summary, to attract new customers, you must give them a special reason to buy. This usually means unusual merchandise or recognizable good values. Merchandise for prospects, however, does not need to be new to the catalog. Space should not be consumed in a catalog going to prospective customers with new, untested merchandise; instead, it should be devoted to the proven winners.

To keep existing customers active, you must restimulate them with new merchandise, which by definition is unproven. They will continue to buy proven merchandise; but, depending upon what it is, with less interest and frequency than before. Unusual merchandise will stimulate the existing customer just as it does the prospective customer, but you can also sell him merchandise that is commonly available.

The implication of this difference between what existing and prospective customers tend to buy is that mail marketers should have two different catalogs, one for each type of buyer. Merchandise should be tested in the catalog for existing customers and when proven to be outstanding it should then be added to list rental catalogs (prospective customers catalog). Furthermore, the computer should print out reports showing the sales for each item to each class of customers.

When a company is small, inventory turnover is a problem, or fresh merchandise is not important to existing buyers, having two separate catalogs does not pay or is unnecessary. But for many larger mail-order houses it makes sense. For them, the catalog going to existing customers should not only contain fresh merchandise and commonly available items that they buy, but it should also be larger and contain more merchandise because it is more productive by far than the catalog going to list rental prospects. It pays to put more pages in catalogs going to existing customers.

the dynamics of copywriting

Copy is the most powerful weapon in the mail marketer's arsenal. It is the great advantage that the mail marketer enjoys over the common retailer. A color photograph and its reproduction in the catalog, if done well, can sometimes equal seeing the product itself; but copy can take the customer far beyond what he will experience in the retail store.

Clerks in a store are sometimes unavailable and often uninformed. But copy can be written thoughtfully, succinctly, and knowledgeably in advance of the sale and be ready in polished form in the catalog for the customer to read when he is considering buying. Copy, sometimes coordinated with diagrams, can highlight features. It can tell the background of the product. It can explain its particular usefulness or reason for being and why it is different from all others. It can assure the customer that the product is made of the materials he expects, as leather in shoes. Copy can create mood, ambience, and enthusiasm. Most important of all, copy can state the theme of the catalog, sell the company as a whole, and in so doing sell every product in the catalog.

Because it can have such great power and because it can highlight selling points, copy can be the key to a merchandiser's success. It permits him to design features into the product and be confident that they will be explained and sold.

For example, at British Isles Collection, we specified unbreakable shoelaces in all our Loake shoes. A shoelace is a small thing, certain not to gain mention by clerks in a shoe store. Yet, who hasn't experienced the frustration of having a shoelace break and wouldn't be delighted to know that the laces on his new pair will give him no trouble? An unbreakable lace costs only a penny or two more than a cheaper one that wears and eventually breaks. Yet, because the shoe manufacturer can be certain that unbreakable laces aren't mentioned in a shoe store, it does not pay for him to build that quality feature into his shoes. But at British Isles Collection, it was one of many quality features that we had built into every Loake shoe style so that we could demonstrate in the catalog the quality of the shoe. It paid to put in his quality feature because we could, through the copy, be assured that the customer would know about it. Thus, the effectiveness of copy in selling the product makes possible merchandise that would not otherwise exist.

Functions of Copy

Copy to express the theme

It was previously discussed in Chapter 1 that copy is one way to express the theme. Indeed, stating the theme of the catalog is the first function of copy. The theme should be stated on the cover, in the institutional section at the beginning of the catalog, and then repeated throughout the catalog. Copy can also state the theme by creating mood.

Creating mood with copy

I draw a distinction between using copy to state the theme and using copy to create mood, which also states the theme. Mood is subliminal and less direct. When a mood is created, the customer is unaware that he is being sold, so he does not raise the barriers that he would normally put up when he is conscious that someone is trying to sell him something. This is what makes mood so effective. It is hard for me to visualize a catalog with mood that is not effective.

How do you create mood? Here are some examples from the British Isles Collection catalog. This first one comes from the institutional section at the beginning of the catalog under the heading of "We love natural materials":

> We love materials at their best, finely made into beautiful shoes and garments. That is, in fact, the whole reason for this catalog. There is nothing so nice, so soft, so luxurious, or so beautiful as a shoe made from English Pebody calfskin. And, when it comes to sweaters and jackets and coats, there is no man-made fiber that is so beautiful and soft as mohair and lambswool. Nor is there any synthetic fiber that rivals wool for warmth in both wet and dry conditions. Cotton is unequaled for comfort and its ability to absorb moisture.
>
> Each of these natural materials has been endowed by its Creator with characteristics which enable it or its host to survive and prosper in nature. It is for these same reasons that each is so good in nature that they serve man so well.
>
> Many of these natural materials are in short supply as mohair and even leather. The availability of some is dependent upon another product, as leather is dependent on the consumption of meat. For this reason, natural materials have been and are becoming increasingly costly.
>
> But we think that the qualities of shoes and clothing made from natural materials are worth their extra cost and that it is better to have fewer and better things, to wear and enjoy them often, than to have something which is not as nice and of which one tires quickly and discards. It is for this reason that every shoe and garment in this catalog is made from natural materials, synthetic being used only when needed for structural reinforcement.

When we wrote the copy for the authentic Wellington boot, we gave some history first to put the customer in a receptive mood. Having done that, we sold him on the boots:

> In February of 1815, Napoleon and a band of 100 followers escaped from the island of Elba and made their way to Cannes on the coast of France. As they

proceeded to Paris, without firing a shot, military units and veterans of his former wars, remembering the glories of France, rallied about him. The government of King Louis XVIII capitulated and all Europe trembled as the greatest general since Caesar marshalled the forces of France anew. Wellington, later known as the Iron Duke, leading a diverse army of British, Dutch, Belgian, and German troops, speaking no common language, handed Napoleon his final defeat at Waterloo and, in so doing, became immortal.

These boots were made for Wellington to his design at about that time. They have changed little since then and have been made continuously for the officers of the military units with slight style variations depending upon the regiment. The styling of our boots, with the shaped top and forest green band, is that worn by all guards regiments.

These Wellington boots have been made by Pollard & Son since before 1857. Today, David Pollard, the great-grandson of the founder, continues to make the boots in the tradition of craftsmanship that has been in the family for well over a century.

Each pair of boots is serial numbered by hand and has calfskin uppers with kidskin shafts. The foot is lined with leather; and, of course, the soles and insoles are all leather. We guarantee the heel to last forever.

Present day customers for Pollard Wellington boots include King Hussein of Jordan and Prince Charles. While originally made for British officers, almost everybody can or does wear Wellington style boots today. Few, however, have access to these authentic ones, which we make available in this country for the first time.

For the authentic reproduction of the World War II R.A.F. flying jacket we did the same thing:

In the summer of 1940, France lay fallen, crushed by the German onslaught; Britain was alone and at bay. Germany readied operation "Sea Lion"—the invasion of Britain across the English channel. The success of this operation depended upon superiority in the air. To this end, Marshal Goering directed repeated Luftwaffe assaults upon the British airfields and upon London. Day after day, the R.A.F., fewer than a thousand fighter pilots, rose to meet their adversaries, inflicting heavy losses. The air battle of September 15, 1940 was the crux of the Battle of Britain, for on September 17 Hitler ordered the indefinite postponement of "Sea Lion." As was said by Winston Churchill, "Never in the field of human conflict was so much owed by so many to so few."

This jacket is the same as worn by those defenders of Britain. It is authentic down to the last detail and is made for us by the only firm licensed to make them from the original patterns. Because flying in those days took place at high altitudes at cold temperatures and in unheated cockpits, these jackets were designed to be warm under severe conditions.

It is constructed with a finished shearling sheepskin, in our opinion one of the finest insulating materials. The collar rolls high to protect the neck and cheeks. Behind each zipper is a layer of shearling to lock out cold. The sleeves are zippered to permit freedom of movement. It is clearly the finest there is.

To introduce the Irish section we devoted a sixth of a page to write about the warm and friendly people of Ireland, Irish music played on old instruments, and Guinness stout:

Cead Mille Failte—one hundred thousand welcomes—that was the greeting we received from warm and friendly people as we traveled about Ireland searching for the beautiful and unusual for our catalog. One evening we went outside of Dublin to a centuries old tavern, looking much as it must have those centuries before, to hear authentic Irish music, played as it always has been played with tin whistles, flute, fiddle and Uilleann pipes, and to capture the mood and spirit of the people. We sat around a long table, family style. A family near us, perceiving that we were Americans, gave us yet another welcome and bought for us a pint of their fabled Guinness stout.

These are the people in the country that make by hand the lovely things that adorn these pages. Handmade—handmade by a warm people—this is the essence of these things. And, because they are handmade, there is an individuality, a beauty of design, often complex, which characterizes them.

In Ireland, as nowhere else in Europe that we have seen, can one obtain so many different things made by hand at so little cost. The knitted things are all made in homes, with the wool being brought and the finished article taken away by a traveler. Normally, a month is required for a woman sitting before the telly in the evening to complete one of her sweater designs. As progress overtakes this largely pastoral country, and manufacturing plants establish themselves, we wonder how much longer we can obtain such lovely things, but, while they last, we offer them here.

In northern Vermont, almost in Canada, Montgomery Schoolhouse, Inc., which started in a building that once housed the school of Montgomery, Vermont, makes a great variety of wooden toys with natural finishes and without nails. The toys are enjoyed by adults as well as children. Montgomery has few people (population: 650) but many covered bridges (five). Montgomery Schoolhouse is the town's only industry. Here is their introductory letter, which could double as a guarantee, written for a catalog to be mailed in late October for Christmas selling:

To our friends and customers:

The maple leaves, which a month ago set our valley ablaze, are all but gone now. The first snows have fallen, precursors of storms that will blanket our fields, roads, and mountains to depths of three feet and more. Route 58 which crosses the Green Mountains through Hazens Notch and connects us to the east is still open but soon will be closed as it is not plowed in the winter. It will be another four months before the sap will begin to run in the maple trees and be harvested.

Our stoves, burning the maple and yellow birch logs we've put away in the woodsheds, are keeping us warm and snug, as they will do for the next six months. Many of our people live close to the building, which we built when the Montgomery schoolhouse, in which we began, burned to the ground. They will walk to work, trudging the snow-banked road. Others living in outlying family farms will, twice each day, traverse hilly roads and the five covered bridges still in use to bring themselves to and from their work.

In this setting, our people at their saws and their lathes make enduring wooden toys all year 'round to bring happiness on birthdays and Christmases to children and grown-ups alike. At their benches they do much of their work by hand, thus assuring the attention to detail and quality in which we pride ourselves.

Nine years ago we were but an idea. Today we are Montgomery's main employer, bearing witness to the ever growing popularity of our toys. Our toys are bought by parents and grandparents for their children and grandchildren. And, they are bought by grown-ups for themselves. They all come back year after year to add a new car to their train or a new truck to their collection.

We hope you will like our toys, but you are the judge. Return anything you don't want or like. We will cheerfully refund the purchase price.

Cordially,

Dan Woodward

This said little about the toys; it described the setting of Montgomery Schoolhouse and in so doing created mood, a mood that would generate toy sales when the customer turned from the institutional section to the main part of the catalog. Here is their guarantee:

Enduring Wooden Toys Which We Guarantee to Last

Like our green, granite hills, which have endured a hundred million years, reluctantly yielding their stature to the erosion of alternating winters and summers and ice ages that have come and gone, our toys are built to last. Ones that we built nine years ago are still in use, being handed from older child to younger. We guarantee that they will always serve your or your child's pleasure. Should a toy break, return it and it will be replaced without charge and with a smile.

Here is what they say about wood, the main component of their toys. They talk about their toys but they create mood at the same time:

Why We Like Wood

Our toys are made almost entirely of wood. Pine, rock maple, beech, and yellow logs are cut in Smuggler's Notch, so named because cattle smugglers once lurked there, in the Green Mountains and are hauled to Jeffersonville where they are sawn to the sizes necessary to make our toys.

We like wood, perhaps because of nostalgia. Our grandfathers made toys of wood for our parents and us too because that was the only material in plentiful supply. Wood is natural and timeless. It is also strong.

We use no nails and almost no steel. Wheels and axles are all wood. One piece of wood is joined to another with a strong glue or with pegs of wood itself. The finish is soft and will never flake or crack, being almost a part of the wood.

This institutional copy consumes much space in the Montgomery Schoolhouse catalog, but the mood developed creates an appreciation of the product, making it easier to sell.

Mood is created through copy, but it can be created graphically through photographs and drawings. Hallie Greer, selling fabrics of a Colonial character, creates mood by photographing a room in a Colonial home furnished with antique furniture and decorated with drapes made of their fabrics. J & F Orr, makers of antique reproductions, creates mood by photographing their furniture inside the Wayside Inn of Sudbury, Massachusetts, where Longfellow wrote *Tales of a Wayside Inn.*

What Copy Should and Should Not Be

Copy must be believable. That is axiomatic; it is pointless that it be written otherwise. Yet it is astonishing that so much copy is patent nonsense. It seems as though many copywriters believe that the more they exaggerate, the more good things the customer will believe about the product.

This leads to the first rule of writing copy to describe products: *Don't use obvious hyperbole.* Don't write that this is the best ice cream scoop there is. The customer knows there are ice cream scoops you have not seen. Write that this is the best ice cream scoop you could find—that is believable and yet carries authority because, presumably, you have seen many ice cream scoops.

The second rule of writing copy to describe products is: *Write NO unbelievable copy*. The emphasis is on the word *no*. An obvious exaggeration in one part of a catalog makes the whole catalog suspect.

The third rule of copywriting is: *Keep your copy meaningful*. If copywriters err by exaggerating, they also err by writing meaningless verbiage. One of the worst cases of meaningless writing that I have seen occurred in the early years of Lawson Hill Leather and Shoe Co. when a copywriter described a shoe with a perforated design as "punchwork perfection." If you have something meaningful to say, say it. But don't go beyond. Don't feel as though you have to do your duty by every item in the catalog and write a lot about each one. Some items require much description; for others, the picture carries them and little needs to be written. Write what is needed and then no more.

The fourth rule of copywriting is: *Make your copy interesting*. Usually, the customer is interested in what you have to say about the product, particularly if he is contemplating buying it. But you can go beyond by introducing historical or background information that romances the product. By keeping the customer interested, you keep him reading the catalog.

Long Copy versus Short Copy

I have often heard it said that people won't read long copy. But Joe Sugarman of J.S. & A. has proved otherwise with full-page magazine ads that are densely packed with copy. If people won't read long copy, they wouldn't read newspapers, which are mostly copy. They read newspapers because they are interested in what is written. They will read copy about products if it is interesting and meaningful. After all, what could interest a customer more than copy about a product for which he intends to spend his money. The key thing is not whether the total number of words written about a product is too great, but that every word counts.

A case in point is the catalog of the Vermont Country Store. It is printed only in one color with rudimentary illustrations, many of which are line drawings that scarcely depict the merchandise. But each item is described with a great deal of copy. It is clear that long copy sells for the Vermont Country Store because the pictures obviously could not. I have watched my wife read the entire Vermont Country Store catalog, her interest sustained by what she read. She said, as she read it, that she loved country stores and enjoyed reading the little tidbits of information such as how they made crackers themselves with an old-fashioned cracker machine, how Gardner Orton founded the company, and how stone-ground cereals retain all their nutritional elements.

Copy may be long if it is interesting and meaningful, sells the product, is not wordy, and is worth the cost of the space devoted to it.

Institutional Copy

Is institutional copy worth the space it occupies? Institutional copy must go on pages two and three of a catalog or else it loses most of its effectiveness. Yet these pages are prime locations on which the very best merchandise might be illustrated. Does institutional copy pay? Many mail marketers apparently feel that it does not, for pages two and three in their catalogs are loaded with merchandise. Others have institutional copy on those pages.

The argument for using such valuable space for institutional copy is that the whole catalog of merchandise is sold by it. My own feeling is that if the space is used for bland copy, which I see written in the front of so many catalogs, then the space is better allocated to merchandise. But if the space is used to state a theme and to build a mood with meaningful, evocative words, then using such valuable space is well-justified to put the customer into a buying frame of mind. And, because pages two and three are devoted to institutional selling, pages four and five take on importance as the first two pages of merchandise.

Elements of institutional copy

In addition to stating the theme and conveying the mood, there are certain institutional elements that should be incorporated in every catalog.

Telephone Orders. Telephone orders should be encouraged in the front of the catalog and on the order form. In addition, many mail marketers repeat their telephone number throughout the catalog to suggest ordering, especially by phone. Telephone orders are to be encouraged because they average much larger sales than written orders and permit additional selling by the order-taker.

At British Isles Collection, we employed the most personable young ladies we had for this important function. We printed their pictures with their names in the catalog so the customers would know who they were. We devoted more than a quarter of a page to a section on telephone ordering, headlined with "About Our Personal Telephone Service" in which we said:

> This spirit of helpfulness is the essence of our telephone service. Our customer representatives, Cindy and Polly, are knowledgeable in our products and are friendly and chatty; and, because we have had so many nice people call, they delight in helping customers. Should you call, they would enjoy helping you, too, and answer any questions you might have. For them a sale does not end with the taking of the order; they give their name and ask the customer to call them personally should there ever be any problem. One or more of these young ladies are almost always on hand between 8 a.m. and 9 p.m., eastern time, seven days a week, ready to assist you.

Credit Card. There was a time when not all mail-order companies allowed payment by credit cards; in those days credit cards were worthy of special emphasis. Even today someone who is buying by mail order for the first time might not know such convenience is available. The logotypes of each card that the company honors should be displayed on at least one of the covers, on the order form, and on page two or page three. This quickly informs the customer which cards he can use and that he has the credit he needs to buy what he wants.

Guarantee. Be sure your guarantee appears on page two or three and on your order form. There is more about the guarantee in the Chapter 4, "Build Confidence."

Retail Store. The catalog is always the most powerful selling tool for the company's retail stores. The more catalogs that are circulated, the more that retail store business grows. I have always been mystified by the fact that so many catalogs put so little stress on their stores. Frequently, as in Eddie Bauer and Talbots, there is nothing more than a listing of store locations. If one thinks of sales of a catalog in terms of sales per square inch, then the space that invites customers to the retail stores is the most productive. Don't just list your stores in the catalog; invite the customer to come visit you, tell him what he might see, and sell him on the pleasures of shopping in your stores.

Express Service. If your service is not good, make it good. Then stress it in the front of the catalog and on the order form. Customers, once they have made the decision to buy, want instant gratification. They part with their money because your products are worth more to them. Good service makes a good impression, creates confidence, and encourages reorders.

A Few Tips on Writing Copy

Seclude yourself while writing copy. Good copywriting demands inspiration and does not come all at once. It requires meditation, which can come only in quiet. Thoughts are elusive things; they can escape before you have a chance to write them down. If someone speaks to you while a thought is coming into your consciousness, it will be lost, and you will have to develop it anew. Good copywriting is much work even though the result is only a few lines.

Make every word count. Long copy can often be justified. Wordiness can never be. Wordiness tires the reader and consumes costly catalog space.

Bibliography on writing. Making every word count is the central theme of the two best books on writing that I have found. I recommend them highly. They are:

> Zinsser, William. *On Writing Well*, 2nd ed. New York: Harper & Row, 1980.
> Strunk, William, and White, E. B. *Elements of Style*, 3rd ed. New York: MacMillan Publishing Co., 1979.

The best handbook on writing that I know of and which I have used for almost 40 years is:

> Hodges John C. and Mary E. Whitten. *Harbrace College Handbook*, 8th ed. New York: Harcourt Brace Jovanovich, 1979.

Have the merchandiser write the copy. Given equal writing abilities, the merchandiser is superior to anyone for writing copy about the merchandise. He understands it better and will be more certain to give expression to the customer appeal he wishes to create. I believe it is so important for merchandising to be coordinated with copy that I recommend an unusual organizational structure. See Chapter 26, "Organize for Success."

If it is not practical for the merchandiser to write the copy, then the copywriter must know what inspired the merchandiser to put the product in the catalog. The copywriter must understand the merchandise thoroughly: its history, something about how it is made, the romance of it, and all the technical details. He or she must know far more than what is finally put down on paper so that he or she can select the best material to write the most effective copy.

Good copy is one of the secrets of catalog mail-order success. It should state the theme, be used to create a mood that is conducive to buying, and bring out the best in a product. Write copy well and use it.

build confidence

If catalog mail order has the great advantage over a retail store of being able to tell the story of the company and its products through well-written copy, it also has the ever-present disadvantage that the customer cannot see the product and must by on faith. In a retail store he or she can see and feel a product and, regardless of the quality of the rest of the merchandise, make some determination of its quality. He can look at the label of a sweater to see if it is wool or synthetic. She can tap a goblet to see if it has a melodious ring or a dull thunk. He can examine a shoe to see if the linings and soles are leather. This the customer cannot do looking at a catalog.

The mail marketer, therefore, must build confidence—not just the customers' confidence that they will get their money back if not satisfied, although this is very important, but also the confidence that they will get what they visualized when they wrote their orders.

Products That Meet Expectations

Almost all catalog mail-order businesses make their profit on existing customers. New customers are rarely gained at a significant profit; if the mail marketer writes off the money spent to acquire customers the season it is expended, as is usually the case, new customers are often acquired at a loss. The cardinal rule of gaining customer confidence, therefore, is that the product must meet the promise of the catalog and customer expectations. If a mail marketer consistently fails to ship good-quality merchandise that meets customer expectations, then he will lose the source of his expected profit.

The quality of all products must be uniformly up to standard. Unlike in a retail store, the mail-order customer does not have the opportunity to

32

see that the poor quality of one product is an exception and that the others are good. One product failure reflects on the entire catalog of merchandise and can destroy the mail marketer's relationship with his customer.

I experienced this personally. For years, I was a customer of a large mail-order clothing company. I still own a top coat and sport coat which I bought from them long ago. Their merchandise was both good quality and good value. But then something happened. I ordered some pants, and they were shoddy. I ordered a jacket, and it was awful. I returned both orders, and the company lost me as a customer. Perhaps the jacket and pants were exceptions, and most of their products were good. But by receiving shoddy merchandise, I concluded that their policies had changed, and I lost confidence in them.

The more poor-quality merchandise one sells, the more customers one alienates. A mail marketer should not retain any merchandise in his catalog that is likely to disappoint his customers, no matter how profitable it might be. This rule seems obvious, but it is often breached.

Gaining the Confidence of Prospective Customers

Shipping goods that meet customer expectations retains and even builds confidence, but how does one gain the confidence of prospective customers so that they order in the first place?

To gain confidence, write believable copy in a sincere fashion. In Chapter 3 I spoke about the effectiveness of believable copy. Believable copy also builds confidence. Here is an example of sincere-sounding copy that builds confidence from the Smith-Hawken catalog.

Garden Spade

Our most popular spade. Although this is not our "strongest" spade, it is by far the most useful tool for the gardener. The blade comes off the shank in a straightforward manner, and the weight and strength are more than sufficient to satisfy all but the most unusual demands. The important point to remember is that the most useful tool is not always the strongest, but the tool that will feel best in the hand and with the work. From our experience of many other gardeners, The Garden Spade shown here is that tool.

The guarantee

A guarantee that the customer will get his money back if he is not satisfied is the usual method mail marketers employ to gain confidence. The guarantee should appear at the front of the catalog and on the order form, where the customer is reassured once again that he is not risking his money. Sometimes the guarantee is written with a certificate border.

Startling guarantees can greatly improve response with prospective customers. At Lawson Hill Leather and Shoe Co. we tested the idea of letting prospective customers wear our shoes ten days before making their decision on keeping them. This astonishing guarantee so increased confidence that we experienced a 25 percent sales increase over the same offer without the guarantee. The consequent reduction in the cost of selling to prospective customers offset many times the cost of the additional returns of worn shoes that we had to discard. But, when we made this same offer to our old customers, the sales improvement was minor, suggesting that they already had confidence in our merchandise.

Introduce the customer
to the guarantor

Your customer will have more confidence in buying from your catalog if he knows from whom he is buying. The customer does not want to buy from a nameless person representing a faceless corporation. The greatest specialty catalog success was built about the personality of Mr. L. L. Bean. Customers knew that Mr. Bean was running the company, supervising the quality of the merchandise, and testing its quality and usefulness during his hunting and fishing trips in the Maine woods. And, because the customers knew that he was a hunter and fisherman, they knew that what he put in his catalog would be right for them. His personality permeated the catalog. Products were often preceded with the possessive *Bean's*, as in "Bean's Camouflage Parkas." He was the authority who said the products were good and, if any of them should prove wanting, the guarantor that made them good. L. L. Bean, Inc. would not be the success it is today if it were not for the projection of Mr. Bean's personality into his catalog. Mr. Bean gave his customers confidence.

Gain confidence
by describing your setting

L. L. Bean was founded in and has always been in the state of Maine. Maine permeates the Bean catalog almost as much as does the personality of Mr. Bean. Shoes are referred to as "Freeport Walkers." Parkas are named "Baxter State Parka" (after Baxter State Park in central Maine) and "Bean's Katahdin Parka" (after the highest peak in Maine). The merchandise is tested in Maine, and the Maine setting coveys an unsophisticated country flavor. No one would say that the L. L. Bean catalog transported to New York City would do as well. The Maine country setting gives customers the confidence that they will not be taken by some sharp city slickers. But it is more than that. By knowing where Bean is located and visualizing the location, customers feel as though there is a place where they can go if things are not right.

French Creek Sheep and Wool Co. gains confidence in a similar manner with great effectiveness. They illustrate their stone barn, their sheep, their pastoral setting, and the people who live and work there. In so doing, they give assurance to would-be customers that they are honest folk living in a community that would have none other. The customers know where to find them if they must.

Don't use a post office
box number by itself

A post office box number in the address goes in the opposite direction of describing your setting. It is as unknown and mysterious as a Swiss bank account and conjures up images of furtive, shadowy men taking one's money and giving nothing in return. If you must use a box number, give a street address as well.

Convey authenticity

Some products are or can be designed to be authentic. When customers know something is authentic, their doubts are removed and they buy with confidence. The success in the British Isles Collection catalog of the R.A.F. flying jacket, despite its high price, can be attributed in part to its authenticity.

Write in the third person

When at British Isles Collection and at Lawson Hill Leather and Shoe Co., we had to make the decision as to what brand we would have put on the shoes being made for us in England; the choice was between our own brand and the manufacturer's. Loake Bros., the manufacturer, was scarcely known in our country at the time. We could easily have taken the opportunity to develop our own exclusive brand. But, if we did, we would have denied ourselves the opportunity of writing about Loake Bros. in the third person. Our enthusiasm about Loake's quality and value would seem to be nothing more than dealer puff if we wrote about ourselves. But writing in the third person about Loake Bros. shoes appeared to be objective and our praise genuine. I attribute much of our success in selling Loake shoes to our promoting their name instead of our own. Writing in the third person about Loake shoes created customer confidence that their quality was good.

Stress your customer service

Your customers may believe your quality is good and you are honest, but a bad experience with you or some other mail marketer may lose a customer for mail order forever. Make sure your order processing works smoothly, avoid out-of-stock situations all you can, and, when you are not able to ship something at once, notify your customer promptly with an apologetic letter. Answer every customer inquiry even if the goods have been shipped and crossed the customer's inquiry in the mail. As soon as possible, set up an on-line computer so you can give immediate answers to customers' order queries when they telephone.

Then, when your order processing and customer service works well, shout about it in your catalog. It gives customers confidence.

Don't let your customer service be nameless and faceless

Don't let your company appear to be a two-hundred-foot sponge upon which a swift kick will produce no effect whatsoever. Let your customers know the name of their customer service representative to write or call. As each new customer is added to the company's list, a letter should be sent from the customer service representative thanking him for his order and welcoming him to the company. In addition, the letter should say that he, the customer service representative, has been asked by the owner of the company to be the customer's own representative and that the customer should write or call him with questions about the merchandise and to solve any problems. To ensure that the customer knows the representative is a real person, I suggest that the representative have a business card with his picture on it and send it with the letter.

Some mail marketers might object that assigning customer service representatives to specific customers would increase costs and cause difficulties when the representatives left their employ. The initial letter, however, can be done by computer; the customer service representative need only sign it. If representatives should change, the company has the options of saying nothing until the customer orders again or writing the customer to notify him of the change. The latter option might be the best because an enclosure featuring some product can be included. The very act of writing customers stimulates activity; the enclosure would give customers a reason to buy once again.

Assigning customer service representatives to specific customers has many advantages. The most important one is that it puts the company's relationship with the customer on a personal basis, eliminating mail order's shortcoming of being impersonal. Customers will be impressed that there is a specific person to turn to for help; someone who will take orders, answer questions about the merchandise, and give them individual attention. It will build trust and loyalty and, consequently, will generate repeat and larger orders. The big payoff is greatly increased sales. The higher the average order and the more responsive the list of customers is, the more sense it makes to give customers personal service.

Another advantage is that the representative is elevated from being a mere representative to being a telephone salesperson as well. The way customers are treated on the phone can make a big difference in how much they will buy. With a computer sales can be tallied by customer service representatives, and bonuses can be paid according to performance.

A third advantage is that customer service representatives, by building up familiarity with their customers, will more speedily solve their customers' problems.

Following is a sample letter which could be generated by the computer and given to the customer service representative to sign. The letter could be combined with a new customer discount offer for a reorder (see Chapter 21, which discusses using the computer as a marketing tool).

Mrs. Robert Smith
25B Escondido Drive
Stanford, CA 94305

Dear Mrs. Smith:

We were happy to receive your order for the lambskin gloves and are delighted to have you as a new customer of British Isles Collection. I have checked with shipping, and they tell me that the lambskin gloves will go out to you today by United Parcel Service.

Traphagen Hill has asked that I personally watch over your account. Here at British Isles Collection we want our customers to feel that they will receive individual attention. If you have any queries about your order, please call me personally. If you wish to reorder by phone, I would be glad to take your order and answer any questions you might have about the merchandise. I am usually in the office Monday to Friday, 9 a.m. to 5 p.m., eastern time. Should I not be in, a fellow customer representative will be happy to help you.

Thank you for your order, Mrs. Smith, and welcome to British Isles Collection. I look forward to serving you again in the future.

Cordially,

Marie Baker

Your customer service
representative

P.S. Enclosed is my card which you can keep handy should you need help or want to place an order with me personally.

Like well-written copy, building customer confidence is a secret of mail-order success. The mail marketer should think of guarding merchandise quality, the guarantee, the portrayal of the guarantor and setting, the writing of believable copy, writing in the third person, and customer service as the factors that build customer confidence, not as individual, unrelated functions. Confidence lowers customer resistance and makes possible the acquisition of new customers. It generates more and larger reorders. The mail marketer should think of building customer confidence as a distinct concept and concentrate on it.

get your customers
to read your catalog
and use the order form

The Covers

As more and more catalogs crowd mailboxes, recipients will inevitably give less and less consideration to each individual catalog.[1] The mail marketer will be increasingly hard-pressed to get customers and prospective customers to look beyond the covers. His first task, therefore, is to gain attention, which can only be done by creating interest on the covers.

This simple statement says a lot. Obvious as it is, it deserves emphasis because so many catalog covers lack interest. Indeed, it appears that many mail marketers give only casual attention, or worse, delegate the design of and decision on the cover to someone whose main concern is something other than its sole function of selling merchandise. The covers are the first thing a customer sees. They determine whether or not he looks inside. Maybe all that is required to create interest is for the customer to identify the name and logotype. Other times, it is what is displayed on the cover. Whatever the case, it is almost always the cover that gets the customer in the catalog. Determining the design of the covers is no casual decision; top management must give the covers close attention and not leave them to someone else to decide upon.

**The center of interest
of the front cover**

For front covers the center of interest is usually one of these types:

1. Abstract designs
2. Pictorial scenes
3. Centers of interest that display merchandise but do not sell it

[1] Total consideration given to all catalogs and buying, however, should go up.

4. Centers of interest that sell merchandise

5. Centers of interest that are often wraps, that have some promotional device as sales, discount coupons, and sweepstakes.

The center of interest of a catalog front cover must be judged upon its ability to generate sales—the sales directly from the front cover plus the sales of merchandise inside the catalog that it generates by interesting the customer in looking beyond the covers.

Abstract Design Centers of Interest. These are designs with no literal meaning. If they are effective, it is because they create an image that possibly suggests the theme and mood of the catalog and interests the customer to look further. For most companies, the design cover is too abstract, its meaning escapes the recipient, and it does not generate sales effectively. One cannot deny that Horchow uses it and Horchow is successful. But for others to copy Horchow may not make sense; Horchow succeeds because of its leadership and many other reasons, of which the design cover is one probably insignificant reason.

Pictorial Centers of Interest. The pictorial center of interest is a picture of some subject matter that usually relates to what is being sold. If it is well-chosen, it will express the theme or create a mood. It is less abstract and more literal than the abstract design cover. In my opinion, they are usually weaker than covers that display merchandise. If it is to be effective, it must be a very arresting picture indeed. Furthermore, it must say "Look inside." I think it is difficult for a mail marketer to consistently find arresting pictures that will suck the customer into the catalog. L. L. Bean uses pictorial centers of interest that reinforce their image as retailers of hunting and fishing merchandise. But L. L. Bean is a special case; their catalog is so well-known that recipients do not need to be told what is inside. Furthermore, L. L. Bean has been using this form of cover for as long as I can remember. While it may be effective for them, there is no assurance that it will be effective for others.

The Merchandise Center of Interest. Merchandise should be the most interesting subject of a catalog. After all, few things interest people more than things they would like to have for themselves. Merchandise has added advantages in that it states what is inside the catalog and that whatever merchandise is illustrated on the cover will sell better when it is repeated on the inside. The dangers are that the merchandise might be atypical or uninteresting. Nevertheless, uninteresting merchandise might be more inviting than an uninteresting picture.

Centers of Interest That Directly Sell Merchandise. I doubt that anyone will write the last word on what makes the best cover, nor do I think that one type of cover is best for all catalogs or even that one type of cover is always best for one catalog company. I do think, however, that the catalog that sells merchandise directly off its front cover, if carefully done, is most often the best choice.

All the reasons for having merchandise on the cover apply. But, because the customer has the immediate opportunity to consider whether or not to purchase the items on the cover, he is in effect already inside the catalog. His interest is heightened because he is able to read the product description and see the price. He might decide that the product is not what he wants, but his interest is aroused in the merchandise and he then looks further.

Another reason is that the best selling space in the catalog is being used for selling. A product on the cover will sell three times as much as it will on the inside.[2] The only reason for not selling on the cover is that whatever is put in its place will confer a benefit to the rest of the catalog, making up for the lost sales.

The argument against selling off the cover is that it degrades the catalog. I admit that some covers from which merchandise is sold do, indeed, look "junky" and degrade the catalogs. Merchandise is randomly arranged, copy is all over the place, and there is no eyeflow.[3] But when it is tastefully done with smooth eyeflow, selling off the cover detracts so little from the catalog that it is more than offset by the additional interest created and sales generated.

This is what we did at British Isles Collection, and few will argue that our sales per catalog were not amongst the highest obtained. Figure 5-1 shows a cover layout that sells merchandise. It has good eyeflow and is tastefully done.

FIGURE 5-1 Layout of a Cover That Sells Merchandise

[2] One consulting client of mine regularly switches merchandise from the inside to the cover and then back again from catalog to catalog. Each time something goes onto the cover, sales go up three times from what they were on the inside.

[3] See Chapter 8, "Does Bad Eye Flow Cripple Your Pages?"

A variation of selling off the cover is to illustrate some merchandise on the cover and then refer the customer to the selling copy block on the inside front cover or to the page inside the catalog where it is repeated. This dresses up the cover somewhat, but the picture of the merchandise is not truly interesting without the price and description, which require some effort to find.

41

get your customers to read
your catalog and use the
order form

The promotional center of interest

The promotional center of interest can be a sale, discount coupon, or sweep-stakes. The sale and discount coupon are effective devices to get a person who already is a customer inside the catalog. They are not effective with list rental prospects because these people are not familiar with the company's values and do not know if the sale or discount is genuine.

Sweepstakes can get people who are addicted to that sort of thing into the catalog but, for many mail marketers, create an undesirable image and repel other prospective customers. People who become customers because they are attracted by sweepstakes do not follow up well unless they are given another sweepstakes offer. Companies that develop too many customers by sweepstakes find that they are trapped into having to offer sweepstakes indefinitely because their customer list does not respond well without it.

Conveying a sense of change with the cover

The cover heralds what follows inside the catalog. For the would-be reader to be interested, the cover must proclaim newness. The thought of seeing something new interests the reader. For this reason, the mail marketer must take care that a cover does not look too much like the preceding one. This is particularly true when the catalog is being mailed to existing customers. Covers can be changed and given a new look by varying the picture (that is, the center of interest), by changing the merchandise, and by changing the background or background colors. The important thing is that the cover be visually and memorably different.

At Lawson Hill Leather and Shoe Co. we could afford to inventory only one line of merchandise for each Fall-Winter and each Spring-Summer season because we had so many stockkeeping units. Yet we mailed our customers three regular catalogs and one sale catalog per season. We varied the covers during the season, but the content remained the same. We changed the merchandise illustrated on the cover for each issue, but since the customer might not remember what merchandise was displayed previously, we also changed the background color that surrounded the photograph. The new color would be far away on the color wheel from the previous color and would, if possible, be suggestive of the season (for example, spring green in the spring). The color change made a great visual impact and, therefore, was more effective than merely changing merchandise.

One time we changed to an entirely different manner of displaying and photographing the merchandise. The change was striking, and what we did was attractive. We split-run tested catalogs having the new cover with catalogs having a cover of the older style. We were flabbergasted to find that the catalog with the new cover outsold the catalog with the older-style cover by 30 percent. While the new one might have been more appealing, my conclusion is that newness, more than anything else, is what contributed to its success. But whatever the reason, let no one doubt the need to pay close attention to the design of the cover.

The cover should convey change. It should convey change of catalog, and it should also convey a change of season. A change of season means that once again a customer has to change his or her wardrobe, purchase gifts, do holiday entertaining, take on new responsibilities, or engage in new sports. The realization that the season has or is about to change is stimulating to the customer and stimulates sales.

Mail marketers know this, and they usually change the merchandise and change the wording on the cover from "Fall" to "Spring" at the very least. But my feeling is that the change of season is often not conveyed with sufficient force. I say this because, as I look back, I feel that the covers of many of my own catalogs did not alert my customers that a change of season was upon them and that they should be thinking of new shoes for the coming season. I changed styles of footwear on the covers from boots to sandals and back again, but often I did little more.

A catalog mailed in November should symbolically say Christmas. Holly and red berries might adorn a catalog—they will say Christmas better than the word *Christmas* itself. By saying Christmas on the cover, the customer is reminded that Christmas is coming, that he had better start thinking about it, and that he had ought to at least save the catalog. He is told that inside the catalog he can find Christmas presents to give and things he can use during the season.

Similarly, saying spring, fall, winter, or summer, both literally and symbolically, stimulates customer thought toward their needs for the coming season. Symbols of spring are flowers; fall, pumpkins and leaves; summer, water and beaches, and winter, snow. Well-chosen symbols exert a strong influence and announce the coming season even better than words.

I must caution, however, that the function of such symbols is to announce a change in season and thus stimulate buying interest. Decoration is not a function or an end. The symbols must not be allowed to dominate the cover, submerging the most interesting thing of all—the merchandise.

Elements of the cover

If the center of interest and the look of the cover must keep changing, there is one thing in the catalog that must not vary. That is the logotype. Visually, it must always be the same: it must always be written the same way, in the same colors, and in the same location on the catalog cover. The logotype retains the identity of the catalog; it is what prevents the customer from confusing it with another catalog. When R.E.I. Coop changes the style of writing its name from catalog to catalog, it condemns itself to anonymity.

Besides the logotype and the center of interest, the elements of the cover should usually include the credit-card-charge availability, the issue such as "Fall-Winter 1983," a statement of the theme, and sometimes the telephone number. Giving the credit-card-charge availability tells the viewer that he has credit and to look further.

Choosing Merchandise for the Cover. Where merchandise is in the illustration on the front cover, great care must be used in its selection. Often, appropriate merchandise is hard to decide upon. Cover merchandise must be representative of broad categories of merchandise and of the catalog as a whole. It should appeal to many people, yet it should be unusual and interesting. It must be appropriate for the season. If the catalog is to be mailed to customers, then the merchandise must also be new. If, however, the catalog is to go to list-rental prospects, then selecting proven winners for the cover reduces risk.

The Back Cover. For most catalog companies, merchandise is sold on the back cover. When one decides against selling merchandise on the back cover, one loses the opportunity of conveying to the prospective customer the type of merchandise on the inside. Interest is lost, and so is the opportunity to sell merchandise. The mail marketer should remember that the back cover should sell twice as much as an inside page. Interesting merchandise on the back cover will not only sell well, but also get customers interested in the catalog merchandise and to look inside the covers. All the considerations that apply to selecting merchandise for the front cover apply as well to the back cover.

43

get your customers to read
your catalog and use the
order form

Get Your Customer Through Your Catalog

Having gotten the prospective customer into the catalog, the mail marketer's next task is to sustain the customer's interest and keep him leafing through. One item of interesting merchandise will quicken his interest in the merchandise that lies in the pages beyond. If the pages are well-organized and not confusing, they will be easy to look at and the customer will not turn away. Headlines that lead the prospective customer into the copy keep the customer going further. If there are subheads, the customer will be drawn through the copy blocks.

Place the most interesting merchandise on the pages where the customer looks first

People look inside catalogs because they want to see if there is anything that they would like to own. More than anything else, the merchandise makes a catalog interesting. The most interesting merchandise, usually the most desirable, should, therefore, be placed on the inside pages where the prospective customer looks first. These pages are the beginning pages where the merchandise is first shown, the back inside cover and the page opposite, and the pages in the center fold. If the order form is not bound in the center but somewhere between the center and the covers, then the catalog may naturally fall open at that point, creating preferred pages opposite the order form on which to put particularly interesting merchandise.

While the merchandiser must use his best judgment in selecting interesting merchandise for these pages, there are some guidelines for him to follow. Obviously, for people who have never seen the catalog before, the best sellers are usually the most interesting; for this reason these should be located on the best pages. Sometimes an item is quite interesting but for some reason, such as high cost or limited practical use, does not sell well. The authentic Wilkinson swords that we carried at the British Isles Collection are an example. Other times an item sells well because it is so utilitarian but is otherwise quite dull. In these cases the merchandiser must decide between interesting items and best sellers, which can be a quandary because it is also a rule, to be discussed later, that the best sellers should also be located on the best pages. In the case of the Wilkinson swords, we decided that they made the whole catalog interesting and located them in the front.

For catalogs going to one's house list, however, the most interesting merchandise is often not the proven best sellers but rather the new items. If a mail marketer has a different catalog going to his house list than to list rental and respondents to media advertising, then the best pages for the catalogs going to customers should have a high proportion of new merchandise, although it is still a good idea to have some proven winners on those pages. If, however, the catalog is going to list rental and respondents to media advertising, then the best pages should have proven winners. If the catalog goes to both the house list and outside names, then the best pages should have a mixture of proven winners and new merchandise.

Make your catalog interesting reading

One comment often made about the British Isles Collection catalog was that it was interesting reading. People claimed that they read it from cover to cover; others said that it read like a novel. We knew that people were reading it because in their correspondence they referred to subjects buried deep in the copy text. We were fortunate, of course, that a catalog on British shoes and clothing lent itself to writing about romance, tradition, and history. We took advantage of this opportunity to weave items of historical interest into the copy to make the catalog more interesting. Copy to describe our kilts, for example, was preceded by copy describing the origin of clans and tartans:

> From just before the Christian era, repeated invasions of the British Isles by the Romans and later the Anglo-Saxons drove the Celts, who had been living there, into the most inhospitable corners of the Isles, such as the northwesterly islands and highlands of Scotland. There, these people were isolated from one another by the mountains and the sea. Each isolated group became a clan, and in the course of time the custom of wearing tartans arose, with chief's pattern, called a sett, being worn by his followers. Originally, the patterns were muted and served as camouflage. These muted types are called hunting tartans. Later, brighter hues were woven into dress tartans. A clan could have both a hunting and a dress tartan. A tartan is always woven from threads of unbroken color, and the pattern of the weft is the same as the warp.

Sometimes we selected products because the story we could tell would make our catalog more interesting. We did this with the Wilkinson swords, which permitted us to tell the story of the last cavalry charge made by the British Army at the Battle of Omdurman, in which Winston Churchill participated, and in so telling allowed us to glorify the source of the shoes and clothing that we were selling.

What we did by writing copy about the story of our product to make our catalog more interesting could be similarly done by other mail-order companies more often than it is. Williams-Sonoma, a mail-order firm selling kitchenware and tableware for the gourmet, writes on page three of their catalog:

> *A Culinary Note from Chuck Williams on Coffee*
> I think it can safely be said that America is a coffee drinking nation, so it is only natural that a good percentage of our coffee drinkers develop a sincere interest in the taste and enjoyment of good coffee as well as the mechanics of making it. Really good coffee depends on the quality of the bean, the roasting, the method of grinding and brewing and even the water. From time to time, new brewing techniques are developed for the home but little has been done about roasting coffee at home. Green, or unroasted, coffee beans keep almost indefinitely but once roasted, they immediately start to lose flavor. This is why some stores specializing in bulk coffee roast beans almost every day. It is something one should be able to do at home, too. A simple home roasting technique has been developed by the Palani Coffee Plantation people (see p. 46) making it possible to blend and roast green beans in your home oven as

you need them, then grind and brew the freshly roasted coffee for the ultimate in coffee drinking pleasure.

Bon Appetit.

45

get your customers to read
your catalog and use the
order form

Here Chuck Williams has talked about the requirements for making good coffee and the need for freshly roasted beans. To the gourmet cook, this is informative and interesting reading. It was placed on page 3 but referred the reader to page 46 where not only were the coffee roasting trays sold but other coffee-related items; thus Chuck Williams adroitly got his reader deeper into the catalog.

Again Williams-Sonoma precedes the copy selling a product with some interesting information about *crème fraiche*:

Almost every other recipe in the "nouvelle cuisine" calls for crème fraiche—fresh cream that has been allowed to thicken, developing a fine, full flavor. (No added sugar is needed when used "as is" with desserts.) It keeps for a long time and does not curdle when added to a bubbling sauce and reduced. It's very easy to make with our SOLAIT™ KITCHEN DAIRY which holds cream mixed with crème fraiche starter at the correct temperature until the thickening and culturing process is complete. Ideal for making yogurt, buttermilk, cottage cheese, sour cream or even cheese. The non-electric, two-piece KITCHEN DAIRY has a 1 qt. glass liner and comes with a dairy thermometer, full instructions, a packet of yogurt, cheese and crème fraiche starter and a recipe book.

Elsewhere in the catalog, Williams-Sonoma gives recipes for *fromage blanc*, broccoli quiche, walnut-apple salad, guacomole, and many others. It is a well-done catalog that must certainly hold the interest of the gourmet throughout its pages. It is not surprising that they are successful.

To get your customer through your catalog, make it easy to read

In a book, one paragraph follows another and chapter follows chapter in a well-ordered pattern. But in a catalog, paragraphs of uneven size are interspersed with pictures of varying dimension and shape. It all can be very confusing, with the eye not knowing where to go next. Confusion tires the reader and, no matter how interesting the product and copy, tends to deflect his attention.

What I am talking about is eye flow. Good eye flow exists when all the important elements of a page gain the reader's attention. Because the reader's attention is gained and held throughout the page, it is also there when the page is turned, and tends, if the products displayed and copy are interesting, to keep him looking at pages and leafing through the catalog. I call attention to eye flow here because of its function of sustaining reader interest, but because of the breadth of the topic and its other functions I treat it separately in Chapter 8.

Some other tips on making your catalog easy to read

Copy blocks should be made easy to read with interesting headlines that also serve the function of showing the reader where to start reading. If the copy block is long, it is wise to break it down into two or more paragraphs that are easier to read. Subheads may also be used to carry the reader's attention through long copy blocks.

Make sure your typefaces are easy to read. Eight-point type is the best compromise between legibility and the need to prevent the type from consuming too much space. Serif types, such as Times Roman and English Times, are much easier to read than the sans serifs, such as Helvetica. Whenever possible, avoid reverse type (where the letters are unprinted and the space around them is printed). White against dark is much harder to read, and should the press registration be off even a few thousandths of an inch, the type space will be filled up with one of the colors that surround it.

Make sure that the copy is easily related to the picture of the product it describes. This can be done by placing the copy near the picture or using a key system, in which a letter or number is placed upon the picture and the relevant copy block. In the key system, the copy blocks should follow in the same sequence that the reader naturally views the pictures. (I've seen catalogs where the eye has had to zigzag back and forth and up and down to follow the descriptive copy in the products' natural viewing sequence.) A good test is to try to order the products from the page yourself to see if it can be easily done.

Make sure stock numbers, sizes, and prices are clear. A format that I like is: **067** Curly lamb coat. Sizes: 6, 8, 10, 12, 14 & 16 **$395**. The extra-bold stock number sets off this part of the copy from the rest, and the price in extra-bold type provides finality to the paragraph.

Speaking of stock numbers, we always had a saying at my companies that we would never let operating convenience interfere with sales. Every now and then one of us would come up with an idea for a stock number that would make it easy to identify the product when reading computer reports or have some other operating benefit. But these stock numbers would inevitably involve many digits. Many digits means more numbers to confuse customers. Furthermore, they consume much valuable space that could be put to better use. Keep your stock numbers down to three or four digits at most.

Make Your Order Form Easy and Pleasing to Use

The object of all one's efforts in the mail-order business is to get the catalog reader to use the order form. It is amazing, therefore, to see that most order forms are not only unattractive, but look like and are as difficult to fill out as the Internal Revenue Service's Form 1040.

Although I doubt that anyone has tested the selling power of a catalog with a difficult-to-fill-out order form against the same catalog with an easy-to-fill-out order form, there is no doubt that a difficult-to-fill-out order form is a sales deterrent and perhaps a significant one. Many people just don't like forms or are just too lazy to use them. This, in fact, is one of the reasons why telephone ordering has increased so much in recent years. Why, then, shouldn't the mail marketer spend considerable effort to design the order form so that it is pleasing and easy-to-use?

I have seen order forms that read sideways and order forms that are hard to find. Gate flaps on the order form (an extra flap on the order form) are often spot pasted down to cover the ordering section, the instructions, or both. A few order forms even require the customer to construct his own envelope. Some order forms are hard to total; others have complex and needlessly long instructions. Many have a poor flow from one ordering step to another and require the eye to zigzag about the form to fill it out. These defects are all needless sales deterrents. It is clear that these forms were designed by the operations department, *not* the sales department.

Order forms should be so simply designed that few or no instructions are necessary. The very existence of instructions suggest a patch effort to remedy a defective order form. Instructions are a bother to the customer; and, even if they are redundant, the customer feels compelled to read them through. Keep your instructions to a minimum.

How else can you make your order form easy to fill out? Besides keeping instructions to a minimum, here are a few suggestions: Have the steps to filling it out go from top to bottom, not both sideways and top to bottom. Tint the areas that the customer does not have to fill out with very pale green (10% screen), leaving in white relief the areas that must be filled out. Number the steps with large numbers (18 or 24 point). Put any instructions near the spot to be filled out. If you mail your catalog in an envelope, bind your order form into the catalog. A loose one will get lost and then your customer cannot order. Don't make your customer make his own envelope; don't make the customer turn the catalog sideways in order to fill it out, and, above all, don't have the instructions located so the customer cannot see both the order blank and the instructions at the same time. When you are finished, give the order form to a young child and see if he can fill it out with ease.

Even when you have made your order form simple, it can still be quite forbidding. For most catalogs the form is a white, antiseptic sheet of paper in sharp contrast to the colorful and attractive catalog that surrounds it.

Why not make the order form attractive too? Couldn't order forms receive the same artistic consideration given to the catalog? Why not use pink paper for the order forms for women's catalogs, or, if that is too expensive, why not print a feminine design on the order form, perhaps a garland of flowers around the border? At British Isles Collection, we had the order form background simulate a piece of parchment. But I have seen no other catalog where any significant effort was made to make the order form look attractive, yet attract the customer to the order form is what the mail marketers must do.

A word about spot-pasting. Printers will have you go to great lengths to make sure that a gate flap does not fall down and jam on the carrying chain of the binder while being stapled into the catalog. Leave it up to the printers and they will have you place a spot of glue on both the top and bottom of the gate flap to securely cover up the order form or whatever else is underneath. The big disadvantage is that whatever is underneath will get no casual attention, for the customer must make a conscious effort to unstick it, sometimes with a considerable tearing action.

My own feeling is that spot-pasting is often a needless precaution taken for the convenience of the printer, and that it is another case where someone's operating convenience has been allowed to interfere with sales. I have had many catalogs printed with gate flaps without spot-pasting that caused no trouble that was ever reported to me. If your printer insists upon spot-pasting a gate flap, have him use only one spot of paste, putting it where it will be cut off when the catalog is trimmed in the printer's bindery.

The Sole Objective of the Mail Marketer

The sole objective of the mail marketer is to induce the catalog recipient to use the order form or, alternatively, to use the telephone. He must think

47

get your customers to read
your catalog and use the
order form

in terms of the steps that the catalog recipient takes to become a customer and what he, the mail marketer, must do to bring this about. In a mailbox that is crowded with other catalogs and other mail, his catalog's covers must attract the attention of the recipient and interest him in looking inside. Once inside, the interest of the recipient, who has now become a reader, must be sustained from page to page. And, finally, the mail marketer must do everything possible to ease the transition from reading to ordering. If the mail marketer thinks in these terms, he will discover one of the secrets of catalog mail-order success.

spending more money on your catalog and making it bigger

Does it pay to increase the catalog size and the number of stockkeeping units? This question should be asked and answered by every mail marketer.

Fixed and variable costs of a catalog

The first step toward finding an answer to that question is for the mail marketer to determine which catalog costs remain fixed and which catalog costs are variable as the number of pages is increased. Table 6-1 shows the costs in the mail of an 8½ × 11 inch four-color catalog printed on 50-ounce paper and what happens to those costs when 16 pages are added to a 32-page catalog and also to a 64-page catalog. The costs in this table are likely estimates based upon my experience. I held the weight of the paper constant regardless of the number of pages. It could be reasonably argued, however, that the bigger catalogs should be printed on lighter paper, possibly keeping the heavier weight on the outer 8 or 16 pages, thus saving on both paper and postage costs.

The important thing to note is that increasing a 32-page catalog by 16 pages results in a 16 percent increase in costs with a 50 percent increase in selling space, but adding 16 pages to a 64-page catalog results in a 25 percent increase in selling space with a 21 percent increase in cost. The principle to be observed is that small catalogs can be helped more than big ones and there is a diminishing relative improvement as catalog pages are added to increasingly larger catalogs.

Does it pay to increase the size of the catalog?

Whether it pays to increase the number of pages of a catalog, however, depends upon (1) the percent business goes up with an increase in selling

TABLE 6-1   Costs of Catalogs in the Mail*

	32-PAGE CATALOG	48-PAGE CATALOG	64-PAGE CATALOG	80-PAGE CATALOG
Printing of catalog	13.0¢	18.8¢	24.6¢	30.4¢
Printing of order form with gate fold	2.7	2.7	2.7	2.7
Cost of putting catalog in mail	1.1	1.1	1.1	1.1
Cost of merging and purging names including piggyback labels	1.2	1.2	1.2	1.2
Postage	9.5	9.5	13.4	18.3
List rental	8.3	8.3	8.3	8.3
	35.8	41.5	51.3	62.0
Percent increase in cost over next size smaller catalog	–	16%	23%	21%
Percent increase in active selling space over next size smaller catalog		50%	33%	25%

*These costs do not include catalog preparation costs.

space, (2) the sales per catalog for the unincreased catalog, (3) the increase in the cost of the catalog, and (4) the variable costs of the business (the cost of the merchandise plus operating expenses, such as shipping cartons and labor, that go up or down with a change in sales).

The percent that sales go up depends upon how effectively one uses the additional space. The rationale for adding space is that one can offer more merchandise, which means there is a better chance a customer will see something that he will buy. Furthermore, there is some merchandise that can be sold proportionately better with increased space. Obviously, to maximize the sales improvement, one must have proportionately more merchandise, or one must use the additional space effectively to better present existing merchandise. In addition, the added merchandise should overlap the appeal of existing merchandise as little as possible while continuing to satisfy the customer's interests toward which the catalog is directed.

So how much do sales go up with more pages? I don't know of any conclusive tests, but the rule of thumb I have always used was taught me by Louis Leber, a consultant who helped me immensely during my early years in mail order. The rule is that when the number of pages is increased by a certain percent, sales will go up by half that percent. This rule of thumb assumes that the additional catalog space is used with equal effectiveness as the rest of the catalog. When we increased the British Isles Collection catalog to 32 pages, I used this rule in making my projections. We came within one percent of projections, which suggests that the rule is not far off but does not prove it because of other variables that affected the results.

To answer our question "Does it pay to increase the size of the catalog?" I have so far talked of percents. I have done so because I wished to show how increased pages act upon a catalog's sales. But a percent cannot be used to pay printing bills. The question is does the percent improvement act upon a catalog with a high-sales-per-catalog or a low-sales-per-catalog? The higher the sales per catalog a catalog enjoys, the bigger it can be made.

Our question "Does it pay to increase the size of the catalog?" is answered if we make a calculation of the expected change in profit by subtracting the additional catalog cost from the additional profit contribution generated by the increased sales. The additional profit contribution is the sales of the unincreased catalog multiplied by the expected percent sales increase and by one minus the percent variable expenses of the business, the percents being expressed as a decimal.[1]

This can be expressed mathematically:

Profit change = Additional contribution − Increased catalog cost
$$\Delta P = (\% \, S) \, S \, (1 - V) - \Delta C$$

where:

ΔP = the change in profit
$\%S$ = the percent increase in sales resulting from the increase in pages
S = the sales of the unincreased catalog
V = the variable business costs as a percent of sales but expressed as a decimal (these costs would be variable operating expenses[2] and merchandise)
ΔC = the increase in catalog costs

Example. The interaction of the factors of catalog size, the percent increased cost of going to more pages, the sales per catalog of the unincreased catalog, and the variable costs of the business is shown on Table 6-2 for a catalog that is increased from 64 to 80 pages. Taking our costs from Table 6-1, the additional cost of increasing a catalog from 64 to 80 pages is

$$\$620/M - \$513/M = \$107/M$$

TABLE 6-2   Change in Profit as a Result of Adding 16 Pages to a 64-Page Catalog

Sales/M 64-Page Catalog	Sales/M 80-Page Catalog	Sales Increase	Variable Costs	Increase in Catalog Contribution	Increases in Catalog Costs	Increase in Profit (Loss)
$ 750	$ 843.75	$ 93.75	40%	$ 56.25	$107	($ 50.75)
750	843.75	93.75	50	46.88	107	(60.13)
750	843.75	93.75	60	37.50	107	(56.25)
1,000	1,125.00	125.00	40	75.00	107	(32.00)
1,000	1,125.00	125.00	50	62.50	107	(44.50)
1,000	1,125.00	125.00	60	50.00	107	(57.00)
1,500	1,687.50	187.50	40	112.50	107	5.50
1,500	1,687.50	187.50	50	97.75	107	(9.25)
1,500	1,687.50	187.50	60	75.00	107	(32.00)
2,000	2,250.00	250.00	40	150.00	107	43.00
2,000	2,250.00	250.00	50	125.00	107	18.00
2,000	2,250.00	250.00	60	100.00	107	(7.00)
3,000	3,375.00	375.00	40	225.00	107	118.00
3,000	3,375.00	375.00	50	187.50	107	80.50
3,000	3,375.00	375.00	60	150.00	107	43.00
5,000	5,625.00	625.00	40	375.00	107	268.00
5,000	5,625.00	625.00	50	312.50	107	205.50
5,000	5,625.00	625.00	60	250.00	107	143.00

[1] There is one factor that is not taken into account in this profit change calculation and that I have avoided in order not to complicate the discussion. Increased pages means more stock-keeping units and usually more inventory, which in turn could mean more expense and lower turnover. Needless to say, one must consider what happens to inventory when one increases the size of a catalog.

[2] Variable operating expenses are expenses, such as shipping, which increase as sales increase. See Chapter 14.

51

spending more money on
your catalog and making
it bigger

We assume that our rule of thumb that sales go up by half the percent increase in the number of pages holds true; this means that in going from 64 pages to 80 pages (a 25 percent increase) sales will go up 12.5 percent. This table was calculated using the formula given above, for the change in profit.

What is made evident by Table 6-2 is that as sales per catalog go up, it becomes more and more profitable to increase catalog size. Similarly, as variable costs go down, it becomes more and more profitable to increase catalog size. What also can be seen from these calculations is that in larger catalogs it is particularly advantageous to lighten paper in order to save on paper and postage costs, thus lowering the increase of catalog costs.

Frequently, the variable business cost percent, the sales of the unincreased catalog, and the cost of increasing the catalog size is predetermined for a mail marketer. What he needs to know is the percent sales increase he must have in order for the increase in the catalog size to break even. Our formula solved for the percent increase in sales is:

$$\%S = \frac{\Delta P + \Delta C}{S\,(1 - V)}$$

Since to break-even with an increase in the size of the catalog means a zero profit change, our formula becomes:

$$\%S = \frac{\Delta C}{S\,(1 - V)}$$

For example, if our increased catalog cost is $107/M, sales of the unincreased catalog is $1,800/M, and variable business expenses are 45%, then:

$$\%S = \frac{107}{1,800\,(1 - .45)} = .108$$

In other words, a decision to increase the catalog size will neither add to nor subtract from profit if sales go up by 10.8 percent.

Spending more money
to make a better catalog

In talking about the economics of increasing the number of pages and how greater sales per catalog justifies more pages, we are actually considering a special case. The general rule is that the more sales per catalog one receives, the more money one can and should spend to make the catalog better.

There are two ways, besides increasing size, one can spend more money to make a better catalog: (1) one can spend more money on catalog preparation, mostly better photography and better color separations, and (2) one can spend more money on paper. My observation is that a business quickly reaches a volume where it does not pay to save money on photography and color separations at the expense of good representation of the product.

Paper is a different matter. Mail-order companies that have large volumes mail more catalogs. Paper costs go up with an increase in sales, so the cost of paper cannot be escaped by a mere increase in volume. It can only be escaped by increased sales per catalog. Costly paper, if it increases sales, can be used when the sales per catalog are high and cannot be used when low.

Paper can increase sales two ways. First, it can increase sales because the luxury, feel, and gloss of the paper subliminally convey an impression of quality and worth that the catalog reader unconsciously transfers to the product. Second, better paper will print better, resulting in a better representation of the product and thus producing more sales. When paper with a high, uniform gloss is used, each printing dot retains its identity and shape; but, when paper with lower gloss is used, the dots tend to merge, creating a muddy effect.

Conclusions on Spending More Money to Make a Better Catalog

It may seem obvious that spending more money in the form of more pages, better preparation, and better paper should be considered in the light of a profit change calculation and that it is hardly worth devoting a chapter to it. Indeed, most mail marketers will give lip service to the concept, and yet very often they do not think through the concept to its ultimate conclusions.

How many mail marketers systematically try to determine the optimum size of their catalog? If there has been a change in the sales per catalog or an increase in the cost per catalog, do they make a new calculation and think through whether they should increase or diminish the size of their catalog? I suspect that many times the size of one year's catalog is chosen because that is what it was the year before.

A logical conclusion is that catalogs mailed to buyers should be bigger and have more merchandise than catalogs mailed to list rental prospects. After all, buyers produce more sales per catalog.

Similarly, catalogs mailed to buyers should be printed on better paper than those mailed to list rental prospects. If one experiences high sales per catalog, then perhaps one's order form should be printed in color instead of black on white. Perhaps the order form paper should be better.

Part

two

Build Strong Dynamics
Through Better Graphics

---

catalog analysis and design

A sound catalog mail-order business is no accident. It is the result of careful planning and design from its inception. Like a well-designed house, it starts with a central idea that develops into a plan. That central idea is the concept of the business and its theme; it constitutes the foundation of the catalog's dynamics—the forces that drive the catalog in the marketplace. It is supported and developed by the merchandise, copy, devices to build customer confidence, methods of getting customers into the catalog and sustaining their interest, and the optimum catalog size.

But, as strong and as well-supported as the concept of the business with its theme might be, it can be emasculated through poor graphics and catalog design. The catalog must be designed so that each item of merchandise gets its optimum share of the catalog space and, taking into consideration the other merchandise, be located most advantageously. Each page must be laid out so all important elements gain the reader's attention. Photographs must show the merchandise to its best advantage, so it jumps right off the page into the reader's consciousness. Color separations, with which the printer makes his printing plates, must closely equal the photograph and, where the photograph is deficient, they should improve upon it. Finally, printing must retain what has been achieved in the color separations.

Catalog Analysis

The starting point of this graphics and design process is the analysis of the sales results of previously mailed catalogs. With that knowledge, one can decide which items to retain or drop, which categories to expand or reduce, and how much space should be allocated to each. The object of this analysis and decision making is the maximization of the profit produced by the catalog. The analysis must, therefore, be so organized as to show how the space occupied by each item of merchandise contributed to or subtracted from profit. When well-organized, the analysis virtually makes merchandise and space allocation decisions for you. The analysis should take into account all catalog costs and all sales produced by it and should, therefore, lock right into the profit and loss statement. The analysis that I use and present here is one that was taught to me by Louis Leber.

The Publicity Cost and Profit
Contribution Analysis of a Catalog

The end results of the publicity cost and profit contribution analysis of a catalog are a study of the sales and the cost of the space allocated to each item and a contribution index, which is the contribution, expressed as a percent, of each item towards overhead and profit. This contribution index takes into account the mark-up in the net sales of each item, from which the cost of its space is subtracted. The index for each item can be compared with the catalog average and with what is needed to operate the business, and decisions can be made as to whether an item is to be retained or dropped and whether more or less space is to be given to it.

The contribution index is shown in the right-hand column of Table 7-1 for four items of a typical catalog page illustrated in Figure 7-1. As can be seen, the down vest contributes the same percent of sales as the catalog as a whole. Something, however, will have to be done about the outdoor jacket because it did not contribute enough to cover the cost of its space. The overcoats are inadequate, but the shooting shirts are far above average. The page as a whole is better than the catalog as a whole.

The first step in making the analysis is to add up all publicity expenses. These expenses are all the costs of putting the catalogs in the mail, including printing, postage, list rental charges paid to list owners, order envelope and order form costs, and preparation costs such as photography, layout, design, color separating, and typography. Added to this should be any media advertising expenses (cost of advertisements in magazines and newspapers) that produce sales in the catalog.[1] If the catalog is the only one mailed during the season, the total of all these expenses should be the same number that appears opposite the item of Publicity Expense on the profit and loss statement. In our example, the total publicity expense is $467,352.

This total of the publicity costs is then divided by the number of pages in the catalog that directly sell specific product. The catalog analyzed in Table 7-1 is a 32-page catalog. However, not all of the 32 pages directly sell product. The institutional pages do not sell specific product—just the catalog as a whole. The logotype and some of the other elements of the cover are general and do not apply to specific merchandise, as does the address block on the back cover. All the space devoted to these general items must be subtracted from the total page count. Added to the total page count, however, is space on the order form that is devoted to selling. In our example, the total page count works out to be 34 pages. When the 34 pages are divided into the total publicity expense of $467,352, we arrive at a publicity cost per page devoted to merchandise of $13,741. If we work out the fraction of a page devoted to each product expressed as a decimal, we can arrive at the cost of its space. The space occupied by the overcoats in our example was 0.32 of a page and cost $0.32 \times \$13,741 = \$4,397$.

---

[1] To avoid needlessly complicating the discussion, I have assumed that no sales are made directly off advertisements in magazines and newspapers.

FIGURE 7-1 Publicity Cost and Profit Contribution of a Catalog Page

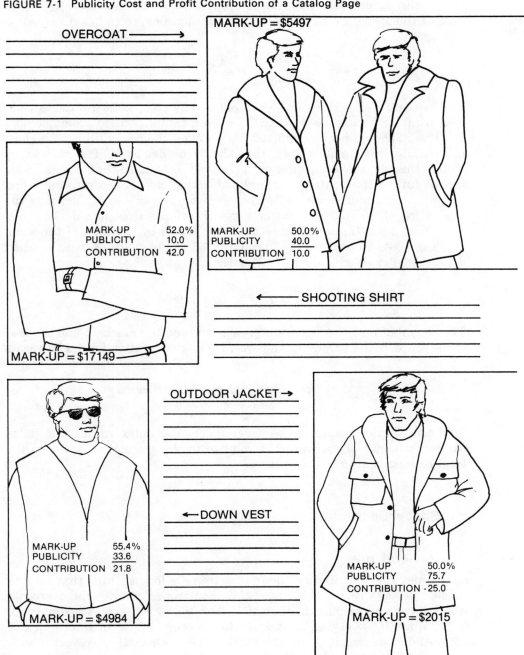

TABLE 7-1 Publicity Cost and Profit Contribution Analysis of a Catalog Page

PAGE	DESCRIPTION	STYLE NUMBER	NET SALES	FRACTION OF PAGE	COST OF SPACE	MARK-UP	MARK-UP %	PUBLICITY COST	CONTRIBUTION %
10	Men's Overcoat	101	6,043	.32	4,397	5,497	50.0	40.0	10.0
	Women's Coat	102	4,950						
			10,993						
10	Tan Shooting Shirt	103	15,080	.24	3,298	17,149	52.0	10.0	42.0
	Blue Shooting Shirt	104	10,500						
	Red Shooting Shirt	105	7,400						
			32,980						
10	Down Vest	106	8,997	.22	3,023	4,984	55.4	33.6	21.8
10	Outdoor Jacket	107	4,030	.22	3,023	2,015	50.0	75.0	−25.0
	Page Total		57,000	1.00	13,741	29,645	52.0	24.0	28.0
	Total Catalog		1,391,868	3,400	467,352	770,646	55.4	33.6	21.8

Sales of the overcoats were $10,993. If we divide this number into the cost of the space, we have the cost of the space expressed as a percent of sales:

$$\frac{\text{Cost of Space}}{\text{Net Sales}} = \frac{4,397}{10,993} = 40.0\%$$

The sales used should be net sales; that is, any returns for refunds should be subtracted from gross demand.[2] However, refunds due to avoidable non-fulfillment should not be deducted. If, however, the nonfulfillment is characteristic of the product, then they should be deducted. The philosophy behind this is that the objective of the analysis is to make the right decisions for the future. If an outage of merchandise that caused nonfulfillment and consequent refunds is avoidable in the future, one should not penalize the evaluation of the item by subtracting such refunds from its sales.

Mark-up is the actual gross profit produced by the sales of the item. The overcoats in our example produced $5,497 of mark-up which, when divided by net sales, is 50% of net sales:

$$\frac{\text{Mark-Up}}{\text{Net Sales}} = \frac{5,497}{10,993} = 50\%$$

The contribution index is the difference between the mark-up and the cost of the space, both expressed as a percent. The contribution for the overcoats is:

$$\text{Mark-Up} - \text{Cost of Space} = \text{Contribution}$$
$$50\% - 40\% = 10\%$$

This contribution, expressed as a percent, is the index one uses to judge the performance of each product relative to the space it occupies, to the total catalog, and to desired results.

Making Merchandise and Space Decisions

The general rule

Sometimes the contribution index is extremely low, such as that for the outdoor jacket with an index of −25%. Sometimes, as with the overcoats which have a contribution index of 10%, it is low but not exceedingly so. Other times it is very high, as with the shooting shirts, with an index of 42%. And, of course, it can be the catalog average, as the down vest is with a contribution index of 21.8%.

Each of these items seems to indicate a different decision. What does one do? *The general rule is that space and merchandise should be planned so that the contribution indexes do not differ widely.*

This means that a substandard item, such as the overcoat, has too much space devoted to it. Assuming that there is no competing merchandise and the merchandiser decides to retain the overcoats for the next catalog, then the space should be reduced for the overcoats. The shooting shirts with an index of 42%, however, are producing too many sales for the space devoted to them. The index suggests that the sales of the shirts are being stunted by inadequate space and that overall sales of the catalog can be

[2] Gross demand is credit-worthy orders received before returns for refunds are subtracted.

maximized by giving more space and promotion to shooting shirts. The characteristic of a well-planned and well-merchandised catalog is that extremes of contribution indexes are minimized.

Alternative decisions
when contribution is inadequate

If sales for an item are extremely low, such as those for the outdoor jacket with a contribution index of −25%, it is easy to decide what to do: you discontinue it. There is nothing that can be done to bring its sales up to an acceptable level.

If we make comparisons with the average catalog contribution of 21.8%, then the men's and women's overcoats, although they contribute a substandard 10%, present alternatives. These include discontinuation, giving them less space, changing their prices, discontinuing competing items in the same product category, or adding stockkeeping units. Reducing space will tend to reduce sales but usually disproportionately less than the reduction in space, thus improving the contribution index. If an item has an excessive amount of space, then the sales reduction might be negligible. Although some sales will be lost, discontinuing items of similar appeal will release space and transfer some sales to the remaining items in the category.

The solution to a problem of inadequate contribution might be changing the price. The item might sell just as many units at a higher price, which would produce more mark-up and more contribution. Or, maybe a lower price will so increase sales and reduce the publicity cost as a percent of sales that the drop in the mark-up percent is more than offset.

Sometimes when the sales of an item are too low, it is not because the appeal is lacking but rather that there are not enough stockkeeping units. For example, at British Isles Collection we had a wool dress that we carried in winter white and turquoise. Sales were substandard but not excessively so. Our method to bring sales up to standard was to add, without consuming any more catalog space, two more colors, Kelly green and magenta. Similarly, at Lawson Hill Leather and Shoe Co. we sustained higher sales on our various shoe styles because we offered a wide range of sizes. Each additional size we offered on a style meant more people could buy the style, yet it did not increase the catalog space. Additional sizes, however, did greatly balloon our inventory.

Alternative decisions
when contribution is excessive

When the contribution index is very high, it usually means that you have an opportunity to increase sales. Perhaps more items should be added in the same product category, as more shirts might be called for in our example. Perhaps more space devoted to the product will increase sales. While merely a larger-sized picture will increase sales by giving more attention to the product and showing detail better, you probably can increase sales even more if the additional space presents something new about the product—for example, diagrams that illustrate particular features, more meaningful copy, additional illustrations to show the product at different angles, or more mood background. Of course, a successful item warrants picturing more of its variations. Our shooting shirt, for example, might be photographed on models in two or three colors instead of being illustrated in just one color. The other colors that have been carried but just listed might be arranged and photographed in a compact group. Furthermore, it would pay to add more stockkeeping units in the form of more colors and more sizes.

Ranking and mark-up

A convenient way to evaluate a catalog is to rank the merchandise items according to their contribution percent, with the best items at the top and the worst at the bottom. This makes it easy to see which items should be cut off. Comparisons can be made with the catalog average and also with what is needed to operate the business.

It is also worthwhile to rank the items by the dollars of mark-up they generated. The purpose of this ranking is to prevent making the mistake of discontinuing an item with substantial dollars of mark-up but low contribution when the real problem is that too much space has been devoted to it. For example, the overcoats are second only to the shooting shirts in creating mark-up, which suggests that illustrating them with less space might be a good move.

Catalog Design

Where to place an item in the catalog

The general rule is that the best items should go in the best locations. The reasoning behind that is, if a particular location increases sales by a certain percent on an item, that percent applied to a high sales figure will result in a bigger increase than if it is applied to a low sales figure.

In Chapter 5 it was said that the best locations, in diminishing order of importance, are the following: front cover, back cover, the first two-page spread of merchandise in the catalog, the inside back cover and the page opposite it, the center spread, and pages adjacent to the order form if the form makes the catalog break open at a place other than the center. These preferred pages are the places to put the best sellers (unless there were items that created unusual catalog interest).

After these locations, the remaining better merchandise should go in the front half of the catalog, and the weaker should go in the second half. This assumes, however, that the merchandise does not also have to be grouped by categories. If the merchandise should be kept together by category, then the better categories should go in the better locations.

There is one special location that I have not discussed so far—the order form. The order form is also one of the most productive locations in the catalog. But, because it is the place to which every customer turns when he or she wishes to order, it is peculiarly suited to displaying add-ons, that is, items which the customer decides to buy after making the main purchasing decision. These add-ons, or impulse items, constitute extra business, which boosts the average order, and should take precedence over items with higher sales. I usually give these items very small spaces and put many of them on the order form.

Homogeneous or heterogeneous merchandise arrangement

Should merchandise be arranged by categories or heterogeneously? There are two schools of thought on this, but I know of no split-run tests that prove one method is better than the other. The answer certainly depends in part upon the product line of the catalog and the merchandise category. All I can do here is to present both schools of thought and let the reader decide what is best for his situation.

One school of thought says that keeping all merchandise of a category together gives the impression of a big selection in the category, attracting buyers. To the argument that doing so makes the merchandise items compete with each other, this school retorts that this is good because the weaker items will be knocked out by the competition, leaving the strong.

The other school of thought says that putting all items of a category together, such as all overcoats, is boring and that reader interest will be lost. An overcoat situated between some sports coats will get more attention because it contrasts with the sports coats. Also, the merchandiser has the opportunity to interest the customer in a greater variety of items as he glances at the page—if the customer is not interested in overcoats, he might be interested in sports coats. Similarly, a woman's cape shown adjacent to a skirt and sweater combination might sell better than a page full of capes. Of course, coordinating items must be shown together. For years L. L. Bean has used the heterogeneous format. Shoes have been sprinkled throughout their catalog rather than grouped together.[3] The obvious advantage is that their customers must keep browsing through the catalog to see what they want and, in browsing, they might become interested in other things. Certainly, the heterogeneous format increases sales among people who like to browse.

Should one use a homogeneous format or a heterogeneous format? I am sure there is no one answer for all catalogs, or for even any one catalog. The answer is a matter of judgment; each situation must be decided on its merits.

Catalog size and shape

The two most common catalog sizes are $8\frac{1}{2} \times 11$ inches and $5\frac{1}{2} \times 8\frac{1}{2}$ inches. These can be formatted upright with the fold going the long way or horizontally with the fold going the short way. There are also some unusual sizes: L. L. Bean's catalog, for example, measures $8\frac{5}{8} \times 7\frac{3}{8}$ inches.

The size to use depends upon the size of the illustrations and how the products are presented. If, in general, the space devoted to an item is very small, then the larger $8\frac{1}{2} \times 11$ inch page will have too many items and look too crowded; it would be hard for an item to gain attention. On the other hand, if a large amount of space is generally devoted to an item, then the larger page size is usually desirable because a group of related items can be put on one page or on a two-page spread. Sometimes, however, the mail marketer wants to give a whole page to each item; the smaller size achieves this without consuming too much space. In general, I would avoid an unusual size, such as the one employed by L. L. Bean, because few printers use it and it is difficult to get competitive price quotations. I would also avoid very large or very small catalogs because they do not handle or store easily. In addition, very small catalogs are hard to look at.

The best choice of format, upright or horizontal, depends mostly on the shape and size of the products. Some product lines will lay out better one way or the other. It is a problem of optimally using the catalog space and yet retaining good eye flow, the subject of the next chapter.

---

[3] Recently they have tended to group shoes together somewhat.

8
does bad eye flow
cripple your pages?

Do your would-be customers weary easily of your catalog pages, turn them quickly because they are hard to concentrate on, and then put your catalog down? This is the costly price of bad eye flow. My observation is that poor eye flow is the most common and most serious defect of mail-order catalogs.

Good eye flow means that all the important elements of a page receive attention. When good eye flow exists, the page is easy to read; the eye goes to a primary point of focus and then from element to element until all the important elements on the page are seen.

I once was only dimly aware of what good eye flow meant. And, then, I did not know the term. I knew only *confused* and *organized, cluttered* and *clean*, and *crowded* and *white space*. It was not until I met Louis Cheskin that I became aware of the significance of eye flow. Louis had received much national attention when Vance Packard published his book *Hidden Persuaders*, in which Packard decried what he described as the attempts of marketers and market researchers to influence subliminally and psychologically the buying habits of the public.[1] Louis Cheskin figured heavily in the book. It was after reading about Louis Cheskin in *Hidden Persuaders* that I made contact with him.

Louis taught me all that I know about eye flow. He taught me that the pages of my catalogs must not be tiring or difficult to look at, that the eye must flow over them in an easy and natural manner. Barriers that brake the eye must be taken down, and poorly-placed elements that disrupt eye flow must be relocated. Sometimes elements must have visual weight added or subtracted. With good eye flow, he taught me, my catalog had a better chance of being looked at by my customers and my shoes gaining their attention.

---

[1] Something that they cannot do; they can only learn what consumer preferences are and exploit them.

The eye moves in certain natural patterns. If the layout accommodates these patterns, it is more likely that the eye flow will be good. In Western countries, people read from left to right. Semitic peoples read from right to left, and the Chinese read from top to bottom. Each of these peoples have been conditioned by their reading habits to view a page in a certain manner. In Western countries, pages that have initial points of focus in the upper left-hand corner are more likely to have good eye flow than those with it at the bottom right. In the Middle East, however, the initial point of focus would be best located in the upper right-hand corner. These locations are usually best because these points are where the eye starts reading. Layouts that counter the habitual movements of the eye require extra effort to view. To the mail marketer extra effort to view a catalog page means that his products will be seen and bought less.

Some Suggestions to Improve Eye Flow

A good layout needs an initial point of focus, that is, something with eye-pulling power that gets the eye started on the page. The eye should then be drawn across the page and down. Visual weight is needed, therefore, at the bottom of the page to attract the eye. All the important elements on the way down should have sufficient visual weight to stop the eye briefly on its path to the bottom, but not so much as to compete for attention with the initial point of focus or the attention point at the bottom that is drawing the eye down.

Eye-pulling power is achieved by size and by contrast. Contrast is black against white, white against black, or pairs of complementary colors, such as magenta pink against spring green. It can be achieved by the simple against the complex. A headline above a copy block is a case of contrast.

Eye-pulling power is needed for every product illustrated on the page. This means that not only must its illustration be well-situated and have enough contrast with its surroundings, but also that within the illustration the product itself must contrast with its background. Therefore, be careful of backgrounds; don't choose a background that camouflages the product but rather one that makes the product stand out in bold relief. Busy backgrounds almost always tend to obscure products as do the wrong background colors, poor product lighting, and even poor color separations and printing. Objects placed with the product to create mood will increase sales if, in fact, they do create mood. But they must be chosen and positioned with care. Irrelevant objects that don't heighten mood should be avoided. Ones that do create mood, as leather and hand tools do with shoes, should be positioned so that they get secondary attention and do not confuse the eye.

Avoid white channels and other borders around pictures within the page. They become additional elements that must be contended with and are likely to confuse the eye flow. We ran several eye-movement tests of pages in which white channels were present. Removal of these channels in each instance improved the eye flow.

If you have two pages opposite each other, one consisting of a single illustration and the other of several illustrations, put the page with the single illustration to the left and on the right-hand page put the heaviest element on top. This arrangement gets the eye started naturally and assures that everything will be seen. Figure 8-1 illustrates this concept and shows how a poor arrangement can be improved with what is known as a "Papa Bear, Mama Bear, and Baby Bear" layout.

FIGURE 8-1 Papa Bear, Mama Bear, and Baby Bear Layouts (Two-Page Spreads)
The eye naturally moves better in (B) because it starts with the large illustration to the left, moves to the half-page on the upper half of the right page, and then to the lower half divided in thirds. (A) is poor because out of habit the eye wants to start in the upper left, yet it is drawn to the large illustration to the right.

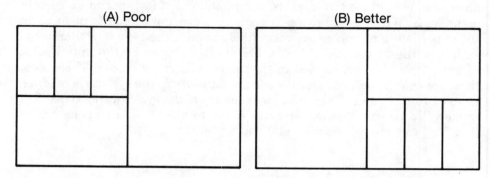

Avoid discontinuous lines. They break up the flow of the eye over the page. Figure 8-2 shows a defective layout and how it can be improved.

Eye-Movement Tests

Fortunately for the mail marketer, the decision as to whether the eye flow of a page or a spread is good does not have to be a matter of judgment. Eye flow can be tested by means of an eye-movement camera, which determines how the eye moves over a page. At Lawson Hill Leather and Shoe Co., we had many eye flow tests done at Louis Cheskin Associates to prove the effectiveness of our pages, our ads, and particularly the covers of our catalogs.

The tests that they did for us during the fall of 1971 on our Marianna layout were typical of the ones that we had done over the years. Figure 8-3 is a drawing of the page as it was originally printed in the Fall 1971 catalog. Louis Cheskin questioned the eye flow of the page and suggested a test, which we had done. His analysis and ocular measurement are shown opposite Figure 8-3. The test confirmed his opinion. The page was hard to look at; the eye hesitated, looked at the left shoe and then the right shoe, and then went up the leg and off the page. The two smaller shoes did not attract attention.

We then had two alternative layouts done, shown in Figures 8-4 and 8-5. Figure 8-4 was found to be lacking in an initial point of focus, with the

FIGURE 8-2 Two Single-Page Layouts
The eye flow in (A) is defective. The eye wants to go along the horizontal line but is jogged up by the break between the pictures. (B) is better because the eye flow is continuous horizontally.

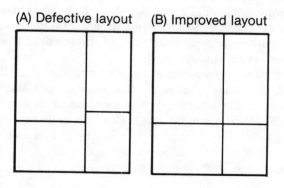

FIGURE 8-3 Marianna, Layout A

Report by Louis Cheskin Associates
Eye Flow Test, Marianna Page Figure 8-3

ANALYSIS

This page is obviously weak. We can only come to the conclusion that the illustrations in the two rectangles do not have enough interest in themselves and detract from the large illustration.

It is advisable not to use a framing device around the shoes.

The larger illustration should always be in front of the smaller ones.

OCULAR MEASUREMENT

Test		Rating
Eye Movement	After considerable hesitation, eyes fell on shoe on model's left foot, moved to shoe on model's right foot, up model's legs and off page.	C (Fair)

FIGURE 8-4 Marianna, Layout B

Report by Louis Cheskin Associates
Eye Flow Test, First Revision of
Marianna Page Figure 8-4

ANALYSIS

Figure 8-4 does not have a primary point of focus; the component elements are fighting for attention, and it is, therefore, a poor layout.

OCULAR MEASUREMENT

Test		Rating
Eye Movement	After considerable hesitation, eyes fell on shoe at upper left, moved to matching shoe below, and, after more hesitation, left page.	D (Poor)

FIGURE 8-5 Marianna, Layout C

Report by Louis Cheskin Associates
Eye Flow Test, Second Revision of
Marianna Page Figure 8-5

ANALYSIS

The eye-movement test of the two page layouts shows clearly that Figure 8-5 has excellent eye flow.

OCULAR MEASUREMENT

Test		*Rating*
Eye Movement	Eyes fell on foot and shoe at upper left, moved to matching shoe just below, down to shoes at lower right, across shoes at lower left, up to shoe at upper illustration, up left leg to *Marianna* and off page.	A (Excellent)

component elements fighting for attention. Figure 8-5 was found to have excellent eye flow. The heavier element on top and the lighter elements on the bottom started the eye with an initial point of focus and then went to the other shoes in a path that is natural to Western readers. All the shoes received attention. The analysis and ocular measurement are shown opposite.

Pay Attention to Eye Flow

As I thumb through the many catalogs that arrive at my home daily, I realize how few mail marketers are aware of eye flow and its importance to them. Pages are confusing and hard to look at. Products are obscured by poor position, insufficent weight, and backgrounds that fight for attention with the product.

A 32-page, 48-page, or 64-page catalog is formidable to look at. Even under the best of conditions and with a patient and persevering reader, it is unlikely that a catalog will be entirely read. But most readers have a short span of attention. When page after page is hard to look at, not only are many items on the bad pages overlooked, but also the catalog itself is likely to be put down with even its good pages unread. The mail marketer must never forget that he competes for the reader's time, and he competes with other catalogs and everything else that makes demands upon the reader. Pay attention, therefore, to eye flow. Good eye flow means that you will gain more reader attention and more sales.

do the wrong background colors cost you sales?*

Mail marketers spend staggering sums on their catalogs, catalog preparation, postage, list rental, and merchandise; then, on a single roll of the dice, they risk all. Yet, at the moment of the roll, they are blissfully unaware that the consumer may not notice their merchandise at all because of bad backgrounds and bad eye flow on the page.

My observation is that bad backgrounds and bad eye flow are the two most common defects in a mail-order catalog. The mail marketer may unfailingly remember such basics as to invite telephone orders, welcome credit cards, and mention the company retail store, but then submerge his product in a background that camouflages it in a page that is so confused that the reader passes it by.

This chapter focuses on background colors; how they are often unwittingly selected to hide the product, and how they can be chosen to give the product greater visibility. In Chapter 8, I discussed background confusion and eye flow.

Why are backgrounds so often bad? There appear to be two reasons: first, the staff artist, jaded by the confinement and dullness of commercial art, seeks to be creative; and, in being creative, he loses sight of his only task of selling the product. The second reason is that the manager of the enterprise and, more often than not, his art director as well are unaware of what constitutes a good background color, a subject that is somewhat arcane because it involves the physical laws of light.

A good background color is one that sets off the product and in so doing gives it visibility. How does the background color give visibility to the product? The answer is by contrast.

On the black and white page, contrast is easy to understand. Black contrasts against white. No greater contrast exists because it is all light

---

* This chapter first appeared as an article I wrote for the February 1981 issue of *Direct Marketing* magazine. It bore the same title as this chapter and is reprinted with the permission of *Direct Marketing*.

against no light. White light contains all colors; black is the absence of the light of any color.

But in color, what do you do? Do you put intense yellow against pale yellow or against nothing at all, which usually means white paper? These answers would be wrong because yellow-appearing light[1] is being reflected back to the eye in both cases. In the first case, it is because yellow ink is printed on the background; in the second case, it is because yellow-appearing light is a component of the white light coming off the white background.

To have maximum contrast with a yellow product requires that there be no yellow at all in the background. This is achieved by printing the background in the remaining printing primaries of cyan (a light blue) and magenta (a pink). The combination of cyan and magenta is violet-blue and is the complementary color of yellow. The definition of a complementary color is white light minus the color. In other words, complete contrast is achieved with a yellow product and a violet-blue background because no yellow-appearing light is reflected from the background, while it is reflected from the product.

The rule, therefore, is that backgrounds for the greatest product visibility should be of a color that is complementary to the color of the product.

The rule that backgrounds should be of a color that is complementary to the color of the product is illustrated by the colors selected for the dust jacket or cover of this book.

The color of the letters in the title of the book is violet-blue and was created by printing the two printing color primaries of cyan and magenta together. If white light is projected onto the letters, yellow-appearing light will be absorbed by the cyan and magenta inks leaving the violet-blue remainder to be reflected back to your eyes.

By printing yellow in the background, maximum contrast and, hence, maximum visibility of the letters was achieved. The yellow ink absorbs the violet-blue light leaving the yellow-appearing components of the white light to be reflected back to your eyes. In other words, maximum visibility of these letters was achieved by having none of the colors of the letters in the background.

Progressive proofs or 3M proofs can guide you in selecting background colors, which is one reason why I insist on progressive proofs (see Chapter 11). Because each color is printed on a separate sheet of paper, one can see at a glance how much of the color is in the product and how much is in the background. If the cyan, magenta, or yellow progressive reveals that its color is largely absent in the product, then for maximum contrast the color should be found in the background. For example, the picture of an orange contains much magenta and yellow but little cyan. Printing cyan in the background, therefore, will increase the visibility of an orange in a catalog.

On the other hand, colors that appear in the product should not appear in the background if maximum visibility is desired. For maximum visibility of an orange in a catalog selling fruit, neither magenta nor yellow should be printed in its background.

These examples are clear-cut because one or two of the printing inks are largely absent in the product. Sometimes all three colors are present in the product in significant amounts, although usually not in equal pro-

---

[1] The term *yellow-appearing light* has been used to aid comprehension. Physicists use the term "minus violet-blue" which is more precise because there is no such thing as yellow light. The yellow-appearing light that we see is, in reality, the light of all the different wavelengths in the visible spectrum with the exception of the violet-blue wavelength, which has been absorbed by the ink on the paper.

portion.[2] In this situation, contrast may be increased by lightening or darkening the background while at the same time using a background of a color that is complementary to the dominant primary colors of the product.

Here are some examples from our experience at Lawson Hill Leather and Shoe Co. Behind white shoes we used a dark background. Behind a black shoe we would use a light background. Behind a bone shoe, which contains a predominance of yellow and magenta, we would use dark blue. Against dark and medium brown shoes, in which magenta and yellow dominate but which contain significant cyan, we used a light cyan background (we could have used white but we felt this was too antiseptic). Behind cordovan shoes, composed largely of magenta, cyan, and black inks, we used light yellow.

Sometimes we increased contrast by using one product as a background for another; for example, a black shoe against a white shoe. Here the photographer is challenged, for he must project a great deal of light behind the black shoe and a little light behind the white shoe while lighting each shoe properly. If the left shoe was the white one, then we would throw strong lighting on the right-hand background, use none or little on the left, and light each shoe individually. In the Talbots catalog, I have often admired the photograph of a woman wearing a spring-green sweater with pink slacks. Here they used each product as part of the background for the other. While they, no doubt, selected these colors because they went well together, they achieved perfect contrast, for green is the complement of magenta.

To summarize: you will gain more sales if you maintain high product visibility on your catalog page. This visibility is achieved, amongst other ways,[3] by contrasting the background with the product.

---

[2] When the primary printing colors are printed in equal proportion, the result is gray or black.

[3] Visibility can also be achieved by size, position, and good eye flow, discussed in Chapter 8.

photographing the product

We must never forget that what the customer sees for a product representation in the catalog is the way he or she thinks it is. This seems so obvious as to hardly bear saying. Yet the merchandiser or creative director can be so conditioned by looking frequently at the product itself that when he or she looks at its illustration in the catalog he or she sees the product, not the way it is illustrated and the customer sees it, but rather the way it actually is. Herein lies the danger that an illustration will be accepted that will have a much different impact upon the customer than upon the merchandiser.

In almost all product lines, the illustration of the product is of great sales importance, but in some lines it is the only thing that sells the product. In clothing, shoes, and food, for example, the color or the appearance of the product in the illustration can make or break it. Often the solution to a problem of poor sales in a product is using a new illustration. In fact, whenever a product does not sell well, you should first see if the illustration is the problem. On the other hand, if a product is selling well, be careful about changing its picture; you could well make it worse. What seems to be a small difference in the color or look could be all the difference to the customer.

At Lawson Hill Leather and Shoe Co., we had a multi-pastel colored shoe, which we called Rainbow and which was our best seller every springtime. For one spring catalog, we got the notion to change the picture; we thought we could improve on it. But to our customers, Rainbow lost its appeal and sales plummeted. The following spring we returned to the former picture, and Rainbow's sales rebounded.

At British Isles Collection, we had a women's coat that had proved to be a best seller for two catalogs. We changed the picture because the men's coat it was pictured with sold poorly. But in the new picture the women's coat did not look as good, and sales plunged.

In another instance, the contrary result occurred inadvertently. The

72

printer failed to run enough ink for the catalog of one of my clients, generally ruining the catalog. The effect of less ink upon one of the products, a women's boot, was to lighten it and change its color slightly. To my astonishment, sales improved, suggesting that our customers wanted the boot lighter in color.

The lessons of these stories are that one cannot devote too much attention to the illustration of the product, and one cannot assume that what one thinks is the best illustration is what appeals to the customer the most. With the staggering costs that the mail marketer must incur in printing, paper, postage, list rental, and mailing expense, the representation of the product in the catalog must be superlative. These costs vary in direct proportion with the numer of catalogs printed, but it is only in small mailings that they do not dwarf preparation costs, as substantial as preparation costs can be. But getting good representation of the product is not so much spending more money (although this may be necessary) as it is taking great pains oneself and knowing what appeals to the customer. One must understand what makes good photographs, color separations, and printing and demand them, rejecting that which is not satisfactory.

Photographs, separations, and printing are the three graphic steps that lead to the representation of the product in the catalog. Although both the separations and the printing must be excellent, their contribution when they are excellent is essentially non-negative; that is, they are doing well if they are faithful to the transparency.[1] The photograph, however, can be poor or can make the product far more appealing than it actually is. The photograph is of paramount importance.

In this chapter on photography, I shall talk little about cameras, equipment, and all things that are dear to a photographer's heart. It is not that these things are not important; they are. But photographers usually have them under good control. What I shall talk about are those things that make a great photograph and in which photographers are often weak.

Lighting

Good photography[2] can almost be equated to good lighting, lighting is so important. It dwarfs all other considerations. Good lighting brings out detail and features, gives the product shape and three dimensions, and makes the product jump off the page into the reader's consciousness. It is surprising, therefore, that so many professional photographers pay such casual attention to lighting and easily satisfy themselves with a few strobe lights, sometimes not even owning tungsten lighting equipment.

Lighting is time-consuming. Lights must be directed to illuminate every detail, dragging out the shot. This, perhaps, tires the photographer, who, being paid by the shot, is anxious to move on. I have never worked with a photographer who consistently lit products to my satisfaction. For this reason, I have always been intimately involved with the photography, almost to the point of okaying every shot.

The photograph is so important that I must confess that at least 25 percent of the time I have thrown out shots that I okayed on set. In most of those instances, it was the lighting that needed to be improved.

[1] However, we shall see in the next chapter that the separation can sometimes improve upon the transparency.

[2] I must acknowledge my debt to Louis Leber, President of Concord Mail Order, who taught me almost all I know about photographing products for mail-order catalogs.

Types of lighting
when shooting stills

There are two types of lighting used when shooting stills, which are almost always shot indoors. One is strobe and the other is tungsten.

Strobe is a flash that is powered by an electrically-charged condenser. Because the flash is not on continuously, the strobe lights have modeling lights within them which are used to light the products while setting up the shot. Because strobe lighting equipment is expensive and only so many lights can be powered off one condenser, photographers tend to have an insufficient number of strobe lights.

Tungsten lights are continuously-burning lights with tungsten filaments. They remain lit during set-up as well as when the exposure is taken. They come in a wide range of wattages and types. Their drawback is that they generate heat, which can be an inconvenience in some situations.

For me, in choosing between the two types of lighting, there is no decision. I belong to the old school—I will use only tungsten lighting. While strobe lights have the modeling lights, what one sees in the ground glass of the view camera is not close enough to what one gets. Furthermore, there never seems to be enough strobe lights in the variety and types that I require to light everything that I want lit in a shot. I need big 2,000-watt lights and often a multitude of "inky-dinks," tiny lights, to bring out details without flooding the whole subject. Between these lights I need lights of a wide selection of intensities. In shots of multiple products in varying colors I require separate lights of differing wattages for each product. I have yet to find a photographer who has this variety in strobe lights.

Types of lighting
for fashion shots

Fashion shots are shots of products, usually clothing, that are taken on human models. The two types of lighting used for fashion shots are strobe and sunlight. Tungsten is not often used because the heat of the lamps causes the models to be uncomfortable.

Outdoor fashion shots in full sunlight are harder to take than indoors with strobe. Faces are often darkly shadowed, and defects, in all their unwanted ugliness, reveal themselves in the full glare of sunlight. Weather delays and clouds intervene, frustrating photographer and mail marketer alike and run up the cost of the models. One forever has the temptation to take the models inside and photograph with strobe under manageable conditions.

But when they are good, outdoor shots are very, very good. Detail shows up in sharp contrast. And colors are at their most brilliant, for only full sunlight has all the colors—all the light wavelengths—of the visible spectrum. Furthermore, pictures taken in sunlight have the cheerfulness that only sunlight can give to enhance the appeal of the products photographed. By comparison, strobe shots are flat and lacking in detail and brilliance of color. I much prefer to struggle with the problems imposed by sunlight and get the best shot possible.

Shooting outdoors on a cloudy day, however, does not achieve anything more than shooting inside with strobe. The clouds filter out many of the wavelengths of light, sharpness of detail is lost, and the somber day tends to induce a somber mood in the viewer.

The purpose of the photograph is to sell the product. It does this by identifying what the product is, by showing features of interest and appeal to the customer, conveying realism, and by making the product appealing. It is through lighting that the photograph does or does not achieve these ends.

The product can be shapeless and uninteresting, or it can be three-dimensional and dramatic. The photograph can lack detail, or product features can be brought out in bold relief. Surfaces can be untextured, or they can have grain and luster. Colors can be dull and lifeless, or they can be vibrant and appealing. All these effects in a photograph are consequences of its lighting.

Getting shape in the photograph

Shape in the photograph gives realism to the product. It takes the product away from the flatness of the catalog page to the three dimensions of real life. Shape, or three dimensions, is achieved in a photograph by light and shadow.

Objects in direct light have brilliant lighting on planes that are directly illuminated and deep shadows on planes that are not. In between, surfaces will reflect light according to how they are angled towards the light source.

The ball is an object with an infinite number of planes. If it is photographed with light coming from many directions, as in Figure 10-1, light will be reflected from all those planes to the lens of the camera. It will appear like a disc and seem flat. If a single source of light illuminates the

FIGURE 10-1 Using Many Light Sources to Photograph a Ball

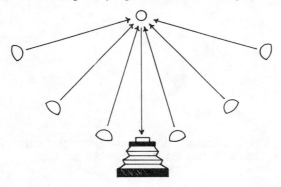

A ball photographed with many
light sources looks flat like a disc.

ball from directly behind the camera, a highlight will occur in the center of the ball and the light reflected back to the camera will reduce towards the edge of the ball. It will still look quite flat. If, however, the light source is angled away from the camera, a shadow will develop and the highlight will follow the light source. The shadows and highlights give the ball shape and depth. People know when they see the highlight on one side of the ball and the shadow on the other side that it is its shape that causes this effect. To them, it no longer looks like a disc but instead like the sphere that it is. Thus, by lighting, a realism can be achieved. Figure 10-2 shows how a ball can be made more lifelike by the way it is lit.

FIGURE 10-2

A ball photographed with a single light
source angled away from the camera.

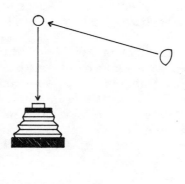

Highlights and shadows have been created;
the ball now has a three-dimensional look.

Suede footwear is a product that more often than not looks flat and uninteresting in a photograph. Where polished leather shoes will have little reflections on the toe to suggest shape, suede looks dead in its non-reflectiveness. But, when skillfully lighted, suede footwear can have a depth and realism that exceeds ordinary shoes. Figure 10-3 shows how, by positioning lights on each side of a women's boot, the sides of the boot will be light and a shadow will be in the center. As the boot gradually darkens from the side to the center, the boot's curved shape is suggested to the viewer.

A cube is a subject that can have three visible planes in a photograph. It can be lit so that each plane appears to be equally lighted. Or it can be lit so that one plane is in direct light, one in partial light, and one in shadow. If it is lighted with the latter method, then the light and shadows create three-dimensional depth and, consequently, lifelike realism. This effect is shown in Figure 10-4.

These are simple subjects, but the principle is the same for more complex ones: *Use light and shadow for a three-dimensional effect that creates realism and makes the product leap off the page.*

FIGURE 10-3 Photographing a Woman's Boot with Two Light Sources to Give It Shape

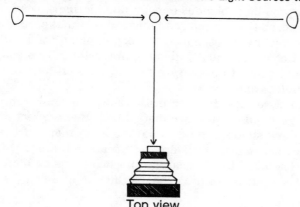

Top view

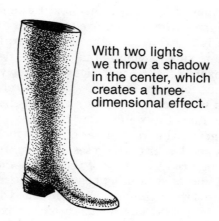

With two lights
we throw a shadow
in the center, which
creates a three-
dimensional effect.

FIGURE 10-4 Lighting a Cube

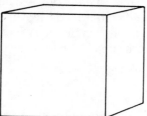

(A) A cube with
equal lighting
on all sides.

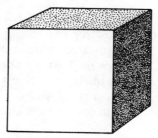

(B) A cube lit with
unequal lighting to
give it depth, that is,
three dimensions.

The concept of using light and shadow to give depth and three dimensions to a product is obvious enough and, perhaps, would not be worth mentioning, except that so many photographers make no effort to use it. Their lighting technique seems to be to put plenty of light all over the subject using flood lamps and reflecting umbrellas.[2] This ensures that the product is well-lit and that everything can be seen, but the product will have a flat, lifeless look.

Of course, care must be used in three-dimensional technique to avoid shadows that go too dark and are disfiguring. By an effect known as tone compression, dark shadows tend to darken even more in the separations; it is sometimes necessary, therefore, to use a small amount of fill light in the shadows. The need for this can be checked by using a spot light meter which measures light in an area that is the size of a small coin.

Lighting to get texture and detail in the photograph

The principle of lighting to get texture and detail is much the same as getting shape—after all, texture and detail are shape on a small scale. The technique is to skim the light over the surface of the subject and, in so doing, create small shadows that etch the detail into the photograph.

For example, at British Isles Collection we had a lovely hand-crocheted blouse made for us in Ireland, which we retailed for $200. Crocheted into the design were scores of Irish roses and shamrocks.

To capture this detail, we positioned the model so that the sunlight skimmed across the front of her blouse, which created tiny shadows behind the petals and leaves of the roses and shamrocks. These shadows, contrasting with the bright lighting of the petals and leaves, brought out in relief the detail and breathtaking beauty of this magnificent work of art.

We used this skim-lighting technique with equal success in other products. We positioned our models wearing handknit Irish sweaters, vests, caps, mittens, and scarves so that the sunlight skimmed across them, throwing shadows behind and setting off each of the complex hand stitches which are the feature of Irish handknits. Suede leather is a similar problem. In most photographs it appears flat, particularly lacking in detail and texture. But by skimming light across suede, the texture of the leather can be seen, giving it realism.

Lighting shiny subjects

The principle of capturing the shine of a shiny subject is just the opposite of getting detail in an Irish handknit sweater. When a beam of light is projected onto a matte subject, the light that strikes any particular point is dispersed in every direction. Some of that light will go into the lens of the camera. Since this is true of every point on a matte subject, it will appear lit all over.

A shiny subject does not disperse the light. The light reflecting from any one point on it goes in only one direction, the angle of reflection equaling the angle of incidence. This means that from a cylindrical shiny subject only a sliver of light will be reflected towards the camera lens, and from a shiny sphere only a point of light. If the subject is perfectly shiny, that is, it disperses no light, then the rest of the subject will go black. As a result, the photographer will fail to capture the shiny quality of the subject.

---

[2] Reflecting umbrellas create an infinite number of light sources and so tend to flatten subjects.

The way to capture the shininess is to increase the number of light sources from one to infinity. This is accomplished by shooting light onto a translucent tent, the surface of which diffracts the light in all directions. Since the surface of the tent thus becomes an infinite number of light sources, each point on the subject will have a light source correctly located on the tent to reflect a beam of light into the lens. This was our solution to the problem we had in lighting the Wilkinson swords. The swords had scores of reflecting surfaces on the curved hilt and scabbards. A few ordinary lights would have resulted in only a few lines and points of light being reflected back to the lens, while the rest of the swords and scabbards would have appeared black. But, by building a translucent tent over the swords and directing light onto the tent, we were able to impart their shiny quality. The principle of tent lighting is shown in Figure 10-5.

Lighting of dark and light subjects

As we shall learn in the next chapter, what appears to be good detail in the ground glass of the camera or in the transparency can, when printed, become indistinct in shadow and highlight areas. This is called "tone compression," a reduction in the density range in these areas. Because there is danger that detail will be lost, it is necessary to pay particular attention to the lighting of light and dark subjects.

Light subjects can have their detail enhanced by skim lighting, as previously described, and by increasing shadows in the detail areas through

FIGURE 10-5 Lighting a Perfectly Shiny Hemisphere

(A) A single light source

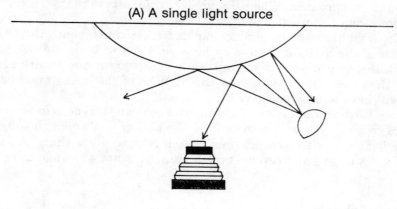

(B) Tent lighting

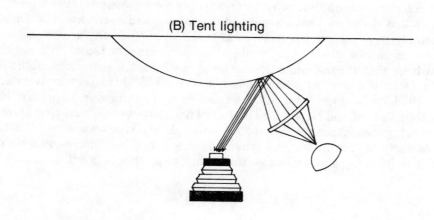

adjustments in the position of the lights. Where both light and dark subjects appear in the same photograph, each should be lit separately, with light-meter readings taken for each. The worst mistake is to try to have one light illuminate both subjects, something I have seen photographers, out of laziness, attempt to do. When one light is used in this situation, there will not be detail in either the light or the dark subjects. The light subject will be "blown out" and the dark subject plugged.

The secret to lighting very dark subjects, such as black or navy blue ones, is to remember that, because of a reduced density range in printing, the detail will be greatly diminished and that one must light the subjects accordingly. Usually, additional lights are required to illuminate details and create shadows behind the details to set them off. Another technique is to direct lights so that reflections define the product's shape and accent details.

Lighting backgrounds

Photographers are usually not attuned to the sole purpose of the photograph. They might be quite concerned with the aesthetics of the photograph and, for example, go to great lengths to eliminate product shadows in the background, which often are harmless, but then lose sight of the photograph's only function of selling the product. They will applaud a photograph as being very beautiful but not notice the fact that the product does not stand out from its background.

Almost as much care should be given to lighting background as to lighting the subject. Very light subjects, such as a woman in a white dress, should have very dark backgrounds, and very dark subjects should have very light backgrounds. When the product contrasts with its background, it becomes much more visible on the catalog page.

Contrast between the product and its background is controlled by both the color of the background and by lighting. Even white backgrounds will be dark if they are not lit. When both a light subject and a dark subject are in the same photograph, then the portions of the background behind each will have to be separately lit.

One further comment on lighting backgrounds. If type is to be printed on backgrounds, you will need to light the backgrounds enough so that it will be legible or plan to print your type in reverse. Everything else being equal, you should avoid reverse type because it is not as legible as printed type.

Outdoor lighting

As I said earlier, nothing can surpass bright sunlight for bringing out detail and color in fashion; but often it creates problems, usually in the form of harsh face shadows. There are a number of ways to overcome this. One is to simply have the models look towards the sun. When this is not possible, reflectors can be used to cast sunlight onto the model's faces. This has the drawback that it may make the model squint, and the reflectors might fill light in on the product where it is not wanted. A third way to overcome face shadows is to use a flash. Care must be taken, however, to assure that the flash is confined to the face and does not flatten out detail that should be accentuated. Another way to get around face shadows is to take the shots early or late in the day when the sun is low and shines directly on the face. If many shots must be taken, however, this is not practical.

What makes fashion photography different from other photography is that the clothing is photographed on live models. Models have facial expressions and poses that are constantly changing. Each model has his or her unique set of body measurements that don't exactly correspond to the clothes that are being modeled. Models can get too warm and perspire in the warm clothing that is being photographed in the summer for a winter catalog or shiver and have goose pimples while being photographed in the winter for a summer catalog. Clothes can hang badly or be distorted and wrinkled by certain positions of the arms, legs, and body. These problems must be contended with by the photographer, his stylist, and the mail marketer. To them are added the problems created by the outdoors: clouds obscuring the sun, the sun at the wrong angle, incongruous backgrounds, and curious onlookers.

All these problems mean that many of the shots can be bad. As nature makes up for so many of her seeds lighting on sterile soil by fecundity, so does the fashion photographer make up for many failures by taking many photographs. Where in a still, three exposures would suffice, in fashion photography the usual rule is 36 exposures for each model in a photograph. Thus, if there are three models in a photograph, 108 exposures are taken. To get this many exposures, usually a 35mm camera with a motorized drive is used.

Even with taking so many exposures, the results can be disappointing. After seeing the slides from one shooting session for British Isles Collection, many of which I found unsatisfactory, I wrote this memorandum to the photographer and models, *Comments on Outdoor Fashion Photography*. It should be a useful guide for anyone doing fashion photography.

After having looked at thousands of slides as the result of the first shooting session of the Fall 1981 British Isles Collection catalog, I have these comments to make. If we observe some of the following guidelines, we shall be able to make a higher percentage of our shots count; that is, give us more shots from which to select, and save film. I have to say that we could have done better on our first shooting.

There is only one object to our photography and that is to present the merchandise so that it will sell. This almost always means good visibility of the detail of the merchandise.

I recommend that in the future we set up each shot, even though it is done outdoors, almost like a still. That is, get everything exactly right before we start snapping off scores of photographs. We should determine such matters as position of arms and hands, how the jackets should be worn, the direction from which we want the light to come—in short, just as if we were doing a still life inside the studio. Once we have done this, then we can take a series of shots in which the models make minor changes in their expression, etc. If we wish to test different angles of position and lighting, then we can do similar set-ups.

Arms and Hands. The position of arms and hands should never distort the clothing and almost never should they be in front of the clothing. This means that they most frequently would lie relaxed at the sides, although they can be akimbo if there is space permitting horizontally in the picture. Women's hands should almost never be in the pockets of their jackets as this tends to distort the jackets. Men's hands may occasionally be in their pants pockets if what is being featured is a sweater or something like that above them.

81

Perspective. Almost always, simple front-on shots should be taken. Shots from an angle rarely show the whole garment.

Hats. We must be very careful that hats do not cast shadows on the face.

Body Position. The weight should be evenly distributed in most instances. One shoulder should never be hiked higher than the other, as this distorts the garments. Any position that causes wrinkles in the clothing should be avoided. There should be no antics going on as we are not interested in photographing these; I mean by this the model standing on one foot, jumping, etc.

Direction in Which the Models Face. Most frequently the best direction for a model to face is directly into the camera, although this can be modified if it's necessary for the model to look a little bit more towards the sun to get shadows off his or her face.

In the case of several models together, for them to appear to be talking to each other is quite acceptable. In any case, if there is more than one model there should be a common point of interest, towards which the models look. One should not be looking to the left and the other looking to the right because this is extremely unnatural. This is sometimes corrected by telling the models to face and look at one particular thing. "Watch the birdie."

Jackets. Jackets almost always should be closed and buttoned. Scarves should hang in such a manner that they do not cover the buttons and closure.

Backgrounds. The backgrounds behind women should be soft. We made a mistake in our last shooting, which was my fault, to photograph hard brick walls behind women. They are not compatible. The other comment on backgrounds is that they should contrast with the clothing being featured. Light clothing should be shot against dark backgrounds, dark clothing against light backgrounds, and the colors of the backgrounds when possible should be complementary to the colors in the garments.

Expression and Mood. A cheerful, pleasant expression with a smile or even a grin is far more preferable than a serious expression. People like cheerful smiles and when they see this it has a positive psychological effect upon them. Therefore, the expression should always be smiling.

Lighting. Clothes with much color should have much direct sunlight. Very dark clothes of course need to have intense sunlight and there should be shadows around lapels and details. Light clothing again should have shadows to get shape. Actually this is true of most clothing, although where color is the feature direct sunlight perhaps is preferable to shading (an example of this would be the tartan vests or tartan sport jackets). Where color is uniform, then shading and shape becomes more important.

Subject Size. The subject and the desired background should fill the frame of the camera to improve detail. (Note: We always did fashion photography with Kodachrome ASA 25 film to maximize detail.)

Determining Position on Set

In a later chapter, I make the preposterous proposal that the merchandiser do his own layouts. This seems to fly in the face of reason because most merchandisers are not artists and so cannot be expected to draw products in their correct position. Ordinarily, the procedure is for the layout artist to determine the locations of the products in the layout and then draw the products in the position in which they are to appear, thus telling the photographer exactly how the picture is to be taken.

But this unnecessarily restrains the photography. The merchandiser knows the product best and what is needed to sell it. What appears to him in the ground glass of the camera as the view of the product that will sell it best is the way the picture should be taken. But whether the merchandiser or the layout artist makes the final determination of the positioning, it should be done on set. When it is done on set not only is the best position obtained, but also the best size is obtained, and background props can be arranged to compose an effective picture.

The layout, therefore, should serve the purposes of allocating space, determining location, and determining the specific area for the photograph. The layout tissues can then be laid upon the ground glass of the camera to see if the product fits. If the product appears small, then the camera can be moved closer to enlarge the site of the product.

This raises the question of the camera. The film expense is a little more, but it is preferable to photograph with a view camera so that the image on the film is the same size as the layout. This enables the photographer to lay the tissues onto the ground glass to check how the product fits in its assigned space.

Exposures

A minimum of three different exposures should be taken. One exposure should be stopped right on the meter reading and the others should be one-third of a stop above and one-third of a stop below. Sometimes it is desirable to take a total of five exposures, one on the meter reading and the others at one-third of a stop above, one-third of a stop below, a two-thirds stop above, and a two-thirds stop below. These ranges of exposures insure against error and also provide a choice of transparencies to balance with other transparencies going on the same page.

11

making great
color separations

No link in the chain of events that leads from the product to its representation in the catalog can be weak. Poorly-made color separations can destroy the best of photographs and result in a representation of the product that costs sales. You should demand, therefore, good transparencies from the photographer and then demand good separations from the separator.

If the color separator shows you a proof (hoping that you will accept it) that is obviously not close to the original color transparency, it suggests that his standards are not high enough and that you may need a new color separator. As I look back, I must confess that my biggest error in dealing with separators was that, rather than insisting upon separations being presented to me right in the first place, I kept trying to improve upon their unsatisfactory work. There was one big advantage to me, however: In the process of trying to improve upon their work, I learned a lot about separating and color correcting.

Except for the density range in the shadow and highlight areas, which you should expect to be less, the separation should look much like the original transparency. If it does not, then it should be rejected. If a color separator says that detail or color cannot be reproduced, then give it to another separator later to see what he can do. Make sure you have plenty of time in your catalog production schedule so that you are not forced to accept poor separations.

Selecting a Color Separator

Two approaches

There are two approaches to separating. One is to have your printer do it, and the other is to have a firm that specializes in separations do it. The argument for having the printer make the separations is that if there is a problem when the catalog is printed, he cannot blame it on the separator

84

because he is responsible for both the separations and the printing. There is the further argument that the printer will not delay delivery of the separations and hold up his own printing presses.

The argument for the independent separator is that the printer might be the best printer but not the best separator. If the printer turned out to be less than adequate or overpriced, it would be less awkward moving separations elsewhere. My personal inclination is to go with whoever makes the best separations. If that person is coincidentally the printer, then go with him. My preference is to have one color separator do all separations so that they are in balance, one with the other.

How to recognize good separations

Often a separator gives you samples of his work but without the original transparency to use to compare fidelity. There are some clues to his ability to separate that you can look for, but you must remember he is showing you his best work, often printed on the best paper.

Look at the whites. Are they clean, white whites, or are they contaminated with one or more of the printing colors? The highlights of white subjects should have no color at all. Contamination of white subjects usually mean the color of the other subjects is off as well. While there should be no contamination, there should be sharp detail in white subjects. They should not be flat or "blown out."

Examine the detail in the shadow area. Is it there, or is it all filled in ("plugged" as they say in the trade)? Are there highlights on the dark subjects? In other words, how is the density range in the shadow areas?

Check the gray subjects. Do they have gray balance? A gray subject is printed with magenta, cyan, and yellow inks (the printing primary colors). But it should not have a pinkish, bluish, or yellowish cast; it should appear gray. If it has a color cast, the colors are out of balance.

Do the memory colors look right? The color of certain things are easily retained in one's memory, such as Caucasian flesh, blue sky, red apples, and green grass. Do these subjects have the right color?

If you have the transparency from which the separations were made, then check color fidelity as well as detail in the highlight and shadow areas.

Which separator is best?

One way to find out which separator is best is to submit a difficult transparency to be separated by competing separators and then compare their work. This transparency should have highlight and shadow areas with detail that is hard to reproduce. Of course, one sample separation made with extra care does not prove that a separator makes consistently good separations. Look at some catalogs that you know have been printed with his separations; if they look good, call the owners and ask how consistent the separator is.

Reviewing Your Own Color Proofs

The first two steps

When you review your separations, you must first check register and fit. Register is the overall alignment of the images of the four printing colors, one on top of the other. For example, the yellow ink could be displaced one hundred of an inch relative to the other three colors. This will result in yellow tingeing the highlight and a yellow cast in the subject areas. Register can be checked by examining the edges of images and the register marks that are on the proof with a magnifying glass. One color should not overhang the others, and the register marks should appear black, not tinged with one or more of the colors.

Fit refers to the register of the individual images within one overall separation. Poor fit of an image exists when the color components of the overall separation are aligned but those of the image are not. Bad fit frequently results from individual separations not being stripped together accurately. It also results from failure or inability to control the stretch of the paper. The control of paper stretch is more difficult with sheet-fed than with web presses.[1] When you review color proofs, it is best to check proofs of the entire form in the printer's imposition. This permits you to check the fit of each separation as it relates to others. (The form is a group of pages, frequently 8 or 16, that are printed together. The imposition is the arrangement of those pages within the form.)

Register and fit are checked first because they affect the color of the images. One does not want to give an instruction to take down the yellow when the problem lies in the fit or register of the yellow image.

The second step is to take the densitometer readings on the color bars for each color across the proof. The densitometer readings indicate the amount of light absorbed by the ink (the balance of the light being reflected back to one's eye), which for a given ink is a function of the ink thickness laid down by the press. They should be to the specifications required by the printer, which will be different depending upon whether the proof is a chromalin or press proof.

These densitometer readings should not vary above or below the printer's specifications by more than 5 percent. If they do and you are not aware of it, then you might call for a color change that should not be called for. If the densitometer readings vary wildly, reject the proof and call for a new one.

Sometimes different densitometers will give different readings for the same sample, indicating that they are not calibrated the same way. In this case the densitometer should be checked against a known standard. If the readings for the known standard coincide with the printer's requirements and with the proof, then the densitometer readings for the proof are satisfactory.

How close to the transparency can a printed separation come?

The mail marketer must recognize that something will inevitably be lost in going from the transparency to the printed separation. That something will be the density range. The density range for an original transparency might be 2.70, but for a duplicate transparency it would be less, maybe 2.60, and for printing on glossy white paper it would be closer to 1.95.[2] As the gloss and grade of the paper become less, the density range will diminish.

---

[1] Sheet-fed presses print one cut sheet at a time, either one color in a pass through the press or four colors in a pass. On sheet-fed printing, only one side at a time can be printed in four colors. On a web press, paper comes off a roll and is printed four colors, top and bottom, in one pass and is sheeted and folded at the end.

[2] Density is the measure of the ink's ability to absorb light. It is the opposite of reflectance (R) or transmittance (T). These are, respectively, the percent of light, measured say in foot candles, reflected to the eye from the printed paper or transmitted through a transparency. The formula to calculate density is:

$$\text{Density} = \text{Log}_{10} \frac{1}{\%R} \text{ or } \text{Log}_{10} \frac{1}{\%T}$$

The significance of this is that one cannot have as good contrast and detail on the printed page as in the transparency and that it will go down as the gloss and quality of the paper goes down.

Viewing conditions

Transparencies and printed sheets should be viewed under the standard conditions used by the printing industry. The transparency viewing device should have 5000° Kelvin color intensity, and transparencies should not be viewed in a darkened room. Masks should not be put around transparencies because it is less like viewing a printed sheet. Printed sheets should also be illuminated with 5000° Kelvin light when being viewed.

Calling for corrections

Ideally you should not have to call for corrections. The color separator should not present his work to you if it does not faithfully reproduce the transparency within realistic limits. From a practical standpoint, you will make some corrections. Here are some suggestions.

When calling for color corrections, it is well to understand the principle of complementary colors. White light is the sum of all the colors of the visible spectrum. When a beam of white light is projected onto a white sheet of paper, all the light is reflected back to the eye and the paper appears white. If that white light is projected onto a white sheet of paper that has been printed with a yellow ink, the light will penetrate the ink and bounce off the white sheet back to your eye. The violet-blue light, however, will be absorbed by the ink and your eye will see what is left of the white light after the violet-blue has been subtracted. This residue of white light after violet-blue has been subtracted is what we call yellow. Yellow is the complementary color of violet-blue; which physicists would call minus violet-blue. If magenta ink (pink) is printed on top of the yellow ink, then green light is also subtracted, leaving only orange light (minus violet-blue and minus green) to be reflected back to your eye. If, finally, cyan (pale blue) is printed, then all colors are absorbed and no light comes back to your eye. Black is included as one of the printing colors only because in practice not all of the light is absorbed by the inks of the three printing primaries. Black is no light at all.

The significance of this is that color corrections can be made by adjusting the problem color or by adjusting the other two printing primary colors. When one of the printing primary colors appear to be wrong, there are two possible corrections: One is to increase or decrease the primary color that seems to be wrong. The other is to increase or decrease the other two printing primary colors. Normally, one would increase or decrease the color that is apparently wrong. But sometimes the separation is weak; raising the other two colors has the effect of canceling out the offending color and increasing density. It is also possible to reduce the ink of two colors to let the desired color come through. When the color problem does not appear to involve just one of the printing colors, two or even three of the colors will have to be adjusted.

Other times, the color of the project is right, meaning that the printing inks are in balance; but the subject has a weak, washed-out look. This means that all the colors are too weak and should be increased. This correction can be applied to part of an image or to the whole separation.

When detail is lacking in shadow areas, a technique to bring it up is to reduce all three of the printing primaries of yellow, magenta, and cyan and to increase the black. Reducing the primaries will decrease the ink laid down in the shadow areas, while increasing the black will accentuate the details.

As in shadow areas, detail is often lacking in white subjects. When detail is lacking on white subjects, then a special black halftone can be done by programming the scanner to bring up the detail. (The scanner is a machine that separates the colors in a transparency and makes the separate sheets of film for each color, called separations, from which stripping negatives are made and from which, in turn, the printing plates are made.)

Improving on the Transparency

Although the printed density range can never equal that of the transparency so that in that respect the color separations cannot improve upon the transparency, it is possible to improve on the transparency by modifying the color of subjects and increasing contrast between the product and its background.

The object of everything that is done is to present the product and, by so doing, sell it. When background colors are too close to the color of the product, the product becomes less visible and will gain less attention on the page. Less attention inevitably means lower sales. The first way to control the background so that the product stands out is to select the right background for the photograph (this was covered in Chapter 9). But if you find that the background was still too dark, too light, or had the wrong colors and contrast could be improved after the picture is taken, then have the background changed on the separation. You will be amazed at how much more the product will stand out. I have often done this with great results. For example, at Lawson Hill Leather and Shoe Co., we often photographed brown shoes against a light blue background, but we would frequently find that the background was too dark and that there was magenta in it as well. We would lighten the blue and greatly reduce the magenta to gain the contrast we wanted. When we photographed shoes on women's feet, we often lightened or darkened flesh tones in the separation in order to increase contrast with the shoes.

Sometimes the background can be psychologically improved. For example, when the photograph of the R.A.F. flying jacket for the British Isles Collection was taken, it was a cloudy day. We changed the sky from dull gray to sky blue to make the picture more cheerful.

Sometimes you have a photograph that you like very much, but the color of one of the subjects is off, or the whole photo has a cast that you do not like. These problems can be corrected in the color separations.

Methods of Separating

Photographs for a catalog can be separated individually, put together in page montage assemblies and then separated, or grouped together by similar densities, separated, and then the separations can be stripped into their page positions.

The individual separating of each photograph produces the best results because the photograph can be analyzed by the separator and scanned according to its particular density. The drawback to this method is that the number of scans is greatly increased, and, since most separators charge by the number of scans, costs are greatly increased. Furthermore, there is a charge for stripping each scan into its page position.

Since only one scan is required instead of several on a page montage and since the separations of the individual photographs do not need to be stripped together, separations of page montages are far less expensive than individual separations of each photograph. The only cost besides the scan is the assembling of the photographs into the montage, which is a small fraction of the cost of stripping. So that the page separation comes out well, the exposures for the page must be selected so that they are in balance with one another. If one is too light and the other too dark, then the separator has to decide whether to favor one or the other or compromise and scan them as they are.

Photographs can also be sorted by their densities into groups and then scanned together. After they are scanned and proofed, they are then stripped into their respective pages. Because photos of similar densities are together, this method has the advantage of reducing the number of scans and increasing the quality of the separations. Because of the additional stripping, however, the cost is greater than the page montage. Furthermore, there is the risk that the fit on one or more of the illustrations will be off because of the increased number of items that must be stripped together. One further advantage to this method is that when illustrations are butted together, the joint is cleaner and less noticeable than when the transparencies are assembled together.

I have always had my transparencies assembled in pages and then scanned. Since I always request at least three and maybe more exposures, I usually have been able to pick exposures that balance well. However, when I look back, I feel that in some instances I would have been better off to pay the price for individual scans. On long press runs, individual scans are unquestionably the best way to go, the extra cost being made up by increased sales.

The Transparency

Choosing the transparency exposure

In addition to the consideration of balancing the exposures when a page montage is to be separated, one should look for detail in the very dark and very light areas when choosing a transparency. These are the areas where the most detail will be lost in printing because of tone compression, which is a reduction in density range. The detail in these areas must be strong, even exaggerated, in order to avoid weak detail in the final separation.

Duplicates versus shooting to size

There are two approaches to getting the right size transparency for making the separation. One is to photograph so that the image on the transparency is the size as it is to be illustrated on the catalog page, usually using a 4 × 5 inch or 8 × 10 inch camera. The other is to photograph with $2\frac{1}{4} \times 2\frac{1}{4}$ inch film and then make a duplicate that is the same size as the illustration. Of course, if each photograph is to be scanned individually, then no duplicate need be made because the scanner will do the enlarging. Shooting with $2\frac{1}{4} \times 2\frac{1}{4}$ inch film saves the cost of the larger and more expensive film but incurs the cost of making the duplicate. I much prefer shooting to size. First of all, I can lay my layout tissues on the ground glass of the camera to check size and position. Second, it has been my experience that the duplicates are often not close enough to the original. And, finally, as mentioned earlier in this chapter, the density range is less in duplicates.

However, fashion shots, that is, shots of clothing taken on models, are better taken with 35 mm or $2\frac{1}{4} \times 2\frac{1}{4}$ inch film because so many shots are needed to catch the right facial expressions and other transient features. For these, duplicates are made, or they can be scanned individually.

If one should have duplicates made, then one should specify RQT (Reproduction Quality Transparencies) duplicates. These are made by a more expensive method (costing almost four times as much) than the alternative method.

Correcting photographs

Photographs often can have the color problems and other defects corrected in the photo laboratory. Detail can also be enhanced there. The method is to have a duplicate made (if the correction is made on the original and the correction is botched, then you are lost) on which corrections are made by applying dyes by hand. In the instances where I have had corrections of transparencies done, I found the result heavy-handed and not to my liking. Knowing that I am going to lose detail in the separations, I must prefer to have plenty of detail in the original transparencies without having to correct them. If broad areas need to be corrected, I prefer to make these corrections in the separations.

Methods of Proofing

There are at least four methods of proofing: (1) 3M color keys, (2) chromalin proofs, (3) 3M match prints, and (4) progressive press proofs.

3M color keys

In 3M color keys, pigment of each of the four printing colors is put onto the images of four light-sensitized layers of otherwise transparent polyester. These are mounted one on top of the other and, when viewed together, give the overall effect of the printed illustration. This method of proofing is the least expensive of the proofing methods, is good for a final check, and tells whether type needs to be reversed in shadow areas (that is, instead of printing the type in black, printing no ink at all in the spaces occupied by the letters so that the letters are outlined by the inks surrounding them). 3M color keys will also tell if final color corrections have been made. They are not accurate, however, and should not be used for making color corrections.

Chromalin proofs

Chromalin proofs are made by laying a layer of light-sensitive acetate sheet over which the separation film of one of the colors is placed onto a highly-coated glossy paper (chrome-coat). It is then exposed to light and dye powders are rubbed onto the surface. Another layer of light-sensitive acetate is laid down and the process is repeated with the next color. When all the colors have been applied in this manner, it is covered with a protective sheet. This type of proof produces a fairly accurate representation of how the printed sheet will look.

3M match prints

More accurate in representing colors are 3M match prints. This method is similar to chromalin except that the dyes are already incorporated into the acetate sheets.

Progressive press proofs

The ultimate proofing method is to prove the separations on the press on which the catalog is to be printed with the paper that is to be used for it. Since the separations are frequently made by someone other than the printer and since the press is often a web press with a high hourly rate, this method of proofing is usually not practical, except that defects noticed after the job has started to run can be corrected by making a change in one or more of the color separations and making a new plate or plates.

More practical are progressive press proofs done by a sheet-fed press. On progressive proofs each color is printed by itself onto separate sheets so that one can see how each color looks by itself. Then each printing primary color is printed with another printing primary; this step is repeated so that each primary is paired with the other two. Then the three printing primary colors are printed together so that they can be seen without black, and finally the three colors plus black are printed together. This method of proofing is the most accurate representation of how the catalog will look when printed. It is, however, the most expensive proofing method.

Choosing a proofing method

I have been told that 90 percent of the proofing is done today by the chromalin method. It is much cheaper and some separators do not have the facilities with which to make press proofs. But I belong to the old school that still prefers press proofs. If I am going to spend enormous sums on catalog, postage, and list rental, I don't wish to skimp on the proofs and take the chance that the representation of the products on the catalog page will cost me sales.

Not only are press proofs more accurate, but, because one can see separately the dot structure of each color, one can make better decisions in making color corrections. For example, one might feel that yellow should be increased, but a look at the yellow progressive proof might show that there is little yellow dot to enlarge. One might want to accent detail by increasing black; a look at the black progressive will tell whether there is a sufficient black dot structure to be increased to produce the desired result. Or one might want to lighten backgrounds; the progressives will show what the component colors are and suggest what corrections to make. These are typical of the decisions that can be improved by being able to analyze with press proofs the components of the color of the subject.

Obtaining Good Separations

For many, the making of separations is an arcane subject best left to others. To me the mystery and challenge of laying on paper the image of the products I wish to sell has been the most absorbing side of mail order. In this chapter I have tried to both make the subject interesting and to give the mail marketer the essentials of what he needs to know and do in order to obtain good separations.

The most important thing the mail marketer must do is to engage a good separator. In order to do this, he must recognize good separations when he sees them. He should also have an understanding of color and be able to call for the right corrections.

Knowing the great impact of good separations upon sales, the wise mail marketer takes advantage of the opportunity to improve upon the photograph in separations. While the density range of the printed page in the shadow and highlight areas never matches that of the original transparency, there are few photographs in which the product cannot profitably be made to project more from its background and there are many in which the detail of the product itself can be enhanced.

The mail marketer must consider cost, and separations are expensive. But their cost is dwarfed by the sales they affect and the other costs of putting a catalog in the mail. Good separations make an enormous difference in the effectiveness of a catalog. For this reason, it is a mistake to try to save a small amount of money, say $50 to $75 per page, on separations and then jeopardize sales. What is the cost/value relationship? That is, how much better a separation can you afford? My answer is that, unless you are mailing very few catalogs, if you can clearly see the difference in quality, you should pay the difference in price.

High cost, of course, does not equate with better separations. Some separators have high overhead and selling expenses and charge more for inferior separations. The key is to recognize good separations and insist on them.

how to get good printing

Printing is the last link in the chain of events that connects the products with their representation in the catalog. If you have managed it well, along with layout, photography, and color separating, you will have a visually strong catalog. Poor printing, like poor separations, will destroy the best photograph. This chapter gives you what you need to know to have a well-printed catalog that will maximize sales.

Types of Printing Processes and Printing Presses

The three types of printing processes that a mail marketer is likely to encounter are offset lithography, letterpress, and gravure. Of these, offset lithography is by far the most common and is the method of printing discussed in this chapter.

Lithography is based upon the principle that oil and water don't mix. Water is used to repel the oily ink from the non-image areas on the plates. The ink from the image areas on the plates is transferred to a rubber blanket wrapped around a cylinder (which is why it is called offset) and then again from the blanket to the paper. In letterpress, raised images are inked and impressed upon the paper. In gravure printing, wells are etched into printing cylinders; on press, these wells are filled with ink which is transferred to the paper. Gravure cylinders are costly to make, but they last for very long press runs. Good printing can be done by gravure on low-grade and lightweight paper, which is an important cost factor for large catalogs where the weight of the paper exceeds the postal minimum and the cost of the paper is substantial, because there are many pages. Catalogs such as L. L. Bean's are printed by gravure.[1]

---

[1] You can identify gravure printing by looking at letters under a magnifying glass. If they appear to be composed of round dots, then the printing is gravure.

The two types of presses that one normally encounters are sheet-fed and web. A sheet-fed press, as its name suggests, has one sheet of paper fed into the press at a time. The press will print one color at a time or as many as four colors at a time, one right after the other, in a single pass through the press. In either case, the sheet-fed press prints only one side at a time.[2]

The web press prints onto a continuous strip of paper, called a web, that is fed from a roll in the back of the press. The web is printed top and bottom each in four colors as it passes through the press. At the end, the web goes through an oven to dry the ink and then is cut into sheets. The sheets are folded into what are known as *signatures*. Because of its lower start-up cost, the sheet-fed press is suitable for short press runs. But on longer runs, the web press is more economical. The successful catalog mail marketer soon graduates to a web press. I have seen web price quotations for a 16-page $8\frac{1}{2} \times 5\frac{1}{2}$ inch catalog be competitive with sheet-fed in runs as little as 25,000 impressions. Sheet-fed printing used to be considered better quality than web, but today the reverse is true.

Choosing the Paper

Other than selecting the printer, there is no printing decision made by the mail marketer more important than choosing the paper. The qualities of the paper greatly influence the quality of the reproduction of the product image on the catalog page.

Types of paper

For catalog printing, there are two types of paper and mixtures of the two. These two types are ground-wood paper and free sheets.

Ground-wood paper, as its name suggests, is made by chipping logs, grinding the chips up into a pulp and laying the pulp along with other additives between two continuous belts, the lower belt being a fine wire mesh and the upper being a felt. A free sheet is made in a similar manner but the difference is that the pulp is first digested in a pressure cooker for a number of hours, which separates the lignins from the cellulose fibers in the pulp. Lignins are the binders that hold the fibers together in the wood; in paper they are impurities. A free sheet means that the paper is free of the lignin impurities.

The ground-wood paper is opaque because of the lignin impurities. But, because the cellulose fibers, which remain in the free sheet, are somewhat transparent, the free sheet tends to lack opacity. Opacifiers, usually of titanium dioxide (TiO_2), are added to make the free sheet opaque and white. The pressure cooking and the addition of the titanium dioxide make the free sheet about twenty percent more expensive. But the lack of lignins makes a much cleaner and whiter sheet, and the free cellulose fibers lie down smoother and result in a glossier finish when coated. Furthermore, the ground-wood paper tends to absorb water from the press, resulting in a puffing of its fibers. The free sheet, by comparison, remains smoother, with the result that the dot is more faithfully reproduced on the paper.

The significance of the two types of continuous belts mentioned above, the fine wire mesh belt and the felt belt, is that the wire mesh belt leaves an impression on one side of the paper. Although the coating is supposed

[2] Except for some sheet-fed presses that can invert the paper halfway through the press and print one or two colors on each side, a process called *perfecting*.

to cover this up, in practice one can often see a difference in the ways the two sides print.

Qualities of paper

The qualities of paper that the mail marketer should be concerned about are (1) printing gloss,[3] (2) weight, (3) whiteness, and (4) opacity. Of these, by far the most important is printing gloss. High printing gloss means that the ink sits on top of the paper in well-shaped dots and does not disperse into the paper causing a gain in dot size. It has what printers call good hold-out. When there is high printing gloss, the white spaces between the dots remain, and there is no fill-in and plugging. The density range, which we discussed in the previous chapter, is the greatest in paper with high printing gloss. Although it is rarely the case, it is possible for the gloss to be so high that the ink will transfer to the printed sheet above it. This is called set-off. It is normally controlled by the oven temperature. Other than this problem, a paper cannot be too glossy. The glossiest of papers are the free sheets.[4]

Because paper that is very glossy has so much free cellulose fiber it is more expensive. And, because it is expensive, the mail marketer must weigh the improved printing quality against its additional cost.

The other expensive quality of paper that the mail marketer must evaluate is the weight of the paper. The cost of paper in a catalog goes up almost as fast as its weight, and postage can go up just as fast if there are so many pages that the weight is over the postal minimum. Unless an extremely flimsy paper is used, a light paper will print almost as well as a heavy one of the same grade. If one lays the same image printed on two weights of the same grade of paper side by side, there will be little visual difference. The register and ink hold-out will be the same. The difference to the consumer with the catalog in hand will be feel. How important feel is in producing sales I don't know. It is of some importance, but, given that increased weight does not greatly improve product representation in the catalog,[5] I think that, if one elects to spend more money on paper, one should go to a free sheet first. Heavier paper, however, is often well-advised for the outer forms as it will stand up better in the mail and, in addition, will provide feel at less cost than printing the whole catalog with it.

In theory, more whiteness means that the colors will be truer. Not only are whites whiter, but, because more light bounces off the whiter paper through the yellow, magenta, and cyan inks, these colors also are more accurate. In practice, however, the difference in whiteness between papers commonly used for catalogs usually produces an insignificant difference in the quality of the representation of the product.

Opacity can be serious if it is wanting. But most papers are opaque enough.

---

[3] I use the adjective *printing* to modify *gloss* because some papers can appear glossy but microscopically they are not and disperse ink away from the dots.

[4] Because a paper of a specific trademark and weight will print differently from printer to printer because of differences in ink, oven temperature, and ink density, the best way to judge a paper is to compare it with other papers printed by the printer you intend to use.

[5] Sometimes the printed results of papers of the same trademark but of different weights will vary significantly because the papers are made on different paper-making machines. Usually, 38-pound through 50-pound papers are made on similar machines, whereas heavier papers are made on different machines. Lightweight ground-wood papers (32- through 50-pound) print better than heavy ground-wood paper (60- through 80-pound). Conversely, lightweight free sheets have less opacity than heavy free sheets. Therefore, you must always judge the printing qualities of paper in the weight you intend to use.

When the day comes that the catalog goes on press, the printer will ask the mail marketer to come down to the printing plant to okay the quality of the printing after the press starts up. There are two stages to bringing the sheet to the point that it can be okayed: (1) gross adjustments and (2) fine tuning.

Gross adjustments

In the first stage, one does not particularly concern oneself with color accuracy. Instead, one steps back from the printed sheet to get an overall impression and asks these questions: Is the ink glossy enough? Is plenty of ink being laid down? Are the register and fit precise?

The ink, as well as the paper, should be glossy. If there is insufficient ink, there will be little ink gloss. Ink gloss is a function of the glossiness of the paper, the sufficiency of ink, the speed of the paper going through drying ovens and the temperature of the ovens.[6]

If insufficient ink is running, then not only will there be little ink gloss, but also there will be low contrast. The sheet will have a flat, dull look. Sometimes, if the ink is very low, it will have a filmy look—as if film were laid across the sheet, making it semi-opaque. I have often seen catalogs printed this way, including my own when I didn't know better.

Before any color tuning can be done, any problems in fit and register must be corrected. A few thousandths of an inch displacement of one color will cause an overall color shift as that color moves into the light areas. The pressman corrects register problems on a modern web press by dialing into the electronics of the press the amount of shift of the plates needed. Problems of fit are corrected by cocking the plates and changing the lateral tension of the web.

Fine tuning

Once ink gloss, ink density, register, and fit have been made right, then one can control the amount of ink laid down for each color and, in so doing, control the color. This is done by adjusting the flow of ink from the row of ink fountains that run along the printing cylinders of each color. If a color is weak, the flow of ink can be increased. If it is too strong, the flow can be decreased. But, remembering the principle of complementary colors explained in the previous chapter, a color can be changed not only by adjusting the flow of its own ink but also by adjusting the flow of ink of the other two primary printing colors. For example, if the yellow is too strong, one can either reduce the yellow or increase the cyan and magenta, depending upon the situation.

One must realize, however, that an adjustment in the ink flow in a certain ink fountain affects every image on the cylinder that passes that point. An increase of ink to one image means an increase in every image on the cylinder passing those fountains that were adjusted. This means that if the separations are not perfectly balanced, that one will have to favor one image over another, or one must compromise the color of both images. This is why it is so important to have accurate separations that

---

[6] Lower temperatures mean the ink will dry glossier, but the danger is that the ink will come out wet and smear. Since the press runs at top speed once the okay is given in order to keep costs down and sharpen the image, the ovens must be long enough to thoroughly dry the ink on the web and still retain the gloss.

are strictly held to specified densitometer readings and why one good separator should be responsible for all separations.

Some printing problems

In addition to bringing the images up to color with good ink density and gloss and with precise fit and register, you should look for and be able to recognize certain printing problems, which you should have corrected before you okay the printing of the rest of the catalog.

Sometimes, instead of being symmetrical, the dot is elliptical or has a tail like a polliwog when examined under a magnifying glass. This is called *slur* and is caused by looseness in the cylinders. Slur will cause a color change and muddiness.

Occasionally, the ink and water balance is off. If the ink is stronger than the water, a weak film will print between the dots. Or, if the water is the stronger, the image will be weak. Sometimes water is so strong that one will keep turning up the fountains to strengthen the image but with no result.

Doubling occurs when a second set of dots, usually weaker, is printed next to the original. This is usually caused by looseness in the cylinder.

Trapping is the ability of the ink to adhere to ink previously laid down. When poor trapping occurs, insufficient ink is laid down for one or more colors, resulting in a color shift. The degree of trapping can be determined by examining the color control bars visually and with a densitometer.

The blankets will also wear. Light areas on the printed sheet, areas of low ink density, or a weak image as if not enough ink is laid down are symptoms of blanket wear. The solution is to replace the blankets.

Sometimes the images will appear blotchy. This usually happens when the rubber blankets pick up paper coating. This condition is corrected simply by washing the blankets.

After the Press Okay

Once the images of your products have been brought up to color, you have seen to the elimination of any printing problems, and ink gloss, ink density, register, and fit are made right, you can give your okay for the job to be run by signing one of the signatures. The pressman will then post the signed copy at the press as the standard by which to check color as the catalog is printed. You also should retain some copies to check the quality of catalogs.

While the process of bringing the printing to the point where it can be okayed is going on, the pressman keeps the presses running at midspeed so not to print too many signatures of unsatisfactory quality. Once the press okay is given, the pressman will speed up the press to design speed. With the speed increased to design speed, the quality of the printing will actually improve. The printing sharpens, as they say in the trade, because the ink laid down on the paper is confined closer to the dot size of the plate rather than spreading. After 40,000 impressions there is further sharpening, which is the result of plate wear making the dots smaller and increasing highlights.

As time passes, a quality deterioration that the mail marketer should expect to see is the dulling down of the ink as the ink dries. The ink has its highest gloss just after printing when it is still a little wet. With the passing of time, its volatile components evaporate and the ink gloss dulls somewhat.

As the press runs, samples of the printed signatures should be taken periodically. A good web offset printer takes and identifies samples every

10,000 impressions. These are kept by the printer for a while in case any question of quality arises. If every sample taken is satisfactory, then the customer knows that any quality problem occurred in less than 10,000 signatures.

Engaging a Printer

The dilemma

Poor printing, like poor separations, can seriously affect the quality of product representation in the catalog and, hence, affect sales. The difference between separations and printing, however, is the vast difference in cost. Printing price quotations, depending upon how competitive the printing market is, can vary widely. The difference between one printing quote and another even in moderately-sized press runs can be enough to buy the separations several times over. The mail marketer, therefore, cannot completely disregard the cost of printing and go for quality, for the improved quality might not increase sales enough to overcome the added cost.

Should you seek quality or cost savings? The magnitude of this dilemma can be lessened by being well-prepared. Good, well-balanced separations that have been proved on press and checked with a densitometer provide the printer with a standard to meet. If, in addition, you specify a paper with a good printing gloss, the printer has a responsibility from which he cannot escape.

Then, if you can recognize the characteristics of good printing, such as sufficient ink and ink gloss, you are in the position to demand it. Demanding good printing does not mean that you will get it, but, if it is clear to the printer that the responsibility is solely his and that you know what good printing is, you are far more likely to get quality. This might permit you to go to a lower-cost printer rather than play it safe by going to the best, but higher-cost, one.

Finding a printer

Of course, even though you are in a strong position to demand quality, you never should knowingly select an inferior printer thinking you can hold the printer to your standards by force of will. You must find out which of the printers whose quotations you are considering will do satisfactory work.

The first test to apply is: Is the printer regularly printing other mail-order catalogs, or is he doing mostly publications? Because catalogs must sell products rather than merely entertain, buyers of mail-order printing are much more demanding than buyers of publication printing. Do not go to a printer that has printed few catalogs. Let someone else be the guinea pig.

If a printer has done a substantial amount of catalog printing, then call the printing buyers of many of his catalog customers to see what they think and obtain samples of their catalogs. Ask the printing buyers about the printer's consistency, his ability to lay down ink, and all the other qualities discussed in this chapter. You will get conflicting reports so try to evaluate their ability to judge printing as you talk to them. Make sure that their problems, if they had any, are not of their own making: Was the problem actually in the separations or in the paper that they selected?

If your separator has had experience with the printer, then he is a good person to call. He knows printing better than you ever will and has an interest in seeing that his separations are run properly. Of course, he has no direct interest in your saving money and so might not factor that in when making a recommendation.

Using the evaluation process just described, narrow down the printers you are considering to about three. Even if his quotation is much higher, one of these printers should be one that you are certain is good. Then visit the plants of all three. Look at the work in progress and take random samples. Compare the work of the two printers you are not sure of to the one you are certain is good.

Then ask yourself these questions: Who prints the best? What is the cost? Who has the best price? What quality is the printing? And, is the difference in quality and consistency worth the difference in cost? Or do you think you can hold the lower-priced printer to your standards?

There are three other questions you should also ask yourself before you make your final decision. (1) How conveniently located are their printing plants? Traveling to out-of-the-way printing plants can be time-consuming and expensive. (2) How flexible are they if you are not able to meet a press date, and does missing a press date set you back three weeks? (3) How good are they at meeting mail dates? This question should be asked of the catalog-printing buyers when you call them. The cost of a missed mail date in lost sales can more than offset the saving in printing costs.

Once you have answered these questions, you can make your decision. This lengthy procedure is worth the effort and time because you will have established the relative merits of the printer, which is information you will use profitably for many catalog printings to come.

There is one precaution you should take. Many printing companies have several plants, some of which might do publication-grade work but clearly are not qualified to print catalogs upon which the sale of your products depend. Be sure you visit the plant in which your catalog would be printed and then specify that plant in your printing contract.

Negotiating printing contracts

Printing quotations are rarely rigid and can usually be negotiated and improved upon. The starting point is to obtain at least a half a dozen quotations to determine what the price should be. Then, when you have narrowed down the field of printers, negotiate lower prices, playing one printer off against the other.

A big part of printing cost is the amortization of the huge investment the printer has in printing presses, equipment, and plant. In order to recover that investment, the printer seeks to keep his presses operating twenty-four hours a day. Buyers of printing that can offer substantial volume can negotiate a significant reduction in price.

One way to offer substantial volume is to enter into a two- or three-year printing contract. Because the printer cannot foresee that his plant will be booked up several years hence and because the total amount of printing offered is so much greater, the multi-year printing contract is of great attraction to him. In a multi-year contract, a base price is negotiated, to which the inflation in the cost of paper, ink, and labor is added each year at an agreed-upon formula. If the contract you are negotiating is with a new printer, it is wise to include an escape clause, so that, if you are not satisfied with the printing, you can terminate the contract after the first run.

The Decision

Selecting a printer is the most important printing decision made by the mail marketer. It is a decision that is made difficult by the facts that printing costs a lot and good printing is so important to the success of the catalog. Is one printer as good or almost as good as another? Should you save money or go with the printer you know is good? The secret to making this decision is to be prepared. Never compromise on separations, and know printing well.

media advertising

The size of a mail-order company can be measured by the size and quality of its mailing list of buyers. There are two ways to build the list: one is by mailing to rented lists, the subject of later chapters, and the other is by advertising in media.

**Ways of Building a Buyers List
by Advertising in Media**

Product advertising

Many mail-order companies, particularly small entrepreneurs, start out by selling products from ads in magazines and newspapers. If the entrepreneur is lucky enough to have picked out the right product and prepared a good ad, he will break even or make a small profit. If he doesn't break even, he will give up or try a different product. If he does break even, he will slowly build a list of buyers. When his customers reach a significant number, he will need other products to sell to them. This need eventually leads to a catalog.

Since the purpose of the ad is to build a mailing list, the ads should generate customers that are likely to buy products that are consistent with the theme and concept of the catalog. The products selected for the ads must, therefore, fit and support the theme and concept.

As an approach to building a mailing list, selling products from an ad has great appeal because, if the ad is successful, its cost is quickly recovered and the money can be recycled into another ad. The problems with this approach are these: If the product has a high ticket and even if sales from the ad are sufficient to break even, few buyers are generated for the mailing list because few sales are required to break even. But if low-ticket items are sold in the ad to generate a large number of names, buyers will be added to the mailing list that by and large do not respond well to high-ticket offers. If the catalog that is sent to these customers consists of high-priced merchandise, then they will follow up poorly. They will follow up better if mailed a catalog of lower-price merchandise, but it must be added that such catalogs are harder to make profitable. Gift and gadget mail-order companies have built their businesses, in part, with the approach of generating many names through the direct sale of low-priced products in media and then mailing to them a catalog of similar and somewhat higher-priced merchandise.

There is a second problem with media-generated customers. Regardless of how much they paid for the product they bought from the ad, they do not follow up as well as customers generated from catalogs. In fact, a criterion of evaluating a list to be rented is how many names on the list are media-generated buyers and how many are catalog-generated. The reason for this poor follow-up of media-generated buyers is that a person buying from an ad has demonstrated only a very narrow interest for a specific product. He has not demonstrated a willingness to browse through a catalog and buy from it.

An interesting example of how narrow the interest of a media-generated customer is can be seen in Old Pueblo Traders, a former consulting client of mine that sells women's ready-to-wear and some footwear. For years, they had a successful media program selling low-price pant boots. In the course of those years they built up a substantial list of customers who bought other low-price pant boots and low-price footwear from their catalog. But Old Pueblo Traders found that only a small portion of their pant boot customers bought their ready-to-wear fashions. They, in effect, had two businesses within one catalog.

This leads us to an important point. Although generating buyers through media ads may be profitable and worth doing, this produces a customer that does not follow up as well as a catalog-generated customer. Therefore, the mail marketer must identify media-generated customers on his file[1] and track their sales separately from catalog-generated ones. He can then mail catalogs to these media-generated customers with less frequency and can stop mailing to them sooner.

A third problem with selling products directly from an ad to generate customers is finding the right product. As I said earlier, the product must be compatible with the concept and theme of the business—that the customer generated by the sale of the product must be interested in the other products offered in the catalog. This sometimes imposes a restriction that makes it hard to find a product that will sell in sufficient volume to break even. At British Isles Collection, we had no product that worked in media ads, and at Lawson Hill Leather and Shoe Co. we had only a few.

One additional point should be made. There are a few notable exceptions to the general rule that high-ticket merchandise does not generate enough names. Among these is J.S.&A., which sells high-ticket electronic gadgetry directly from ads. The secret of their success is that through skillful product selection, ad preparations, and copywriting they have been able to make full-page magazine ads work and sometimes have had several full-page ads running in the same issue of a magazine.

It is interesting to note in passing, however, that when one rents J.S.&A.'s list, one does not usually do as well with it as with Markline, a catalog of electronic gadgetry, whose customers are catalog-generated. The difference between the two lists is that Markline's customers are people who have taken the trouble to browse through the Markline catalog to see

---

[1] *Customer file* is mail-order jargon for the mailing list of customers.

if there is anything they might want to buy. J.S.&A. customers, on the other hand, have only shown that they buy when their attention is arrested by an ad for a very specific product with a very specific copy approach. The difference in the responsiveness of the two lists demonstrates once again the difference in follow-up between media- and catalog-generated customers.

Advertising for catalog requests

Advertising for catalog requests is a two-stage approach to building a mailing list of buyers. An ad is run asking prospective customers to send for a catalog. The catalog is then mailed to these catalog requests, as the persons who request a catalog are known in mail order. Some of these catalog requests will buy when they receive the catalog, becoming catalog-generated buyers.

Disadvantages to this approach are that it takes longer for one to get back one's money and one must have an effective catalog to send out. For the small entrepreneur starting out, not having ad money coming back quickly might cause a cash flow problem, and having an effective catalog with a broad selection of merchandise might be impossible.

There are, however, some big advantages. By advertising for catalog requests, one usually generates a great many requests because the customer outlays little or no money. Then these catalog requests often can be mailed catalogs many times before they cease to be profitable to mail. How often they can be mailed depends upon the original medium and the catalog. At Lawson Hill Leather and Shoe Co., we were profitably mailing catalogs to requests more than six years old. Other companies mail catalog requests only a season before they drop them.

The big advantage to this approach is that the request who becomes a buyer is a true catalog buyer who will usually pay more for his products and respond well to future mailings of the catalog.

A third advantage of advertising for requests is that, if the ad clearly communicates what the catalog sells, the respondents will be responsive because their interests will closely parallel what the catalog offers.

Advertising for catalog requests and sending catalogs out to them was the way Marcia and I started Lawson Hill Leather and Shoe Co. For two or three years until we got into renting lists, that is the way we built our business.

Advertising to support
a list-rental program

For most mail marketers, mailing to list-rental names eventually dominates their publicity expense[2] budget and the response to media advertising for requests appears to atrophy. As more and more catalogs are mailed to rented names, the advertising program seems to produce fewer and fewer requests for catalogs. What is occurring, of course, is that the catalog is arriving before the recipient has an opportunity to send for it. Furthermore, many people, because they received the catalog one time, feel that they are on the cataloger's mailing list, even though they may not be.

The poorer, increasingly unprofitable results would suggest to the mail marketer to abandon advertising for requests and to advertise only products to be sold from the ads if the right products can be found. To do this, however, would be to ignore or dismiss as insignificant the effect the media ad has on improving the response to catalogs mailed to rented names.

[2] Publicity expense is any expenditure to generate sales, such as advertising, catalog, postage to mail catalogs, and so on.

That this effect occurs there is no doubt. At British Isles Collection during fall 1981, we had excellent results when we mailed catalogs to the subscribers list of *British Heritage* magazine. We also placed a catalog request ad in the August issue, before we mailed our catalog to their subscribers list in September, and again in the October issue. We received excellent response to the ad in the August issue and virtually none from the October ad, indicating that the mailing of the catalog to the entire subscribers list preempted the October ad. What was really interesting, however, occurred the following year: The owners of British Isles Collection, who had bought out my interest, failed to place any ads in *British Heritage* magazine and, as a result, response to the catalog mailed to the subscribers lists plummeted.

What happened was that the ads in the magazine had created recognition for the catalog, which resulted in the catalog being looked at and ordered from. The October ad, unproductive as it was in generating catalog requests, was very productive in boosting sales when the catalog was mailed to the subscribers list.

This case, of course, is exceptional because the magazine's subscribers list and the list to which the catalog was mailed were one and the same. But it clearly demonstrates the fact that advertising improves the response to catalogs mailed to rented lists. The imponderable is not qualitative but quantitative: How much do mail-order ads improve response to catalogs mailed to rented lists?

I know of no studies that have quantitatively established the correlation. Indeed, such studies are probably impossible to structure. But, judging from the severity of the impact of the failure to advertise in *British Heritage* magazine upon the mailings of the British Isles Collection, I feel certain that a correlation is strong and that an advertising program of some extent, for this reason alone, is warranted. Even though ad response goes down with increased catalog circulation, the larger the circulation, the more an advertising program is advisable to support the catalog.

Mail marketers, by long conditioning, are not disposed to spend money on publicity efforts that don't produce a measurable result. And this caution saves them from making many big mistakes. In the name of institutional advertising, one could well spend too much money in an ad support program. But although one must be careful, one also must not overlook this opportunity.

One alternative is to develop a program of selling products from mail-order ads. If these ads are at least self-liquidating, then the favorable impact upon list-rental mailings is a free benefit. This idea is easier to suggest than to execute, however, as it is usually pretty difficult to find products that sell well in ads and that also characterize well the product line of the catalog.

How to Put Together a Mail-Order Ad

Getting attention

The first thing an ad must do is get attention. This means the ad must be conspicuous on a page of ads and the headline must interest the targeted customer.

If the ad is small and likely to be located anywhere on a page of similar, small mail-order ads, all of which will be fighting for attention, the problem is how to increase its visibility. There are several ways. Frequently the headline can be put in extra bold type in white reverse in a black background. This can also be done with the logo type at the bottom of the ad.

A second way is to put a heavy black border around the ad. But, since many mail-order advertisers do this, the ad may become just another ad with a black border in a sea of ads with black borders. In this case, doing the opposite by having no border at all will make the ad contrast with the others and give it greater visibility. Another advantage to no border is that not having a border will free space for a few more lines of copy or allow the illustration to be larger.

Whether the ad is small or large, however, there is one characteristic it must have in order to gain and hold attention: good eye flow. If the ad layout is confusing, the casual reader will not make the effort to read the ad and will pass it by. The ad must be laid out in such a manner that it is easily read. The eye should naturally rest upon the product or the headline first, and then after viewing these two elements be easily drawn down through the ad so that all the important elements are read. The principles of eye flow, as described in Chapter 8 for catalog pages, apply with equal force to mail-order ads. If the same ad is to be run many times, it may pay to have eye flow tests done.

The headline

The headline determines whether or not the ad is read by the right prospect. It is, therefore, the most important element of an ad. It must interest and stimulate that prospect to read further. If the purpose of the ad is to solicit catalog requests, then the headline must convey what is inside the catalog, or it must appeal to the interest that the catalog is designed to satisfy. If a product is being sold, then the headline should convey what the product is and its unique benefits. When the reader does not know what the product is, and the picture is not certain to communicate it at first glance, the reader will have no interest. Headlines, particularly in small ads, therefore, can rarely afford to be oblique—they must be direct.

Here are some examples. An ad in *Smithsonian* magazine was headlined "There's a Cry," a rather cryptic headline. The body copy was not much more illuminating; it ran "for the worthwhile, the different, the truly memorable—Here it is!" Not until the end of the ad was there a clue to what was being sold when only the three words *Covered Wagon Vacations* appeared. I presume they were selling vacation trips taken in covered wagons. How much more effective that ad would have been if it were headlined "Relive the Old West on a Covered Wagon Vacation." It is a long headline, but at least it would inform the prospect of what was being offered and possibly interest him in the vacation. And, if space were a problem, all copy except the imperative *Send for brochure* could be eliminated.

In another instance, Richlee Shoe Co., a consulting client of mine that sells height-increasing shoes called "Elevators," had an advertising program of four ads with these headlines:

1. Take on a whole new image in Elevators
2. Make people look up to you
3. Don't wait until she brings it up
4. It's second nature to want to be taller

Only in the fourth ad is there a hint of what is being sold.

When the new owner and manager, Bob Martin, came on board, he changed the headlines to:

5. Be Two Inches Taller
6. Height Increasing Shoes

Although at this writing it is too early to know the results, there is no question but these headlines will stimulate more ad readership and more response because they are direct rather than indirect. Headline number (5) might get more readership if it were changed to: How to Be Two Inches Taller.

Picture of the offer

The purpose of the picture in the ad of the product or catalog is to aid recognition of what the offer is. It also increases ad readership because people like to read captions that explain pictures.

If the offer is to send a catalog, then the mail marketer must decide if the picture is to be of the catalog or a representative product. When the product line is broad, as with L. L. Bean, then a picture of the catalog is best, because any one item would create the impression that that item typified the whole product line. Richlee Shoe Company, on the other hand, wisely illustrates a shoe because that best says what they are selling. But even when the product represents the whole catalog, as shoes do with Richlee, there is the weakness that its picture does not communicate to the reader that he should send for the catalog. The first impression is that the reader should send for the item illustrated. If there is room, the ad would be improved with an additional illustration of the catalog.

Some thoughts on copy

Copy clinches the headline. Pay close attention to the first sentence; it must sustain the interest aroused by the headline so that the rest of the copy is read.

Mail-order ads are usually small, so it is doubly important that every word count. Sentences should be recast so that the same thing is said in fewer words. Concepts of marginal value should be eliminated to make room for ones that are important.

If the purpose of the ad is to solicit catalog requests, then the functions of the copy are to establish the worth of the product line and the broad selection of the line within its limits. Selection can be demonstrated by a representative list of the products available followed by the words "and much more." If the product line is for both men and women, make sure that is clear. Here is how we tried to express in a one-column 2½-inch ad that our catalog had a broad selection:

Headline:	SHOES & CLOTHING from the BRITISH ISLES
Subhead:	Men and Women
Copy:	Send $1.00 today for your catalog. Superb Loake English shoes, authentic WWII R.A.F. flight jackets, Wilkinson swords, kilts & ties in your tartan, cavalry twill trousers, gamekeeper jackets, Liberty print dresses, beautifully tailored clothes of handspun and handwoven fabrics, color coordinations, Irish handknits, and much more. Most never offered in U.S. before. Stocked in N.H. for Christmas ordering.

Picture: Catalog
Logotype: British Isles Collection

This ad ran in the *Wall Street Journal*. If the ad had run in a women's magazine, then the mix of goods listed in the copy would have been shifted to include more feminine items.

Coupon

Although only a small percentage of respondents fill out a coupon, the coupon does serve the purpose of suggesting action be taken and, in so doing, increases response. But the coupon takes space and space costs money. A one-inch ad that has a one-inch coupon added to it doubles in size and doubles in cost. A ten-inch ad with a one-inch coupon added goes up in cost by only 10 percent. If a coupon, by stimulating action, increases response by 10 percent, then it pays for itself in the ten-inch ad and not in the one-inch. Each mail marketer, if running larger ads, should split-run test an ad with a coupon and without. If he is running smaller ads, three or four inches or less, he may still want to test; but it is a pretty safe bet that the coupon will not pay.

Other considerations
in preparing a mail-order ad

If your catalog is free or you are selling a product, be sure to give your telephone number so you can get impulse orders or requests for the catalog. Even if your number is not an 800 number, you should list it. Many people use their business phones and are not concerned about the cost of the call. Although the catalog may not be free, it may pay to list your telephone number and let people charge the catalog to their credit card. Alternatively, you could *not* charge for phone requests for catalogs. With the main purpose of the charge for the catalog being to filter out respondents with only mild interest in the product line, the cost of the phone call would provide the filter.

If you are selling products from the ad, don't forget to list the charge cards that you accept.

If you can, make your logotype bold enough so that it draws the eye down through the ad.

Use the word *complimentary* instead of *free*. Louis Cheskin taught me long ago to describe our free catalog as a *complimentary catalog* rather than a *free catalog*. The word *free* connotes little value.

Use the word *subscription*. If you are charging for the catalog, you might express your catalog offer as a subscription. This makes the respondent feel as though he is getting more.

Department number

Many beginners in mail order fail to code their ads and consequently don't know what results each ad produces. Each ad in each issue should be coded separately. Coding systems include a department number, such as British Isles Collection Dept. 12, or a change in the street address number, such as 12 Main Street.

Some mail-order firms use a code, such as Dept. Y2, which tells them that the respondent came for the February issue of *Yankee* magazine. This method, however, makes manual sorting and tallying difficult, particularly when the code becomes BHG 12 for the December issue of *Better Homes & Gardens*. Simpler to handle is a straight numerical system, such as Dept. 12. In this system, pigeon holes can be marked in sequence for rapid sorting.

If the results are keyed into a computer, then the difference is only a few key strokes, although again the numerical code usually takes fewer strokes.

To Charge or Not to Charge for the Catalog

Charging respondents to one's ads a price for the catalog serves two purposes: it creates a small amount of revenue (in some cases a significant amount) and it filters out respondents who are not likely to order. Of the two reasons, the second is the most important, for if the list of catalog requests is loaded with people who are only mildly interested in the product, not only is money wasted in sending out catalogs unnecessarily, but also the life of the mailing list is shortened because the response to mailing the list falls below the break-even point sooner. Thus the mail marketer, by the presence of uninterested respondents in his list, is denied by below break-even costs the opportunity of continuing to mail to his list of catalog requests.

Charging for the catalog, however, also filters out some potential respondents who would order from the catalog. They viscerally dislike paying for a catalog that they think they ought to receive free, they don't have a dollar in their wallets, or it is too much work for them to write out a check.

So what should the mail marketer do, charge or not charge? The question ultimately should be answered by split-run testing in magazines. But, in a situation where an immediate decision is necessary and there is no time to test, there are some guideposts. If sales received from the catalogs mailed to requests are very high, one can afford to mail to both interested and uninterested respondents. But if the sales response to the catalog is low, not too far from break-even, then a charge should be made.

For example, one of my clients, although he does not charge for his catalog, gets very few requests for his catalog from his ads. But, he receives almost $15,000 of sales for every thousand catalogs he mails to these requests. It would be folly for him to charge for his catalog to save a small amount of postage when the catalog requests produce so much business.

On the other hand, if he were receiving many requests but sales from the requests were close to his break-even point of about $800 per thousand requests, then he would be well-advised to filter the requests by charging for the catalog.

If one decides to test whether one should charge for the catalog, the ad results should be tracked over successive mailings until they cease to be productive. Thus one will be able to compare their life expectancies. The Life-Time-Value (LTV) method of evaluation, which ascertains the present value of a future stream of income from a list segment, should be used. It is described in Chapter 15.

Should the response of catalog requests acquired in a particular season weaken to an unacceptable point, one can mail a letter to the requests asking if they still wish to receive the catalog.

Mail Requests First Class or Third Class?

The answer to this question is similar to that of whether to charge for a catalog. When someone writes in for a catalog and you send it to him third class, the catalog is delayed two or more weeks by the slowness of third class and delay in your office as you do the sorting and accumulate the two hundred name minimum required by the post office.[3] This slowness costs

[3] This delay is much less for firms that mail many thousands of requests daily. For them,

sales. The longer someone waits for a catalog, the less likely it is that that person will order.

But first-class postage can add substantially to costs. The decision, first class or third class, can be tentatively made by analyzing the responsiveness of the names: the more sales per catalog the names produce, the more desirable it is to mail first class. Since the names produced by some media are more responsive than names produced by others, the decision must be made on a medium-by-medium basis. Ultimately, each mail marketer should test to determine whether first- or third-class postage is the most cost effective.

There is one other factor to consider when deciding between first class and third class. If it is close to Christmas or some other date that cuts off sales, then one must mail first class.

Small Ad Versus a Large Ad

If an ad is big enough to effectively communicate the whole message, then, there are usually diminishing returns in increasing the ad size. Nevertheless, greater visibility and amplification of the message will be achieved, which will increase response, but not in proportion to the increase in ad size. If the ad is very profitable, then it is likely that it would be worthwhile to increase the ad size or run it more frequently in the same medium. On the other hand, if the ad is marginal, it should be kept as small as possible.

Best Time to Advertise, and Shaking the Tree

If there is one concept of advertising that advertising salesmen like to push that is pure nonsense in mail order, it is that repetition is necessary in order to get results. In mail order, the reverse is true: the more times you shake a tree, the fewer apples will fall with each succeeding shake. Each succeeding ad in a medium produces fewer responses than the ad preceding it.

For this reason, many mail marketers find it necessary to limit the number of request ads that they put in a medium during any one season. If they sell merchandise and can vary the merchandise offer, then they can increase the number of ads. When they are limited as to the number of ads, then they must decide which issues are the best ones to go with. While it may vary somewhat from product line to product line, the best issue in the fall is the September issue (although for products that sell better in early fall, August may be the best). In the spring, it is the January or February issue that is best for most products. These issue dates are early enough in the season to allow time for the ad to be seen, the catalog sent for and received, and the merchandise to be ordered and received. The later the ad is run, the less time there is for the catalog to work before the season expires.

Testing and Evaluating Advertisements

Which is the most effective ad, ad A or ad B? This question can be answered by split-run testing in magazines. This is possible because two copies of an

---

there is no wait to accumulate the minimum number of names and, because the catalogs can be presorted and sacked at least by postal sectional center and sometimes by zip code, the catalogs travel quickly through the mails. For these firms, first class rarely pays.

issue of a magazine are printed with each revolution of the printing cylinder. One copy can contain one version of an ad, and the other copy the other version. In effect, each ad appears in every other copy of the magazine, which assures statistically equal distributions of the ads. Furthermore, the two versions of the ad occupy the same location in the magazine, and, of course, they reach the public at the same time. In other words, the only variable is the difference in the ads. Within the statistical limits of the response, a good comparison of the two ads is assured.

Readers wishing to know which magazines offer split-run testing should check the Standard Rate and Data Service for magazines for an up-to-date listing. (See Bibliography.)

How do you measure ad results and how do you compare one ad with another and with what you should be doing? So far we have talked much about the various types of ads and how to put them together but have said nothing about how to measure their results. Having the right method for measuring results, however, is almost as important as having the right ads, for it tells you how well you are spending your money and allows you to plan for the future. Yet, there is no more serious and common a weakness among beginners and often mail marketers of considerable longevity than improper accounting for the results of publicity efforts. All publicity efforts must, at least, be evaluated in terms of how they contribute to profit. That is the important subject of the next two chapters.

Part
three
The Basics of
Catalog Mail Order

controlling the business with the profit formula

The experienced mail marketer should not pass by these chapters on the basics. I do not call the basics *basics* because anyone who has been in mail order for any period of time is familiar with them. They are basics because they are basic to running a catalog mail-order business. That a company is successful is no assurance that its management has achieved mastery of the basics. Indeed, many or even a majority of mail marketers are weak or lacking in one or more of them. Often I have seen mail-order companies with dynamics so powerful that they are successful in spite of a virtual disregard of the basics. I have seen other companies with moderately strong dynamics that could be successful if they were not overlooking so many basics. In either case, the companies could have been much more profitable.

The Profit Formula

Nothing is more basic than how one views one's operating results. They can be so presented on the profit and loss statement that management is confused by a welter of illogically grouped, miscellaneous accounts and cannot distinguish the forest from the trees. Or, operating results can be seen, as they should be seen, in their simplest terms.

There are just three categories of mail-order expenses. All expense accounts should be arranged on the profit and loss statement so that they are components of these categories of expenses. These categories of expenses are cost of goods sold, publicity expenses, and operating expenses. Together with sales, they comprise the profit formula. The profit formula for a company might look like this:

Sales	100%
Cost of Goods Sold	45%
Publicity Expenses	25%
Operating Expenses	20%
Profit	10%

The usual component accounts of these categories are shown in Table 14-1.

TABLE 14-1   Chart of Accounts in a Catalog Mail-Order Company

SALES are net sales after returns and allowances are subtracted. It does not include money sent in by customers for shipping and handling, which is an offset to shipping expense.

COST OF GOODS SOLD includes:

Purchases
Inland Freight
Markdowns

PUBLICITY EXPENSES encompasses all money spent to generate mail-order sales either through media advertising or catalog. Publicity expenses include:

Media advertising costs net of any income received from requests in payment for catalogs
Cost of mailing catalogs to catalog requests
Catalog preparation including photography, separations, typography, layout, and so on
Catalog printing
List rental expense net of list rental income
Postage to mail catalogs
Cost of service to mail catalogs
Cost of merge-purge
Any other expense incurred for the purpose of generating sales

OPERATING EXPENSES include all other expenses:

General and administrative personnel (F)
Operating personnel (V)
Payroll taxes (V)
Group insurance (V)
Legal expenses (F)
Accounting expenses (F)
Rent or building expenses (F)
Insurance (F)
Property taxes (F)
Electricity (F)
Heat (F)
Maintenance and supplies (F)
Telephone and Telex (V)
Shipping supplies (V)
List maintenance (F)
Computer (F)
Travel (F)
Samples (F)
Credit card fees (V)
Office supplies (V)
Office postage (V)
Depreciation and amortization (F)
Miscellaneous expenses (V)
Merchandise shipping expense net of shipping charges received from customers (V)
Interest (F)

PROFIT OR (LOSS)

(F) Signifies an operating expense that is usually fixed with variations in sales
(V) Signifies an operating expense that usually varies with sales

The reason for reducing the plethora of accounts to only three is to give the mail marketer perspective. Of course, he or she will want to examine the many expense accounts in detail, but first he or she must always look at the main categories, for they disclose major problems and opportunities and make major decisions possible. When I undertake a consulting project for a client, my first step is always to look at its profit formula to see what it reveals. But before we study some examples of profit formulas, we must first investigate the nature of these main expense categories.

Publicity expense is the dominant expense of a mail-order company. It is the expense over which the mail marketer has the most control before the catalog is printed and the least control afterwards. Once a print order is given and the catalog printed, not only is the expense fixed but sales are determined and many of the other expenses are committed for as well. For most catalog mail-order companies, catalog expense dwarfs media advertising expense. Catalog expense should always be viewed in its two main parts:

1. Those catalog expenses that are fixed regardless of how many catalogs are printed, such as photography, typography, separations, and press start-up; and
2. those catalog expenses that are variable with the number of catalogs mailed, such as printing, catalog postage, order form, merge-purge expense, mailing service, and list rental expense.

It is in the variable expenses of the catalog and in the media advertising program that the mail marketer has the greatest latitude to change the profit formula. List rental programs can be expanded or contracted; ads can be placed or dropped. But changing the quality of photography or separations produce much smaller cost changes and greatly affect the productivity of each catalog mailed.

Operating expenses, like catalog expense, should be divided into fixed and variable; the variable expenses, however, are variable with sales. The expenses that are usually fixed are shown in Table 14-1 and are marked with the letter (F), variable expenses with (V). The significance of this is that, within limits, fixed expenses do not go up and, therefore, do not need to be taken into consideration when making "go" and "no-go" decisions on publicity efforts. Because there are so many operating accounts and many of them are intractable, considerable management effort is required to reduce these expenses sufficiently to produce a significant effect upon the profit formula. Because operating costs vary with the number of orders and the number of items on those orders, the operating expense percentage tends to be small with companies with high average orders. Conversely, operating expenses tend to be a high percentage with companies with low average orders. These companies are compelled to streamline their operations to stay profitable.

Merchandise can be changed as a percent of sales by increasing prices. But raising prices has its limits because it almost always reduces demand.

Applying the Profit Formula

Now let us look at the profit formula in different situations and see what should be done with each of our expense categories to improve profit. A consulting client of mine in the clothing and footwear field had this profit formula:

Sales	100.0%
Cost of Goods Sold	46.3%
Publicity Expense	40.2%
Operating Expense	15.8%
Loss	(2.3%)

For a company in shoes and clothing, the cost of merchandise was good. Increasing mark-up could well have been self-defeating by lowering sales and increasing the percent of publicity expense and fixed operating expenses. Operating expenses looked a little high; an analysis of fixed and variable operating expenses revealed that a third were fixed, which would go down if sales went up. But what was clearly out of line was the publicity expense.

What was happening? Why was publicity expense so high? The answer would be one of four things: (1) The response to the buyers list was low; (2) there were not many buyers; (3) the company was small and fixed catalog expenses constituted a high percentage of total publicity expenses; or (4) the company was buying sales with a heavy publicity program. As it turned out, the company was new and had few buyers of its own and was investing heavily in publicity to get itself up to a profitable level. Little correction was necessary. As the company's own list of buyers, which was expected to respond very profitably, grew, publicity and operating expenses could be expected to come down and the company become profitable.

If, however, the company had been established for a long time and had a substantial buyers list, the correction to make the company profitable would have been to mail fewer catalogs to submarginal[1] rented names. If the company had a very heavy list rental program with many submarginal names, then this correction would be successful. If it did not, then the company would have a fundamental weakness in its dynamics that would have to be remedied.

Another consulting client of mine had a profit formula that looked like this:

Sales	100%
Cost of Goods	42%
Publicity Expense	14%
Operating Expenses	35%
Profit	9%

For the product line (footwear) the cost of goods looked good. Operating expenses were extremely high, but what was really significant was that publicity expense was very low, considering the mark-up. That means they were not spending nearly enough money on media advertising and list rental. The prescription for them, therefore, was to increase sales by renting more names and placing more media ads and to attack operating costs, which were high by at least twenty percent. By increasing sales through

---

[1] By submarginal rented names, I mean names which, if rented, would result in a reduction of profit or in a greater loss.

spending more money on publicity expense, fixed operating costs, as a percent of sales, would go down and thus lower overall operating expenses.

For another client, the profit formula looked like this:

117
controlling the business
with the profit formula

Sales	100%
Cost of Goods Sold	40%
Publicity Expense	15.5%
Operating Expenses	26%
Pretax Profit	18.5%

By almost anyone's standards the profit of this company looked very good. The company, however, had been stagnating for a number of years with little sales growth.

Publicity costs looked low. An examination of their publicity program suggested an expansion of their list rental efforts. Furthermore, they were not mailing their house list sufficiently. These greater publicity efforts might reduce publicity as a percent of sales but so increase sales as to greatly increase the dollars of profit.

Their operating expense percentage looked high, which reflected their low averge order. A program designed to upgrade their average order without decreasing their pull (the percent response to the number of catalogs mailed) was prescribed.

Thus we see in these examples how the profit formula in its simplicity permits the mail marketer to have perspective of his business and gain direction for remedial action. The profit formula prevents the mail marketer from becoming so engrossed in the expense details that he fails to see the big moves that he must make. Most action needed to correct a profit formula weakness requires modification of the publicity cost. To do this, we must first learn how to record properly and to measure the results of our publicity efforts. This we learn in the next chapter.

15
measuring the results of publicity efforts

Too often, the results of publicity efforts are summarized at the end of a season in an incomplete, confused, and inaccurate manner. As the entrepreneur seeks the right method to present them, publicity results are frequently expressed differently from one year to the next, thus making comparisons difficult. Worse still is that the entrepreneur tends to focus on the wrong measure of the results. Often I hear people say "We received a 2 percent response on this mailing." This means nothing unless one knows the average order, the incremental cost of the mailing piece, the percent returns, and whether unknown orders are allocated back to coded orders. Even then one must make some calculations to know the significance of the remark. But, if someone says "The cost of mailing to this list was 25 percent of the sales of the mailing generated," then one can immediately relate the fact expressed to the profit formula and determine if the results were below break-even, at break-even, or contributed to profit.

Reporting the Results of Publicity Efforts

This is the feature of the format that I advocate for analyzing publicity costs. It presents the results of each publicity effort (an advertisement or mailing) in a single number, the publicity cost percent, which tells what the cost of an effort was relative to the sales it generated. Then, if one knows the percent merchandise and the percent variable operating expense, one can tell at a glance whether an effort contributed to profit, reduced profit, or broke even by using the profit formula.

Furthermore, this publicity cost format locks right in to the profit and loss statement, as the total of the sales and publicity costs of all the efforts for a season or year and the publicity percent of the totals is what appears in the profit and loss statement.

How publicity efforts act upon profit when merchandise and variable operating expense percents are known can be seen in the publicity cost analyses shown in Tables 15-2 through 15-5 for the first year of operation of the Mayflower Gift Co., a fictitious company. The last column, marked "publicity cost percent," gives the publicity cost percent of sales for each effort. In the September mailing, Table 15-3, for example, the publicity cost of list A was 55.5 percent, and for list K it was 23.3 percent. From a calculation that we shall make later, we know that for the Mayflower Gift Company, additional publicity efforts break even at a publicity cost of 39.1 percent. The Mayflower Gift Company, therefore, lost money on list A and made money on list K.

The publicity program for the Mayflower Gift Company during its first year consisted of the September mailing reported in Table 15-3, an October mailing reported in Table 15-4, and an advertising program reported in Table 15-5. All the individual efforts reported in these exhibits are summarized in Table 15-2. The total sales, the total publicity costs, and the publicity cost percent shown in this exhibit are the same numbers that appear in their profit and loss for this first year of their operation. Thus, the reporting of the results of all the individual publicity efforts lock into their profit and loss statement.

Fixed and variable costs

For the purpose of simplifying the previous discussion, I glossed over an important distinction in the types of costs. The purpose of this format for reporting the results of publicity efforts is to enable the mail marketer to make the right decisions. He or she must decide whether each publicity effort should be continued, rolled out,[1] or dropped. List K clearly should be rolled out. List A should be dropped or retested. Therefore, to make a decision on each publicity effort, the mail marketer must know what occurs when a change is made. If he rolls out a mailing, he must know how much sales will go up and how much publicity and other costs will go up.

This requires the mail marketer to distinguish between costs that don't go up with an increase in a mailing effort and costs that do. That is, he must distinguish between fixed and variable publicity costs and between fixed and variable operating costs. Fixed publicity costs are those such as costs of photography, separations, and press start-up that don't increase or decrease if more or fewer catalogs are mailed. Variable publicity costs are those such as printing and postage that increase as more catalogs are mailed. Fixed operating costs are those that, within limits, do not change with a change in sales, such as rent and electricity. Variable operating expenses are those such as the cost of shipping an order that change with a change in sales.

Fixed and variable publicity costs

Since only variable publicity costs change when a publicity effort is rolled out or dropped, only variable publicity costs are included in the reporting of the individual publicity efforts in Tables 15-3 through 15-5. The publicity cost percents in the last column of these exhibits, therefore, reflect what will happen if a change is made. For example, if list K is rolled out, publicity costs will increase by 23.3 percent of the sales increase.

Fixed costs, because they do not change, are treated as a separate item in the summary of publicity expenses, which for Mayflower is Exhibit

[1] Roll-out is mail-order jargon for the continuation of a mailing effort in larger numbers.

16-1. They, therefore, do not influence the decisions that the mail marketer makes with respect to individual lists.[2]

The variable publicity costs of a mailing consist of postage, printing of additional copies of the catalog, printing of additional copies of the order form, merge-purge expense, the cost of mailing the catalogs, and list rental expense. Fixed publicity costs of a mailing program consist of layout and design, photography, typography and paste-up, color separations and stripping and press start-up. For advertising, the mail marketer's decision is whether or not to repeat an ad; the variable publicity costs of an ad, therefore, are the cost of the ad and the variable publicity costs of the catalogs sent to respondents to the ad, less any money sent in for the catalogs by the respondents.

Variable operating costs and the profit formula

Just as he or she must consider only variable publicity costs, so must the mail marketer consider only variable operating costs in evaluating a publicity effort. Table 15-6 shows the second year budget for the Mayflower Gift Company and a breakdown of its operating expenses into fixed and variable. Variable operating expenses are expected to be 8.6% of sales. That is, if sales go up or down, operating expenses will go up or down by 8.6% of the change in sales.

From Table 15-6, we also see that the Mayflower Gift Company anticipates that the cost of merchandise will be 52.3% of sales. With this information we can now construct their profit formula for evaluating their individual publicity efforts. For list A the profit formula looks like this:

Sales	100.0%
Merchandise	−52.3%
Publicity	−55.5%
Operating	− 8.6%
Loss	−16.4%

In other words, list A reduced profit by 16.4 percent of its sales. List K, however, increased profit by 15.8 percent of its sales, as shown by its profit formula:

Sales	100.0%
Merchandise	−52.3%
Publicity	−23.3%
Operating	− 8.6%
Profit	15.8%

In the media program, for example, the Smithsonian ad contributed 12.9 percent of its sales to profit, as shown by its profit formula:

Sales	100.0%
Merchandise	−52.3%
Publicity	−26.2%
Operating Expenses	− 8.6%
Profit	12.9%

[2] Some mail marketers allocate fixed publicity costs to the list of customers who have bought within one year. Since one always mails catalogs to customers who have bought within one year, no decision to mail is influenced by this allocation. By allocating fixed publicity cost to the list of one-year-old customers, one can see if the sales from these customers are sufficient to overcome them.

The variable break-even publicity percent

Often the mail marketer makes his decision to roll out a list or repeat an ad based upon whether or not it breaks even. While there may be a sound argument for continuing an effort at less than break-even because of the value of the customers acquired, for many mail marketers the most important considerations are to prevent a negative cash flow and not to reduce profit.

What is the break-even publicity cost percent? This can be quickly calculated from the profit formula. For the Mayflower Gift Company it is

Sales	100.0%
Merchandise	−52.3%
Variable operating	− 8.6%
Available for publicity to break-even	39.1%[3]

Knowing this information, Mayflower's management can quickly scan the publicity cost percents given in the last column of Exhibits 16-2 through 16-4 and determine if an effort contributed to profit or reduced it. If an effort had a publicity percent of less than 39.1%, it increased profit; if the percent was greater, it reduced profit.

Explanation of the Reporting Forms

Publicity cost analysis of a mailing program

There are two forms for doing publicity cost analyses, one for analyzing the results of mailing programs, the other for media programs. The analysis of mailing programs is shown in Table 15-2.

The first five columns of this analysis require little explanation. The *source code* is the code that appears on the mailing label and identifies which effort generated the sale. *Circulation* is the number of catalogs mailed to each list.

$$.391S = \$291/M$$

$$S = \frac{\$291/M}{.391} = \$744/M$$

The number of orders that have been identified as resulting from each mailing are recorded in the column marked *Raw Orders* opposite their respective source codes. In addition, unknown orders, both mail and phone, are recorded in this column. We recognize, however, that the unknown orders are, in fact, generated by the various mailing efforts; but, since we don't know from which efforts the unknown orders result, we make the assumption that the unknown orders are generated by the various publicity efforts in proportion to their known orders, and we allocate them pro rata. When the orders are so allocated, they are given under the heading *Weighted Orders*. For example, in the September mailing there were 799 coded orders, 147 unknown phone orders, and 162 unknown mail orders for a total of 1,108 orders. The 147 unknown phone orders and 162 unknown

---

[3] The corresponding break-even net sales per thousand catalogs mailed (S), where the cost of a catalog in the mail to a rented list is $291/M, is arrived at by equating the percent of sales available for publicity to the publicity cost ($291/M) and solving for S.

mail orders are allocated back by multiplying the number of raw orders for each effort by the ratio of $\frac{1,108}{799}$. List A had 30 raw orders, so its weighted orders become:

$$(30)\left(\frac{1,108}{799}\right) = 42 \text{ orders.}$$

Weighted Pull is the number of weighted orders divided by the circulation and expressed as a percent.

Raw Gross Sales are the coded sales, expressed in dollars, plus unknown phone and mail sales before any returns and allowances are deducted. The unknown phone and mail sales are allocated to the coded sales, in the same manner as unknown orders, to give us *Weighted Gross Sales*.

Average Order is Weighted Gross Sales divided by Weighted Orders.

As much as we would like all orders to stick, inevitably some orders are cancelled and merchandise is returned. *Net Sales* are Weighted Gross Sales from which cancellations and returns have been deducted.

Net Sales Per Thousand are net sales divided by the catalog circulation expressed in thousands. For example, list A had weighted net sales of $2,715 and a circulation of 4,971 catalogs, or 4.971 thousand catalogs. Its net sales per thousand, therefore, are:

$$\frac{2,715}{4.971} = \$546/\text{M.}$$

Catalog Cost is the total of the variable costs, excluding list rental, to mail the catalog to the list in question.

List Rental Cost is the cost of renting the list.

Total Publicity cost is the sum of Catalog Cost and List Rental Cost.

Publicity Cost Per Thousand is Total Publicity Cost divided by the catalog circulation expressed in thousands.

Publicity Cost Percent is the Publicity Cost Per Thousand divided by the Net Sales Per Thousand. This is the index by which we measure each individual publicity effort. For list A the calculation is:

$$\frac{\text{Publicity Cost Per Thousand}}{\text{Net Sales Per Thousand}} = \frac{303}{546} = 55.5\%.$$

Publicity cost analysis
of a media program

A media program, as shown in Table 15-5, is analyzed much the same way as a mailing program but with these differences.

There are no columns for Sales Per Thousand, Publicity Cost Per Thousand, and Catalog Circulation.

Space Cost replaces List Rental Cost and is the cost of the ad in the medium.

Sales of Catalogs is a new column in which money sent in for catalogs is recorded.

Raw Catalog Requests and *Weighted Catalog Requests* handle coded and unknown catalog requests in the same manner as orders.

Raw Orders and *Raw Gross Sales* reflect orders that come directly off the ad and orders that come in as a result of mailing catalogs to the requests.

Catalog Cost is the complete cost of catalogs sent to requests. *Total Publicity Cost* is Catalog Cost plus Space Cost less money received from the sale of catalogs.

Publicity Cost Percent is obtained by dividing Total Publicity Cost by Net Sales. The Publicity Cost Percent for *Smithsonian* magazine, for example, was calculated as follows:

$$\frac{\text{Total Publicity Cost}}{\text{Net Sales}} = \frac{1,265}{4,819} = 26.2\%.$$

The significance of weighted pull, average order, and net sales per thousand

Weighted pull is a number that is often used by people in and out of mail order. But, without knowing average order, it says little. If a mail marketer obtains a one percent pull in a mailing with a one-hundred dollar average order, almost everyone would consider that he did well. But if the one percent pull is joined with a twenty-five dollar average order, the results are below break-even for everyone. Pull can be useful when one tries to think of ways to increase pull without decreasing average order. For example, if one offers additional credit cards, more people will respond, thus increasing pull.

Pull is also useful in determining the amount of risk associated with a given sample size in a test mailing. Raw pull, rather than weighted pull, however, must be used in this determination. This will be discussed in the next chapter.

Average order has considerable significance. If a catalog produces a high average order, the mail marketer must look for other lists of high average order when seeking list rentals. The higher the average order of one's catalog, other factors remaining equal, the more restricted the universe of responsive names. But a high average order has its compensations. Once a buyers list has been built up, it usually produces far more sales per thousand catalogs than do lists of low average orders. Usually, lower operating cost percents are associated with higher average orders because fixed order processing costs are a smaller percent. Weighted pull tends to be lower with catalogs that produce higher average orders.

Low average order, on the other hand, is accompanied by higher pulls. With a low average order, one's list builds faster and there is a larger universe to prospect. Low average order, however, requires an efficient shipping plant in order to be profitable.

Sales per thousand is useful because it tells you how much business you are going to get if you multiply it by the number of thousands of catalogs you are going to mail. For example, if you roll out list B the following September and mail 15,000 names you can expect to do in sales, assuming no other factors have to be taken into account:

$$15M \times \$927/M = \$13,905$$

The sales per thousand is the basis for making all budgets.

Reducing the number of unknown orders

Unknown orders are inevitable, and, when they are a high percentage of the total orders as they are in the case of the Mayflower Gift Company, they put in doubt the accuracy of the publicity cost percents. For this reason, the mail marketer should take whatever steps he can to reduce the number of unknowns.

First of all, the mail marketer can increase the likelihood that the piggyback labels are used by making obvious on the order form that the label should be used. The method that I have used is to print the following legend diagonally in the name and address section of the order form using a gray screen: *Please Peel Off Address Label From Back of Catalog and Place Here.*

Second, the mail marketer can make sure that his telephone order-takers religiously ask the customer to give the source code from the catalog label.

Third, the mail marketer can ask the computer center that did the merge-purge to retain a "short record" tape of the match codes keyed to the source codes and to run the match codes of the unknown orders against it, thus identifying the unknown orders. This is practical, however, only if there are a large number of unknown orders; otherwise, it is too expensive to be worthwhile. About half the unknown orders can be recoded this way.

Fourth, the mail marketer, if his catalog is printed at certain web offset printers, can have the customer's name, address, and source code ink-jet imprinted on the order form before it is bound into the catalog. The ink jet imprints both the order form and the address block of the catalog. After imprinting, the order form is bound inside.

Fifth, if the order form wraps the catalog, then the source code is automatically returned with the order.

Sixth, some mail marketers insert the order form between the covers and the pages opposite and die-cut a hole into the cover so that the label can be attached directly to the order form and show through the hole. In my opinion, this method is using a sledgehammer to kill an ant. Not only is the cover often mutilated in the mails as a result of the weakness created by the hole, but the method necessitates putting the order form in what is often not the best location.

Lifetime Value of a Customer

The value of the calculation of the incremental break-even publicity cost percent is that it enables the mail marketer to decide which publicity efforts can be safely rolled out without contributing a loss. For most small companies, often marginally capitalized, the ability to avoid loss in the current year is a necessity. For them it is difficult to explain to their bankers that the company has a hidden asset of so many customers, and, if the mail marketer decides to capitalize his customers on the balance sheet, which is definitely not conservative accounting, the banker is likely to discount the asset, and tax problems are created as well.

But, if a company is well-financed and can afford to "buy" customers, the question arises: What is the lifetime value (LTV) of the customers being bought? The answer to this question allows the mail marketer to decide what the maximum anticipated incremental publicity cost percent can be and still mail the list.

Lifetime value analysis serves another function. Some sources of new customers will produce customers that last longer than others. For example, at Lawson Hill Leather and Shoe Co., we generated new customers by advertising a low-priced suede casual shoe in the *Wall Street Journal,* the *National Enquirer,* and other media. But these customers had demonstrated only that they would buy a particular bargain from an ad. They did not respond to mailings of our catalog as well as customers who had originally bought from the catalog itself. The question we had to ask ourselves was, "Where should we spend our publicity dollars in the future—in these ads or by increasing catalog circulation?" This question can be asked of all list rental efforts; some rented lists produce customers that last longer than customers that come from other lists.

Calculation of lifetime value

The lifetime value of a customer is the present value of future income to be generated by the customer. Present value means that a dollar received a year from now is not as valuable as a dollar received today. The difference in value between the two dollars is the rate of interest or return on investment at which the dollar received today can be invested. The value today of a dollar received a year from now is $\frac{\$1}{1+i}$ where "i" is the rate of interest or the return on investment. The present value of a dollar received two years from now is $\frac{\$1}{(1+i)^2}$ and "n" years from now is $\frac{\$1}{(1+i)^n}$. Thus, if the Mayflower Gift Company can alternatively earn ten percent by investing its dollar in a money market fund, the present value of a dollar received five years from now is $\frac{\$1}{(1+.1)^5} = \$0.62$. To calculate lifetime value of a customer, therefore, we need to anticipate what the interest rate will average during the life of the customers.

In addition, we need to know the sales per thousand customers to be expected in the next mailing, the number of mailings made each season or year, the decay rates from mailing to mailing within the season and from year to year, the percent the cost of goods and variable operating expenses are to sales, the cost of a catalog mailed to a customer, and the average order. For the Mayflower Gift Company, the values for these are as follows:

Sales per thousand customers	$6,250
The number of mailings next season	3
Decay rates within the season	
First mailing	100%
Second mailing	75%
Third mailing	$(.75)^2 = 56.25\%$
Decay rate from year to year	80% of previous year
Cost of goods sold	52.3%
Variable operating costs	8.6%
Cost of catalog in mail to customers	$236/M
Average order	$ 82

In other words, Mayflower will continue its practice of mailing just in the fall but will have three mailings to its buyers list each fall season. Each second mailing in the fall seasons is expected to do 75% of the first mailing. The third mailing of each season is expected to do 75% of the second mailing, or 56.25% of the first mailing of the season. Each year the mailings will be 80% of the mailings of the preceding year. The cost of goods and variable operating expenses are 52.3% and 8.6%, respectively. The variable catalog cost is $236/M. Mayflower expects on the first mailing to its customers during the year after they were acquired that they will produce $6,250 in net sales per thousand customers. Their average order from Tables 15-3 and 15-4 averages $82.

What then is the lifetime value of one thousand customers? The sales for each mailing are shown below with the second and third seasons reflecting their mailing-to-mailing decay of 75%.

First Year

Sales/M	1st Mailing $6,250 (1.00)	$ 6,250
	2nd Mailing $6,250 (.75)	4,688
	3rd Mailing $6,250 (.75)^2	3,515
	Total Sales	$14,453

From these sales we subtract costs to get the contribution to profit. Merchandise and variable operating expenses are arrived at by multiplying the total sales ($14,453) by their respective percents. Publicity cost is the cost of mailing catalogs to one thousand customers.

Merchandise (0.523) ($14,453)	−7,559
Publicity cost	− 236
Variable Operating Expenses (0.086) ($14,453)	−1,243
Income to be received the first year	$ 5,415

This future income must be multiplied by $\dfrac{1}{1 + .1}$ to arrive at a present value based on 10% interest

$$\$5,415 \left(\frac{1}{1 + .1}\right) = \$ 4,923$$

The calculation for the second year is similar except that we must take into account the decay that occurs from year to year.

Second Year

Sales/M	1st Mailing (0.8) ($6,250)	$ 5,000
	2nd Mailing (0.8) ($6,250) (.75)	3,750
	3rd Mailing (0.8) ($6,250) (.75)^2	2,812
		$11,562

Subtracting Costs	
Merchandise (0.523) ($11,562)	−6,046
Publicity cost	− 236
Variable Operating (0.086) ($11,562)	− 994
Income to be received in second year	$ 4,286

Present value of second year income equals:

$$\frac{4,286}{(1 + .1)^2} = \$ 3,542$$

The third year is similar to the second year except that once again the sales decay by an additional 20% of the previous years sales. We, therefore, must multiply them by 0.8.

Third Year

Sales/M	1st Mailing (0.8)^2 $6,250	$ 4,000
	2nd Mailing (0.8)^2 $6,250 (.75)	3,000
	3rd Mailing (0.8)^2 $6,250 (.75)^2	2,250
		$ 9,250

Subtracting Costs	
Merchandise (0.523) ($9,250)	$ 4,838
Publicity	236
Variable Operating (0.086) ($9,250)	795
Income to be received in third year	$ 3,381

Present value of third year income equals:

$$\frac{3,381}{(1 + .1)^3} = \$\ 2,309$$

If we repeat these calculations until the sales become so small that the profit contribution is overcome by the publicity cost, which is unchanging, we find that in the fifteenth year the total income received will be $23,719 and that the present value of $23,719 is $16,879. This is summarized in Table 15-1.

TABLE 15-1 Lifetime Value of One Thousand Customers, Mayflower Gift Company

YEAR SINCE ACQUISITION	INCOME	PRESENT VALUE OF INCOME	
		i=25%	i=10%
1st	$ 5,415	$ 4,333	$ 4,923
2nd	4,286	2,743	3,542
3rd	3,380	1,731	2,539
4th	2,658	1,089	1,816
5th	2,079	681	1,291
6th	1,616	424	912
7th	1,245	261	639
8th	948	159	442
9th	712	96	302
10th	521	56	201
11th	370	32	125
12th	249	17	80
13th	152	8	44
14th	75	3	20
15th	13	1	3
	$23,719	$11,634	$16,879
LIFETIME VALUE OF ONE CUSTOMER	$23.719	$11.634	$16.879

The important variables in the lifetime value calculations are the sales per thousand customers during first year and the decay factor from year to year. These will be different for every company, and every mail marketer should determine what they are for his company. Both variables should be established for each source of customers (source code) and, of course, for the business as a whole. For companies with computer operating systems, these lifetime value calculations, once a program is written, are easily done. The computer could calculate the decay factor for each source code and then calculate its expected lifetime value. But for companies with manual operating systems, a complete lifetime value calculation for each source code is probably too arduous. Furthermore, source codes with low circulations would yield statistically unreliable results. But calculating them for one or two years will yield some very interesting results, and calculating them for the business as a whole will help the mail marketer decide whether or not he wants to subsidize the acquisition of customers and, if he does, by how much.

How much to subsidize the acquisition of customers

One must be careful when one decides to subsidize the acquisition of customers. If the estimated decay is wrong or changes, one could find that the recovery of one's investment, from a cash flow standpoint, is intolerably long, or could even be never. The longer it takes to recover the investment, the more likely it is that the decay rate changes adversely. It makes sense, therefore, that the decay rate used for calculating lifetime value be conservative.

The decision of how much to subsidize the acquisition of customers depends upon the return on investment (ROI) the mail marketer wishes to make, the cost of mailing catalogs to list rental names, and the other factors for the calculation of lifetime value that were mentioned earlier in this chapter. While a 10 percent return on investment would compare favorably with a money market fund, it was altogether too low a target for the employment of the assets of the Mayflower Gift Company. Mayflower's management desired, instead, a return of 25 percent on assets employed.

What, then, was the sales per thousand rented names that would have provided Mayflower with a 25 percent return-on-investment, assuming that the cost of a catalog in the mail to rented lists was \$291/M. The investment that Mayflower made to buy customers was the portion of publicity costs that were unrecovered by the response to the rented list when it was mailed. If we equate the unrecovered publicity cost to the present value of the customers acquired based on a return on investment of 25 percent, we can solve for the net sales per thousand rented names that will produce this return.

The present value of the customers acquired is $-\$11.634C$, where C is the number of customers acquired and \$11.634, from Table 15-1, is the present value of one customer based upon a return on investment of 25 percent. The negative sign is necessary because the amount is an unrecovered portion.

The unrecovered publicity cost is the difference between net sales and merchandise, variable operating expenses, and publicity cost. For Mayflower, for one thousand rented names, this is $S - .523S - .086S - \$291$ where S is the net sales received in response to renting one thousand names.

Equating the two expressions we have:

$$-\$11.634C = S - .523S - .086S - \$291$$

We have two unknowns in this equation, which means that it cannot be solved unless we have another equation. If we divide the sales per thousand rented names (S) by the average order for Mayflower, we can calculate the number of the customers acquired. From Tables 15-3 and 15-4 we know that the average order for Mayflower averages \$82. Therefore:

$$C = \frac{S}{82}$$

Substituting this expression for C in the above equation we reduce the equation to one unknown and have

$$-\$11.634 \left(\frac{S}{82}\right) = S - .523S - .086S - \$291.$$

Solving for S we have

$$S = \$546/M.$$

The corresponding publicity cost percent is

$$\frac{\$291}{\$546} = 53.2\%.$$

This means that the Mayflower Gift Company will achieve a return on investment of 25 percent if their net sales per thousand rented names is $546. The publicity cost that they must have is 53.2%.

Increasing the Lifetime Value of Customers

These calculations of the lifetime value of customers make clear an important point. Whatever is done to increase the lifetime value of customers will lower the net sales per thousand list rental names needed to achieve a required return on investment. This, in turn, broadens the universe of names to which the catalog can be mailed and thus enlarges potential size of the business.

There is an exponential effect because the methods of increasing the lifetime value both increase sales and profits and make it possible for more lists to be rented. These methods include active renting of the list to others and, particularly, more mailings. Mayflower planned for only three mailings a year to their customer file, but nine or ten are not unreasonable and many companies can mail much more. As can be seen, maximum utilization of one's customer mailing list is a secret of mail-order success. We shall discuss this further in the next chapter.

TABLE 15-2   Publicity Cost Analysis of a Mailing Program:
Summary of First Year Publicity Program

				MAYFLOWER GIFT COMPANY			
SOURCE CODE	LIST SEGMENT	MAILING PIECE	MAIL DATE	CATALOG CIRCULATION	RAW ORDERS	WEIGHTED ORDERS	WEIGHTED PULL %
	September Mailing	Fall Cat.	Sept. 1	129,940	1,108	1,108	0.9
	October Mailing	"	Oct. 25	160,608	1,862	1,862	1.16
	Fixed Catalog Expenses						
	Combined Mailing Program			290,548	2,970	2,970	1.0
	Media Program			2,228	175	175	
	Combined Publicity Program For Year			292,776	3,145	3,145	

TABLE 15-2   (cont.)

AVERAGE ORDER	RAW GROSS SALES	WEIGHTED GROSS SALES	NET SALES	NET SALES PER THOUSAND	CATALOG COST	LIST RENTAL COST	TOTAL PUBLICITY COST	PUBLICITY COST PER THOUSAND	PUBLICITY COST PERCENT
81	90,117	90,117	79,303	610	30,682	7,907	38,589	297	48.7
83	154,706	154,706	136,107	847	37,917	8,865	46,782	291	34.4
					36,400		36,400		
82	244,823	244,823	215,410	741	104,999	16,772	121,771	419	56.5
68	11,961	11,961	10,166				4,423		43.5
	256,784	256,784	225,576				126,194		55.9

TABLE 15-3 Publicity Cost Analysis of a Mailing Program: September Mailing

SOURCE CODE	LIST SEGMENT	MAILING PIECE	MAIL DATE	CATALOG CIRCULATION	RAW ORDERS	WEIGHTED ORDERS	WEIGHTED PULL %
	MAYFLOWER GIFT COMPANY						
800	List A 0-6 mos + $50	Fall Cat.	Sept. 1	4,971	30	42	0.8
801	" B " "	"	"	4,986	48	67	1.3
802	" C " "	"	"	4,516	15	21	0.5
804	" D " "	"	"	5,003	27	37	0.7
805	" E " "	"	"	5,014	33	46	0.9
806	" F " "	"	"	5,008	24	33	0.6
809	" G " "	"	"	5,096	34	47	0.9
810	" H " "	"	"	5,028	23	32	0.6
811	" I " "	"	"	4,881	32	44	0.9
815	" J " "	"	"	9,970	35	49	0.5
817	" K " "	"	"	4,995	71	98	2.0
818	" L " "	"	"	4,990	19	26	0.5
819	" M " "	"	"	4,984	62	86	1.7
822	" N " "	"	"	4,995	17	23	0.5
824	" O " "	"	"	4,905	33	46	0.9
826	" P " "	"	"	5,018	39	54	1.1
827	" Q " "	"	"	5,013	44	61	1.2
829	" R " "	"	"	4,998	16	22	0.5
830	" S " "	"	"	5,350	39	54	1.0
831	" T " "	"	"	5,050	13	18	0.4
833	" U " "	"	"	5,117	18	25	0.5
834	" V " "	"	"	5,024	45	63	1.3
835	" W " "	"	"	5,392	41	57	1.1
836	" X " "	"	"	4,622	19	27	0.6
837	" Y " "	"	"	5,035	22	30	0.6
	Subtotal			129,940	799	1108	0.9
898	Phone	"	"	—	147		
899	Unknown	"	"	—	162		
	Total			129,940	1108	1108	0.9

TABLE 15-3   (cont.)

AVERAGE ORDER	RAW GROSS SALES	WEIGHTED GROSS SALES	NET SALES	NET SALES PER THOUSAND	CATALOG COST	LIST RENTAL COST	TOTAL PUBLICITY COST	PUBLICITY COST PER THOUSAND	PUBLICITY COST PERCENT
75	2,117	3,085	2,715	546	1,174	335	1,509	303	55.5
78	3,605	5,254	4,623	927	1,177	337	1,514	303	32.7
81	1,143	1,665	1,465	324	1,066	135	1,201	266	82.1
92	2,345	3,418	3,008	601	1,181	350	1,531	306	50.9
76	2,421	3,529	3,106	619	1,184	276	1,460	291	47.0
80	1,787	2,604	2,292	458	1,183	275	1,458	291	63.5
87	2,810	4,096	3,604	707	1,203	382	1,585	311	44.0
90	1,997	2,911	2,562	509	1,187	251	1,438	285	56.1
85	2,548	3,714	3,267	669	1,152	342	1,494	306	45.7
86	2,903	4,231	3,750	376	2,354	449	2,803	281	74.7
76	5,104	7,439	6,546	1,311	1,180	350	1,530	306	23.2
87	1,618	2,358	2,075	416	1,178	399	1,577	316	76.0
67	3,945	5,750	5,060	1,015	1,177	324	1,501	301	29.7
85	1,361	1,984	1,745	349	1,180	300	1,480	296	84.8
86	2,743	3,998	3,518	717	1,158	417	1,575	321	44.8
74	2,729	3,978	3,501	698	1,185	251	1,436	286	41.0
93	3,867	5,636	4,960	989	1,184	451	1,635	326	33.0
89	1,345	1,960	1,724	345	1,180	375	1,555	311	90.1
105	3,882	5,658	4,979	930	1,263	401	1,664	311	33.4
79	957	1,394	1,226	242	1,193	354	1,547	306	126.4
80	1,349	1,966	1,730	338	1,208	192	1,400	273	80.8
79	3,439	5,012	4,410	877	1,186	213	1,399	278	31.7
78	3,051	4,447	3,913	728	1,269	242	1,511	281	38.6
71	1,296	1,889	1,662	359	1,091	254	1,345	291	81.0
72	1,469	2,140	1,884	374	1,189	252	1,441	286	76.5
81	61,831	90,117	79,303	610	30,682	7,907	38,589	297	48.7
	15,092								
	13,194								
81	90,117	90,117	79,303	610	30.682	7,907	38,589	297	48.7

TABLE 15-4 Publicity Cost Analysis of a Mailing Program: October Mailing

				MAYFLOWER GIFT COMPANY			
SOURCE CODE	LIST SEGMENT	MAILING PIECE	MAIL DATE	CATALOG CIRCULATION	RAW ORDERS	WEIGHTED ORDERS	WEIGHTED PULL %
838	List A 0-6 mo. + $50	Fall Cat.	Oct. 25	10,060	75	144	1.4
840	'' B '' ''	''	''	5,097	28	53	1.0
841	'' D '' ''	''	''	4,989	34	66	1.3
842	'' AR '' ''	''	''	4,937	31	60	1.2
843	'' E '' ''	''	''	4,993	70	134	2.7
844	'' G '' ''	''	''	5,049	17	32	0.6
845	'' I '' ''	''	''	5,001	51	98	2.0
846	'' M '' ''	''	''	4,940	39	75	1.5
847	'' AS '' ''	''	''	4,985	26	50	1.0
848	'' V '' ''	''	''	5,061	49	95	1.9
849	'' W '' ''	''	''	5,067	35	67	1.3
850	'' P '' ''	''	''	5,092	31	59	1.1
851	'' S '' ''	''	''	5,342	44	85	1.6
852	'' Z '' ''	''	''	4,914	50	97	2.0
853	'' AA '' ''	''	''	5,000	50	59	1.2
854	'' AB '' ''	''	''	4,948	12	24	0.5
855	'' AC '' ''	''	''	4,956	16	31	0.6
856	'' AD '' ''	''	''	5,023	46	89	1.8
857	'' AE '' ''	''	''	4,950	17	33	0.7
858	'' AF '' ''	''	''	5,032	9	18	0.4
859	'' AG '' ''	''	''	5,004	13	25	0.5
860	'' AH '' ''	''	''	4,943	34	66	1.3
861	'' AI '' ''	''	''	5,005	24	46	0.9
862	'' AJ '' ''	''	''	4,972	29	55	1.1
864	'' AK '' ''	''	''	5,029	21	40	0.8
865	'' AL '' ''	''	''	5,240	24	46	0.9
869	'' AM '' ''	''	''	4,964	12	23	0.5
870	'' AN '' ''	''	''	4,984	33	64	1.3
871	'' AO '' ''	''	''	5,000	34	65	1.3
872	'' AP '' ''	''	''	5,000	14	27	0.5
873	'' AQ '' ''	''	''	5,001	19	36	0.7
	Subtotal			160,608	987	1862	1.16
	Phone				499		
	Unknown				376		
	Total			160,608	1862	1862	1.16

TABLE 15-4 (cont.)

AVERAGE ORDER	RAW GROSS SALES	WEIGHTED GROSS SALES	NET SALES	NET SALES PER THOUSAND	CATALOG COST	LIST RENTAL COST	TOTAL PUBLICITY COST	PUBLICITY COST PER THOUSAND	PUBLICITY COST PERCENT
75	5,161	10,817	9,519	946	2,376	639	3,015	300	31.7
81	2,045	4,286	3,791	740	1,204	324	1,528	300	40.3
82	2,588	5,424	4,773	957	1,178	349	1,527	306	32.0
92	2,632	5,517	4,855	983	1,166	321	1,487	301	30.6
85	5,426	11,372	10,007	2,004	1,179	275	1,454	291	14.5
83	1,258	2,636	2,320	249	1,192	389	1,581	311	68.1
78	2,634	7,617	6,703	1,340	1,181	353	1,534	307	22.9
97	3,487	7,309	6,432	1,302	1,167	326	1,493	302	23.2
96	2,284	4,787	4,213	845	1,177	464	1,641	329	39.0
86	3,903	8,180	7,198	1,422	1,195	278	1,473	291	20.5
84	2,691	5,640	4,963	979	1,197	256	1,453	287	29.3
87	2,456	5,147	4,529	889	1,202	306	1,508	296	33.3
83	3,375	7,074	6,225	1,165	1,261	347	1,608	301	25.9
82	3,784	7,931	6,979	1,420	1,160	511	1,671	340	23.9
88	2,495	5,229	4,601	920	1,181	318	1,499	300	32.6
89	1,152	2,414	2,124	429	1,168	203	1,371	277	64.5
81	1,213	2,542	2,236	451	1,170	228	1,398	282	62.5
80	3,389	7,103	6,251	1,237	1,186	229	1,415	282	22.6
78	1,242	2,603	2,291	462	1,169	328	1,497	302	65.3
79	673	1,410	1,241	246	1,188	332	1,520	302	122.5
82	999	2,094	1,842	368	1,182	230	1,412	282	76.7
76	2,394	5,017	4,414	893	1,167	180	1,347	272	30.5
74	1,628	3,412	3,002	600	1,182	Exchange	1,182	236	39.4
82	2,141	4,487	3,942	792	1,174	308	1,482	298	37.6
83	1,567	3,284	2,890	574	1,186	Exchange	1,186	236	41.0
91	1,994	4,179	3,678	702	1,237	249	1,486	284	40.4
85	929	1,947	1,713	345	1,172	203	1,375	277	80.3
84	2,554	5,353	4,710	945	1,177	281	1,458	292	30.9
80	2,472	5,181	4,559	912	1,181	255	1,436	287	31.5
78	1,023	2,144	1,887	377	1,181	178	1,359	272	72.0
73	1,241	2,601	2,293	459	1,181	205	1,386	277	60.4
83	73,792	154,706	136,107	847	37,917	8865	46,782	291	34.4
	49,588								
	31,324								
83	154,706	154,706	136,107	847	37,917	8865	46,782	291	34.4

TABLE 15-5   Publicity Cost Analysis of a Media Program

MAYFLOWER GIFT COMPANY						
SOURCE CODE	MEDIUM AND ISSUE	AD DESCRIPTION	RAW CATALOG REQUESTS	WEIGHTED CATALOG REQUESTS	RAW ORDERS	WEIGHTED ORDERS
21	*Smithsonian* September	Request	772	1,003	48	67
22	*New Yorker* September 8	Request	276	359	18	25
23	*Colonial Homes* September	Request	177	230	7	10
24	*House Beautiful* September	Request	132	171	4	6
25	*House Beautiful* October	Product	66	86	31	43
26	*Yankee* September	Request	159	206	16	14
27	*House & Garden* September	Request	133	173	7	10
	Subtotal		1,715	2,228	131	175
	Unknown		513		44	
	Total		2,228	2,228	175	175

TABLE 15-5 (cont.)

AVERAGE ORDER	RAW GROSS SALES	WEIGHTED GROSS SALES	NET SALES	SALES OF CATALOGS	CATALOG COST	SPACE COST	TOTAL PUBLICITY COST	PUBLICITY COST PERCENT
84.62	4,244	5,670	4,819	802	699	1,368	1,265	26.2
58.84	1,101	1,471	1,250	287	240	557	520	41.6
125.60	936	1,256	1,068	184	160	557	533	49.9
82.50	371	495	421	137	119	718	700	166.2
21.70	698	933	793	69	60	1,389	709	89.4
62.07	651	869	739	165	144	335	314	42.5
126.70	948	1,267	1,076	138	121	399	382	35.2
	8,949	11,961	10,166	1,782	1,543	5,323	4,423	43.5
	3,012	11,961	10,166	1,782	1,543	5,323	4,423	43.5
68.35	11,961							

TABLE 15-6   Second Year Budget and Variable and Fixed Cost Analysis, Mayflower Gift Company

	BUDGET	Percent	Fixed	Variable
SALES	$1,349,600	100		
COST OF GOODS				
Purchases	674,800			
Freight	4,080			
Markdowns	27,030			
Total	705,910	52.3		
GROSS PROFIT	643,690			
PUBLICITY EXPENSE	399,689	29.6		
OPERATING EXPENSE				
General and Administrative Personnel	28,900		28,900	
Operating Personnel	57,200		7,000	50,200
Payroll Taxes	11,700		4,878	6,822
Outside Labor	1,300			1,300
Legal	2,000		2,000	
Accounting	6,500		6,500	
Rent	12,000		12,000	
Electricity	1,700		1,700	
Heat	3,000		3,000	
Maintenance and Supplies	2,000		2,000	
Telephone	9,600			9,600
Insurance	1,700		1,700	
Shipping Supplies	16,000			16,000
List Maintenance	5,000		5,000	
Travel	3,000		3,000	
Samples	4,000		4,000	
Credit Card Fees	18,273			18,273
Bank Charges, other	400			400
Office Postage	2,500			2,500
Office Supplies	9,300			9,300
Depreciation	2,200		2,200	
UPS and Parcel Post	-0-			
Miscellaneous	2,000			2,000
Interest Expense	7,000		7,000	
Total Operating	$ 207,273	15.3	90,878 (6.7%)	116,395 (8.6%)
PROFIT	$ 36,728	2.7		

16
planning for a profit

A profit is rarely bestowed upon those who fail to plan. How is a profit to be made? What is the mail marketer's plan? If the business is not making a profit now, when will it? Are the underlying dynamics of the business strong enough, and does he have the financial resources to realize his dreams? These are the questions a mail marketer must ask of himself and seek to answer.

The three-year plan gives the mail marketer an answer. It tells him or her if there will be enough cash. It tells the mail marketer that, although he or she may not be making a profit now, the dynamics of the business, given time, will build at an acceptable cost a customer list that will make profits.

The bases of the three-year plan are the budgets and publicity plan. The budget shows if the relationship of costs and sales is such that a profit can be made. The publicity plan tells how much sales to expect, how much the sales will cost, how many customers and requests will be acquired, and how the business will be built. The foundation of all planning is the publicity plan. But the publicity plan is even more, for it signals management when the catalog is not on target.

The Publicity Plan

Staying on target

An advantage of mail order is that one deals in large numbers. Individual lists are rarely mailed in quantities of less than five thousand. Tests, which for most catalog companies are five or ten thousand names, are rolled out in quantities of twenty-five and fifty thousand; and proven "workhorse" lists are mailed to the limits of their availability, which often exceed a hundred thousand names. Small tests and mailings are put together with roll-outs and mailings to workhorse lists to make, along with media programs, publicity plans of hundreds of thousands or millions of names. These large numbers, the large number of lists mailed and the large number of names within each list, confer a statistical reliability to mail order that is enjoyed by few other businesses. Only when a new force, such as a change in the catalog or a change in economic conditions, affects every list mailed should there be a major difference between forecasted and actual results. For example, the laws of probability dictate that 95% of the time, when there are no new forces having an impact on the sales of a catalog and where a 2% response is expected, a deviation in excess of 2½% will not occur in mailings of 212,000.[1]

This statistical reliability of a mailing program bears much more thought than is usually given to it. What it means is that, if actual results stray far from what is forecasted, then there is a reason for the difference and that management had better investigate. Does the difference result from a change in the economy, or is there a weakness or strength in the catalog or merchandise that was not there before? Was there a failure in the elimination of duplicate names or in the delivery of the catalog? Was there an error in the logic of the forecast? These questions bring out a few of the reasons why a catalog's results will differ from the forecast. If the results were better than expected, then management needs to know why so it can repeat its success. If the results were worse, then management must learn how to avoid a repetition of errors. The point is that a difference of 10 percent and 15 percent and even more should not be disregarded as a statistical aberration, but rather must be analyzed for its meaning.

The publicity plan, which is the plan of all mailings and advertising for the season, should be drawn up, therefore, with care and in full detail. It should not be a rough approximation, such as, "We will mail 750,000 names and average $800/M and, therefore, do $600,000 in sales." Instead, each list segment should have the number of its names to be mailed multiplied by its expected rate of response to determine its expected sales. Then, list by list and ad by ad, the mailing plan should be constructed. It should be accurate to within a few percentage points.

Building a publicity plan

The Four Main Elements. The publicity plan of a catalog company typically consists of four main elements: mailings to the house file, roll-outs of rented lists, tests of rented lists, and the media program.

These main elements are shown in the publicity plan for the Mayflower Gift Company for the three mailings they planned for the first roll-out year (the first year after the test year) in Tables 16-2 through 16-4. The house file element of the plan consisted of mailings to the few buyers and catalog requests acquired during the test year and, in later mailings, the buyers and requests acquired during the current year. The tests were largely concentrated in the first mailing so that if any exceptional lists were discovered, they could be included in the second and third. The lists that were rolled out were those that came close to or did better than breaking even during the test year. The media program was repetition of the test year, as shown in Table 16-5.

The Mailing Dates. The plan consists of three mailings—a mailing on September 1 designed to hit just after Labor Day, October 25 aimed at Christmas business, and December 22 designed to arrive in the recipient's mailbox just after Christmas for the start of spring business. Two of these

---

[1] See the probability tables in Table 16-6.

mailing times, September 1 and October 25, had been tested the previous year and sales-per-thousand figures for the various rented lists were available for making the forecast. But for the third mailing, that of December 22, no experience was available. The lists for this mailing, being the same ones that were tested previously, had known results; but how they would perform in December was unknown. For this reason, Mayflower's management reduced the sales-per-thousand figure by 25 percent for each of the lists that were mailed in December.

Selecting Lists and Calculating Sales. Having decided upon their mailing dates, Mayflower's management then selected the lists to be mailed on those dates. They had previously determined, as shown in Chapter 15, that additional catalogs mailed at a 39.1% publicity cost do not have an immediate adverse effect upon profits. This criterion was applied to the results of the test year and they planned to mail to all lists that were better plus a few that were close.

To get the sales to be expected from each of these lists, they multiplied the net sales per thousand that each experienced during the test year by the number of thousand names on its list. Similarly, they multiplied the cost per thousand to mail each list by the number of thousand names on its list. The sales products were totaled and the publicity cost products were totaled to obtain the publicity costs and, *tentatively*, the sales for the first roll-out year.

New Forces that Might Affect the Forecast. The sales forecast was tentative because Mayflower's management still had to consider whether the conditions would be the same in the first roll-out year or whether there would be new forces that would affect results.

Would there be more inflation? Would there be a change in the economy for better or for worse? Would there be more competition? Would the catalog or merchandise be better? They decided that there would indeed be more inflation but decided to disregard it because it would affect both costs and sales and cancel out. They foresaw no change in the economy or their competition.

They did, however, decide that the catalog should produce 5 percent more sales because they would eliminate merchandise that failed in the test catalog and replace it with new merchandise, some of which could be reasonably expected to sell well. They did not increase the size of the catalog; if they had, they would have planned for more sales, using the rule of thumb described in Chapter 6, which says that an increase in the number of pages and stockkeeping units of X will produce a sales increase of 1/2X.

Mayflower's management anticipated, however, that there would be a fall-off in sales because they were rolling out tests. Experience had taught them that when tests are rolled out, the roll-outs often do not do as well as the tests and that this sales reduction is about 5 percent, sometimes 10 percent. Mayflower's management decided to plan for a 5 percent fall-off. Having reviewed all the new forces that might influence the mailing results, Mayflower's management determined that they would cancel out and that they did not need to modify the expected total sales that they had tentatively estimated.

Reasons Why Results Fall Off When a Test Is Rolled Out. It happens so often that roll-outs do not consistently perform as well as tests, as Mayflower's management had anticipated, that it bears some investigation. Of course, many times a roll-out does not do as well as a test because there is simply a statistical deviation in the test. But beyond that, there are a number of other reasons why the sales of a roll-out can be depressed. Sometimes list owners are not honest and send out better names in order to sell a later roll-out of their list. Sometimes a computer operator is lazy and sends names from a tape of recently acquired names rather than get an nth name selection[2] from the main file. When either one of these situations occur, the results of the roll-out can be drastically different from the test.

A more common reason for the fall-off in sales in a roll-out is that a test, if the tested names are properly selected from the list, will miss the duplicates in the owner's list because the owner avoids adjacent names as he skips through his file selecting names. Yet most duplicates are adjacently located in the file.

Tests in the publicity plan

Tests are a necessary evil. Their publicity cost is high, but without them there is no future for the company. Tests discover the new lists that can be rolled out to generate new customers and build the business. I have seen mail marketers hold back and even eliminate testing with the object of increasing profits. But, like a high technology company that cuts out the expense of research and development in order to present a good statement to its bankers and stockholders, cutting back on testing in one year lowers profits in the years beyond.

Testing Strategies. The first thing to consider in testing is one's strategy. Is the company small, just starting out, with a management that wishes to play it safe? Is the company well-financed, as one of my clients is, with a management that desires to expand as rapidly as possible? Or is it a well-established company seeking new lists to mine profitably for names? Each of these companies requires a different strategy in testing lists.

The first concern of the mail marketer of a fledgling company with limited capital is the success of his venture. He is only secondarily concerned with how big his business might become. His catalog and merchandise are most likely unperfected, incapable of making marginal lists profitable. He should not risk large mailings. His strategy, therefore, is to be highly selective in his tests.

The fledgling mail marketer should first test lists that were built by the sale of merchandise closely related to his own product line. For example, someone starting a catalog of women's ready-to-wear should test women's shoe lists and, of course, lists of women's ready-to-wear catalogs if their list owners will rent to that person. Within these lists only the very best names should be tested, such as customers who have spent more than a certain amount on their last order and who have bought recently. By being selective, the mail marketer maximizes his chances of success and risks the least capital. Only when he has proven the sure bets should he test marginal lists and marginal selections within proven lists.

There is a different strategy for management of the fledgling venture of a large, well-financed company whose desire is either to build a large

---

[2] nth name selection means a uniformly even selection of names from the entire list:

$$n = \frac{\text{number of names in the list segment}}{\text{number of names being rolled out}}.$$

One can sometimes identify a failure to receive nth name selection when all the names received are from one part of the country.

mail-order subsidiary or not to trifle with it. The management of this company will test a broad spectrum of list categories, testing the lists thought to be the best within each category. Within the lists themselves, they will test less narrow selections of several selections, both narrow and broad. They will seek out lists with the possibilities of large roll-outs. For example, a consulting client of mine, which was a division of a Fortune 500 company and had a large budget, wished to move ahead on all fronts to develop a mail-order shoe company. The first category for them to consider was high-ticket clothing and shoes. Since this category was so sure to be good, all the possibilities within it were tested. Then the best possibilities were tested within the categories of high-ticket general merchandise, high-ticket electronics and tools, golf, business, gourmet foods, credit car mail-order buyers, medium-priced clothing, sporting goods, and, finally, narrow selections within the very large general merchandise lists, such as Lillian Vernon and Spencer Gifts. The following season, once a category was proven, the client would test the other possibilities within the category.

This same strategy will eventually apply to the company whose original object was just to prove the success of the venture. Once the sure categories and lists have been exhausted, the management of this firm should expand its testing by testing what are expected to be the best lists in the different categories and then developing in depth the categories that prove themselves. This category approach should be used for all new catalogs.

The list-testing strategy for the mature mail-order company, once again, is different. This company has tested most of the categories and has tested most of the lists within the good categories. It, therefore, must test deeper into the lists that work, trying different selections, and it must watch for new companies to be tested and be alert to changes in old companies.

Factors to Consider in Selecting Tests. What factors does one consider when selecting lists and list segments to meet the needs of one's testing strategy? We have already discussed product similarity: lists of product lines similar to one's own identify people who are interested in one's type of product and will respond better to one's catalog than lists of unrelated product lines.

We have also alluded to recency: The more recently a customer has bought from a list owner, the more likely it is that he will respond to the catalogs of other mail marketers. As time passes, customers tend to disappear, but their names remain on the mailing list. They also lose interest in buying by mail order, their financial circumstances change, or other things occur that make them cease being good mail-order buyers. The very act of buying, however, identifies those people who will still buy by mail order. The people who have just bought have proven that they are still alive, still live at the address on the list owner's file, still have money, and still buy by mail order.

The names on mailing lists, therefore, are usually grouped in six-month segments, that is, customers who have bought in the last six months, customers who have bought between six months and a year ago, and so on. In addition, there is what is known in the trade as hot line. These are customers who have bought very recently, usually within six weeks or three months. Being very selective, companies will rarely rent names more than six months old and will even concentrate on hot line. Companies looking for many names, however, will rent names as much as a year old, but it is exceptional for them to go beyond that.

Frequency is another criterion for selecting a test. Has the customer bought many times from the list owner? If he has, it is a sign that he is a confirmed mail-order buyer. Frequency applied to a six-months segment, however, greatly narrows the available names. For this reason, it is a criterion that is better applied to a large list. Furthermore, many list owners do not keep track of frequency and cannot provide the selection.

A more useful criterion is the dollar value of the last order. A high dollar value of the last order demonstrates that the customer is able and inclined to spend a large amount of money by mail order. If the average cost of the items in one's catalog is high, then one should seek out lists with a high average order, and then, just to make sure one receives responsive names, one can specify customers who have bought over a certain amount. Alternatively, one can specify a high dollar amount on lists with a low average order to net those customers who will spend enough money to buy one's product. It is not necessary and is even perhaps counterproductive to specify a high dollar selection when one's own average order is low.

A word of caution when specifying a high dollar selection: There are two interpretations of what high dollar selection means. For some list owners, it means that the accumulated purchases during a season by a customer exceed the specified amount. For others, it means that the last purchase was over that amount. Obviously, customers who have taken several orders to spend a certain amount are not worth as much as customers who have demonstrated that they can spend it all at one time. Be sure that the dollar selection you are getting is the amount of the last order placed.

Another factor to consider is how clean and up-to-date the list is. Some list owners are slow in making address corrections, and they may have many duplicates in their file. List brokers often know which lists have this problem and can warn their clients. Check on this before you test a list.

One must also watch out for lists loaded with customers who have bought only products sold directly from media ads or customers generated by sweepstakes or from low-priced solo mailings.[3] None of these customers is as responsive as customers who have bought directly from a catalog without an inducement. Customers who have bought a specific product from an ad or a solo mailing have yet to prove that they will browse through a catalog and buy from it. Customers who bought from a catalog with a sweepstakes offer have been "hyped"; without the hype they usually respond weakly. Be sure the names you rent are catalog-generated.

One must also consider the roll-out potential of the list one is thinking of testing. If a list is small, say ten or fifteen thousand names, there is little point in testing it unless the product line is so close to one's own that one is certain that it will work. On the other hand, when a company has reached a certain maturity and is concerned with expanding its business more than with proving that it is a success, its management must make every effort to test and make the large lists work.

Credit card buyers are another criterion. People who habitually pay with their credit cards are more responsive than customers who pay cash. There are a number of reasons for this. The credit card puts off the immediacy of making payment, and the customer avoids the bother of getting out the checkbook, thus making him or her more inclined to buy. Furthermore, the file of credit card customers has more customers who order by phone. People ordering by phone spend more because, among other reasons, they tend to lose sight of how much they are spending as they

---

[3] A solo mailing is a mailing that sells just one or two closely-related products by featuring their selling points in depth.

place their order. People who order by phone also tend to be more impulsive buyers.[4] For these reasons, mail marketers looking for high selectivity should consider selecting only credit card buyers, perhaps even specifying a particular credit card like American Express.

You can test lists restricted to certain ZIP codes, sectional centers of the post office distribution system, states, or parts of the country. Mailing to selected states or parts of the country makes sense for product lines that have regional or climatic appeal. Specifying ZIP codes is a way of reaching desired income groups. There also is an income selection available on a few large lists, such as Fingerhut, which is derived from the U.S. census. Unless the census information has been recently received, however, the income selection tends to be stale.

One can also consider testing catalog requests, which most mail marketers offer for rent. But since requests are not yet buyers, they respond nowhere nearly as well as buyers. If one finds that the buyers of a list respond extraordinarily well, then it might pay to test their requests.

The house file
in the publicity plan

The biggest and most common error made by new mail-order companies is to mail insufficiently to their own file. The house file is the least costly to mail because there is no list rental expense; yet, because of its high response, it is the most profitable of all lists. The more times the mail marketer can mail to his own list, the more profitable his publicity plan will become.

Neophytes in mail order tend to refrain from mailing their own lists often because they feel that what one mailing gains will be stolen from another. This a fallacy. While it is true that one mailing to customers will steal from another, the total amount of business done and, most likely, the profit made will be greater with repeated mailings during the season. The test is not whether one mailing will steal from another but rather whether the publicity cost of a marginal mailing to buyers is more than offset by the contribution to profit made by the increased sales caused by it.

But there is a further advantage to additional mailings to the house file: The customers who respond are upgraded to the file of most recent buyers, the most productive segment. The very act of stimulating them to buy makes them more responsive to future mailings. It is like an allergy: More exposures to the allergen make one more susceptible to the allergy. It is the same with customers. The more often they buy, the more loyal they become.

The rationale behind repeated mailings is this: At the time a mailing is made, only certain customers are ready to buy. When the catalog arrives, the other customers are away, don't have the money, are distracted by other matters, or have no interest. The catalog is at least put to one side and often forgotten by most customers or, worse, is discarded. But later the situation changes, and another group of customers in one's list become ready to buy. If a catalog arrives at that later time, this group of customers orders. Thus, additional mailings generate additional sales.

How often the mail marketer can mail to his customers depends upon how responsive the customers are and how varied the mailings are. The more responsive the customers are and the more varied the mailings, the more times they can be mailed. Even if the catalog is not changed or has

[4] It is not being done now to any great extent, but mail marketers should keep track of which customers order by phone and which by mail.

only a cover change, mailings every six to eight weeks during the active season should not be too frequent for most cataloguers.

In addition to providing for multiple mailings to the house file, the house file in the publicity plan should be segmented by the recency of the names, with the segments being by the time period acquired, usually a six-month seasonal interval. This recency segmentation is shown for the Mayflower Gift Company in Table 16-8.

Media in the publicity plan

The ads chosen for the publicity plan are chosen the same way as for roll-outs of successful tests. An acceptable publicity cost percent is decided upon and those ads that meet that criterion are repeated. In addition, test ads are run to develop new ads and new media.

An acceptable publicity cost percent for advertising, however, is not necessarily the same as for list rental. Given the same average order and the same publicity cost percent, a dollar spent for publicity in media will produce the same number of customers and the same profit as list rental. But the difference is that media advertising will also produce catalog requests that might be profitably mailed for many seasons to come. If one adds the lifetime value of requests to the lifetime value of customers obtained through a media program, given equal publicity costs, there is a great advantage to the media program.

There is the exception to this, however, to which I alluded previously. Media ads that sell products directly from the ad produce fewer requests and customers of a lower lifetime value.

Test sample size
and roll-out quantities

Having completed the testing program and read the results, the mail marketer is faced with the questions of how reliable the test results are and how much he should roll out each list on the next mailing.

Each test is subject to statistical error. While mailing to the entire list (known as the universe) might produce, say, a 2% return (disregarding the fall-off that occurs in a roll-out), the names actually sampled might result, for example, in a $1\frac{3}{4}\%$ or a $2\frac{1}{4}\%$ return. This inherent statistical error must be taken into account by the mail marketer when deciding upon sample sizes and roll-out quantities.

How much statistical error might occur? To guide the mail marketer, the Direct Marketing Association publishes the probability tables shown in Table 16-6. These tables show the sample sizes for various percentages of expected response necessary for a confidence level of 95% for comparing the results of a test mailing to a fixed percentage point, such as the break-even point. For example, DMA Table 2D shows that if the expected response is 2% and the test sample size is 5,893 names, then there is a 95% chance that the 5,893 test will not differ from a roll-out of the whole list by 0.3%. In other words, if the break-even point is 1.7%, there is a 95% chance that the results of the whole list will equal or exceed it.

If we assume that the mail marketer does not want his list rental program to be less than break-even, what quantities should he mail? If he is rolling out many lists with no one listing dominating the mailing, then the mail marketer can mail those lists that test at the break-even point with the confidence that the lists that tested too high will be compensated for by those that tested too low. But a list comprising a high percentage of the total mailing must be approached with caution. Obviously, the higher it tests above break-even, the more names that can be safely rolled out. In fact, a test response of 2.20% can be assumed to be safely above the break-even point of 1.70 more than 95% of the time. But if the mail marketer wants to be 95% confident that the mailing won't fall below 1.7% and the test quantity was 5,893, then he must accept no less than a 2% response for a large list.

The mail marketer, however, should test a large quantity where the possibility of a large roll-out exists or, alternatively, expect to roll out the list in stages. For instance, while in our example a 5,893 test would require a 2% response to be 95% certain that the roll-out would not fall below break-even, the results of a 12,609 test could be as low as 1.9%.

There are, however, many other reasons for a fall-off. As discussed previously in this chapter, roll-outs always tend to fall off. In addition, the lists themselves can change because of a change in the list owner's customer recruiting program. Expanded direct sales through media, low-price promotions and sales, and sweepstakes all, as we have discussed, generate customers that do not respond well. Other reasons for a fall-off include a change in list maintenance methods and a failure by the list owner to update his file. All these reasons, besides the inherent statistical unreliability of the test, should be taken into account by the mail marketer in planning roll-outs for his publicity program.

Mailing dates

The mail marketer should thoughtfully schedule his mailing dates and then adhere to them. Missed mailing dates occur with the best mail marketers, but they are particularly prevalent among neophytes. Beginning mail marketers are not aware of the enormous cost in lost sales that result from them. If there are several mailings to buyers, as there should be, a delay in the first mailing to buyers compresses the amount of time in which the mailing has to work before the next is sent out. If a mailing to rented lists goes out late, then there is less time for the mailing to work before the close of the season and it is even possible to miss the best buying period. If the results of one list rental mailing are to be read before a second list rental mailing is to be made during the season, then a delay in the first mailing means that its results cannot be read before the final decisions are made on the second mailing. For example, the Mayflower Gift Company did the main part of its testing in the September mailing. If the mailing went out promptly on September 1, there was time to read the results of the tests and make corrections in the October 25 mailing. But, if the September mailing were late, its management would not be able to benefit from reading the results. Make your schedule and stick to it.

Tracking mailing results: the orderline

Once the catalogs have been dropped in the mail, the mail marketer usually cannot contain himself as he awaits the verdict of his customers. Will the mailing be stronger or weaker than anticipated? Besides just plain curiosity, there are good reasons for knowing as early as possible whether or not a mailing is on target: The mail marketer has to plan cash flow and bank borrowings. He or she has to plan the order processing staff. Even more crucial, he or she has to plan the buying of merchandise. Is he or she under-bought or over-bought? If the replacement time in buying merchandise is long, the mail marketer must know early that more merchandise must be bought.

Knowing the results of one mailing will affect the decisions being made on other mailings. If a mailing is coming in strongly, the mail marketer might be emboldened to expand a later mailing. On the other hand, he or she will prune marginal lists from a later mailing if the first one is not coming in well. Knowing how a mailing is coming in will tip one off as to whether or not there is a delivery problem in the mails.

The question of how well a mailing is doing is answered by the orderline. The orderline is the anticipated arrival of orders, expressed as a percent, on a day-by-day and a week-by-week basis and is based upon the previous history of the company. The orderline for the Mayflower Gift Company for mailings made September 1 is shown in Table 16-7. The first week an order is received for a mailing coincides with the start of the orderline. Then each week the accumulated sales correspond with the percent complete given in the orderline table. Mayflower's orderline shows, for example, that at the end of the third week they should expect that 26.8% of the total dollars of sales will be in. This means that if they have received $100,000 in gross sales by the end of the third week, that $100,000 is 26.8% of the total expected sales and that the total expected sales equals:

$$\frac{\$100,000}{.268} \text{ or } \$373,134.$$

It should be noted that forecasts made from early results are subject to error because the catalog may travel in the mails differently from one year to the next and that the early orders, which mark the start of the orderline, may come in early or late with respect to the rest of the mailing. A difference of a few days will make a big difference in the forecast. For this reason, while it may be necessary that the mail marketer draw conclusions, great care should be taken in doing so during the early stages of a mailing.

Many factors influence the shape of an orderline. The mail marketer should be alert to its being different for mailings made at different times of the year. The type of mailing can also influence its shape. A solo mailing, for example, will have a sharp early peak and then fall off rapidly. Catalogs have a longer life, and catalogs with many offerings last longer than catalogs with few. And, of course, catalogs will have their life cut short if another of the mail marketer's catalogs is mailed to the same list a few weeks later. Orderlines will also differ from one company to the next.

The size of the mailing and where it is mailed from also affect the orderline. Large mailings will have more of its catalogs sorted and bundled into postal carrier and ZIP code sacks. Because these sacks travel directly without intermediate sortings at various postal ceners, they move much faster, thus causing an early and sharp peak. Too, mailings made from the center of the country will be distributed and have response sooner than mailings made from either end.

The Budget and Three-Year Plan

Most entrepreneurs are long on inspiration and short on capital. The great danger is that at the end of one, two, or three years the entrepreneur will not have enough money to continue even though he might have an idea with sound dynamics. Therefore, he must determine at the outset that he not only has a sound idea but also that there will be sufficient financial resources to carry it out. The budget and the three-year plan show what will happen to capital and cash at various times in the future. By planning ahead and foreseeing cash difficulties, the mail marketer has the opportunity of adjusting the plan before it is too late. Furthermore, by setting targets, it is immediately apparent whether he is ahead or behind and midcourse corrections necessary to stay solvent can be made.

Many entrepreneurs do not even make a one-year budget, to say nothing of a three-year plan. Yet they may be in grave danger of running out of cash. Often, I have suggested to clients that they make a three-year plan, a recommendation that is invariably greeted with groans and the argument that it would not be accurate anyway. But, even if it is wrong by several fold, it will still give the entrepreneur a sense of proportion. He may think he can launch and sustain his project for an investment of $25,000, yet his three-year plan might show that nearer $100,000 will be required.

Planning, of course, must include considerations other than just financial. The entrepreneur must ask questions like these: How long will the building be adequate? If it is a new venture and management is starting with a manual operating system, how long will it be before the manual system becomes too cumbersome and the company will need to shift to a computer system? What personnel will the company need, and what functions will they perform?

Most important of all is that the entrepreneur must plan the concept of the business. I have people come to me for help who are trying to market one or two items through media ads. My first question to them is "Where do you think the marketing of this product will take you?" Is this product a part of an overall plan that will lead them to a catalog, or is it a single, unrelated item? The profit of almost all mail-order companies depends on being able to mail repeatedly and profitably to one's own customers. But, for a repeat mailing to be truly successful, it must, as we discussed in Chapter 1, appeal to the same interest that first attracted the customers. Selling unrelated items in ads will not develop the homogeneity of customers that will permit this. Establishing a concept of the business with its attendant merchandise plan avoids such errors, but, more important, it guides the way for the development of the merchandise and catalog.

The budget

The budget is the financial planning for the year. It is developed in as much detail as possible, with each expense analyzed for its extent and whether it is fixed or variable or both. Detail in a budget is necessary, not just to improve the accuracy of the forecast, but also to enable the mail marketer to spot expenses that are out of control and to take corrective action. Fixed and variable analysis makes it possible to foresee the consequences of missing one's sales estimate. In making the budget, one should be neither optimistic nor pessimistic but realistic.

The budget of the Mayflower Gift Company is shown in Table 15-6 of the previous chapter. Its sales and publicity cost were developed in the publicity plan shown in Tables 16-2 through 16-5 of this chapter. This budget is Mayflower's best estimate of their costs and sales for the year. If they miss their target, it gives them the opportunity to see what went wrong.

Monthly Budgets.   However, annual budgets are not enough. One does not want to wait until the end of the year to learn that one has completely missed one's budget. The purpose of a budget is control—control of revenue and expenses to make a profit. With the business controlled by a budget, the mail marketer can, when deviations occur, make corrections that will keep his business on course. Control should be exercised continuously, which, for practical purposes, means that the annual or seasonal budget should be broken down into monthly budgets.

For the experienced mail marketer, monthly budgets are a matter of course and are not a great burden because, although they are time-consuming, he can assign the task to his controller. But for the beginning mail marketer, who must select and buy merchandise, plan the marketing, prepare the catalog, maintain contact with vendors, and oversee order processing, shipping, customer service, and accounting, taking on monthly budgets is forbidding indeed. Nevertheless, he should undertake the task. Not only will he gain a measure of control and not lose sight of what is going on, he will also gain a consciousness that he would not otherwise have of those factors that influence the ultimate object of the business—its profit. Mayflower's management recognized the need for monthly budgets. Theirs is shown in Table 16-8.

Contingency Planning. Although the budget is as realistic as possible, neither optimistic nor pessimistic, the mail marketer should realize that something could go wrong: Sales could be less than forecast or expenses could be greater than expected. When expenses get out of line, the monthly budget, if it has been prepared in detail, provides the means for making corrections or at least knowing what is going to happen to profit and cash requirements. When sales are substantially less than expected, the impact upon profit and cash requirements can be severe. The mail marketer should be prepared.

Mayflower's budget showed a modest 2.7% profit—pretty good for the first roll-out year. But Mayflower's management thought their sales estimate could be off by as much as 15% and wanted to know what the effect upon profits and cash would be. Since they had divided their costs into fixed and variable, they were able to calculate this quickly. (See Table 16-1.)

TABLE 16-1   The Effect of a 15% Fall-Off in Sales

	BUDGET		15% FALL-OFF	
Sales	1,349,600	100 %	1,147,160	100 %
Cost of Goods	705,910	52.3%	600,024	52.3%
Publicity Expense	399,689	29.6%	399,689	34.8%
Fixed Operating Expense	90,878	6.7%	90,878	7.9%
Variable Operating Expense	116,395	8.6%	98,936	8.6%
Profit (Loss)	36,728	2.7%	(42,367)	(3.8%)

A 15% fall-off in sales would mean that their slim profit of $36,728 would change to a $42,367 loss and their cash requirements by the end of the year would increase by at least $79,095 ($36,728 + $42,367 = $79,095). Yet this assumes that they can keep variable operating expenses and inventory, which tends to balloon when sales decline, in line with the reduced sales.

Knowing in advance that their cash requirements could exceed their plan by as much as $79,095, Mayflower's management was able to forewarn their bankers of the possibility and arrange for the necessary additional line of credit.

Accounts in the Mail-Order Budget. A few words need to be said about the accounts in a mail-order budget. The budget for Mayflower, shown in

Table 15-6, contains the accounts most often needed in mail order. The amounts in each account are based upon my experience in operating mail-order companies and are in proportion to what any mail-order company might experience. The most important thing to note is the arrangement of the accounts. All operating expenses are together and have their own sub-total. Similarly, publicity expenses are all together. This arrangement fits the profit formula, which gives the mail marketer the perspective needed to view the business.

The balance sheet contains some accounts that are peculiar to mail order. One is Prepaid Publicity. For statements given to bankers and creditors, money spent on publicity should be capitalized as prepaid publicity and then amortized over the life of the catalog, which is usually not more than six months. To expense the publicity all at once could result in deep monthly losses followed by high monthly profits, alternately causing alarm and elation among one's bankers. For the Internal Revenue Service, however, publicity should be expensed when incurred. This gives rise to the Deferred Taxes account. Although the mail marketer will not have to pay taxes for income offset by the expensing of publicity costs, the accounting profession views that there is a tax liability. One other balance sheet account peculiar to mail order is Prepaid Mail Orders. Money that comes in with orders that cannot be immediately shipped must be credited to Prepaid Mail Orders instead of Sales, thus creating a liability on the balance sheet.

The three-year plan

Having completed their budget, the management of Mayflower proceeded with their three-year plan, which included their month-by-month cash requirements for the three years, their forecasted profit and loss statements, and their balance sheets for the yearends.

Their first step was to develop their publicity plan for the two additional roll-out years, their first roll-out year having been already planned. To develop the publicity plan, shown in Table 16-9, they had to decide upon the size of the list rental and test mailings for the second and third roll-out years and the size of the media program. These decisions predetermined the size of the house file that they would also mail. To make this publicity plan, they assumed that the average sales per thousand that they experienced for list rental in the test year would be repeated but that they would experience poorer results in their tests. They thought that their one-year-old buyers would produce $6,250 per thousand. For catalogs inserted in their own packages they thought that $2,000 per thousand would be reasonable. Variable publicity cost for the house file would be $236 per thousand and for list rental $291 per thousand. They assumed that repeat mailings to their buyers list would fall off 25 percent with each successive mailing within the season. As the house file aged, they assumed that each year it would fall off 20 percent of the previous year.

They also planned for one additional mailing designed to hit just after Christmas. Since they had no experience, they reduced the sales per thousand for each list by 25 percent.

To determine the size of the house file they would have for each mailing, they did a forecast of buyers and requests, which is shown in Table 16-10. The reader should note that when customers acquired in a previous mailing buy, they should be upgraded to become current season buyers. The number of buyers and requests upgraded in each mailing was estimated by Mayflower's management by dividing the anticipated sales of each segment for a particular mailing by the anticipated average order of $82. For example, the 3,320 buyers acquired in the test year were expected to do $20,750 in sales the first year:

$$(3,320) \left(\frac{\$6,250}{1,000} \right) = \$20,750.$$

$20,750 divided by $82 meant that 253 buyers, as shown in Table 16-10, would be upgraded to current year buyers during the September mailing of the first roll-out year, leaving 3,067 buyers in the segment.

Calculation of the size of the various segments of the house file at the end of each mailing permitted Mayflower's management to complete their publicity plan. This in turn allowed them, using their known merchandise and variable operating costs and their known publicity and fixed operating costs, to project profit and loss statements for the remaining two years of the three-year plan. This is shown in Table 16-11.

Their next step was to forecast their cash requirements. To do this, they first had to forecast their monthly revenue by applying an estimated orderline to their estimated income statements. This is shown in Table 16-12.

They then estimated their cash requirements, as shown in Table 16-13. To do this, they recorded their estimated revenue for each month in their forecast of cash requirements, as determined in Table 16-12, and their expenses according to when they thought they must pay for them. They thought they could get 60-day terms from their merchandise suppliers and also from their printers and other publicity suppliers. Postage had to be paid at once. Operating expenses were assumed to have to be paid during the month in which they occurred. In addition to purchases of merchandise to cover cost of goods sold, they also provided for the cost of goods that would have to stand by in stock for orders. Finally, they had to provide for the money required to buy the fixed assets needed for operating shown in Table 16-14. The monthly cash balances were then calculated.

Having completed their cash requirements estimate, Mayflower's management then did the forecasted balance sheets, shown in Table 16-15, which they knew their bankers would wish to see.

Some Conclusions on Making a Profit

The Mayflower Gift Company described in this chapter was a fictitious company. But it was not a company created in a vacuum. The publicity plan, the budgets, the three-year plan, and all the steps shown here to construct them parallel the steps I took to launch the British Isles Collection. They were steps I thought essential to the success of the company to which I was about to give birth.

The three-year plan foretold to Mayflower's management, as a similar one did for me, what order of magnitude their cash requirements would be and demonstrated that their business had a good chance of succeeding. The first roll-out year's forecasted profit was uncertain; the smallest miscalculation in the forecast would mean it was unattainable. But in the following years, as the house file became bigger and bigger and the proportion of the mailings shifted from marginally profitable rented lists to very profitable house lists, the profit of Mayflower was foreseen to become more and more secure.

The basis of these forecasts was the sales per thousand from rented lists and from the house file. A test had been made and the sales per thousand of rented lists was determined. What was unproven was sales per thousand for the house file, in particular the $6,250 per thousand for first-year buyers. For most mail-order companies this is a high figure. But the response to Mayflower's catalog by rented lists was also high and that fact was proven. And, since response to rented lists and house file move in tandem, it was reasonable for Mayflower's management to assume that response by the house file would be high as well.

The three-year plan for Mayflower is significant because it demonstrates what is necessary to make a profit in mail order. Rarely can a mail-order company make a profit without a house file. Mayflower forecasts one in the first roll-out year when it has no significant house file but this profit is unreliable. But they had a strong response to their catalog when it was sent to rented lists, and they did not need to rent lists that were below break-even in order to build their lists of buyers. Furthermore, they could reasonably be expected to have a strong response to their catalog by their house file, thus contributing substantially to overhead and profit as that list grows. Their success was assured by the strong response rates of the catalog; when they developed their own list, they most surely would be profitable. Substantial house file, strong list rental response, and strong house file response: These are conditions that almost guarantee a mail-order profit. They, in turn, result from strong dynamics, discussed in such detail in the early chapters of this book.

TABLE 16-2 Publicity Plan First Roll-Out Year, September Mailing, Mayflower Gift Company

LIST SEGMENT	MAIL DATE	MAIL QUANTITY	SALES/M	SALES/$	PUBLICITY COST/M	PUBLICITY COST/$
Buyers	Sept. 1	3,320	6,250	20,750	236	784
Catalog Requests	Sept. 1	2,053	2,000	4,106	236	485
Total House File		5,373		24,856		1,269
LIST RENTAL,						
List B	Sept. 1	15,000	927	13,905	303	4,545
List G	"	15,000	707	10,605	311	4,665
List K	"	25,000	1,311	32,775	306	7,650
List M	"	25,000	1,015	25,375	301	7,525
List O	"	10,000	717	7,170	321	3,210
List Q	"	20,000	989	19,780	326	6,520
List S	"	20,000	930	18,600	311	6,220
List V	"	20,000	877	17,540	278	5,560
List W	"	10,000	728	7,280	281	2,810
Subtotal		160,000	956	153,030	304	48,705
TESTS	Sept. 1	150,000	600	90,000	291	43,650
Total List Rental		310,000		243,030		92,355
MEDIA	Sept. + Oct.	2,228		10,166		4,423
Subtotal		317,601		278,052		98,047
PACKAGE INSERTS	Sept. + Oct.	3,391	2,000	6,782	157	532
Total September Effort		320,992		284,834		98,579
FIXED PUBLICITY COSTS FOR SEPTEMBER, OCTOBER, AND JANUARY MAILINGS						42,612

TABLE 16-3 Publicity Plan First Roll-Out Year, October 25 Mailing, Mayflower Gift Company

LIST SEGMENTS	MAIL DATE	MAIL QUANTITY	SALES/M	SALES/$	PUBLICITY COST/M	PUBLICITY COST/$
Test Year Buyers	Oct. 25	3,067	(.75) 6,250	14,376	236	724
September Buyers	Oct. 25	3,391	6,250	21,193	236	800
Catalog Requests	Oct. 25	2,003	(.75) 2,000	3,005	236	472
8,461		8,461		38,574		1,996
LIST RENTAL						
List A	Oct. 25	11,333	946	10,722	300	3,400
List B	Oct. 25	10,000	740	9,460	300	3,000
List D	Oct. 25	14,464	957	13,842	306	4,426
List AR	Oct. 25	20,000	983	19,600	301	6,020
List E	Oct. 25	29,368	2,004	58,854	291	8,625
List I	Oct. 25	50,000	1,340	67,000	307	15,350
List M	Oct. 25	50,000	1,302	65,100	302	15,100
List AS	Oct. 25	20,000	845	16,900	329	6,580
List V	Oct. 25	40,000	1,422	56,880	291	11,640
List W	Oct. 25	30,000	979	29,370	287	8,610
List P	Oct. 25	30,000	889	26,670	296	8,880
List S	Oct. 25	40,000	1,165	46,600	301	12,040
List Z	Oct. 25	20,000	1,420	28,400	340	6,800
List AA	Oct. 25	30,000	920	27,600	300	9,000
List AD	Oct. 25	30,000	1,237	37,110	282	8,460
List AH	Oct. 25	15,000	893	13,395	272	4,080
List AJ	Oct. 25	15,000	792	11,880	298	4,470
List AN	Oct. 25	15,000	945	14,175	292	4,380
List AO	Oct. 25	14,677	912	13,385	287	4,212
Subtotal	Oct. 25	506,010	1,193	566,943		145,073
TESTS	Nov. + Dec.	40,000	600	24,000	291	11,640
Subtotal				629,517		158,709
PACKAGE INSERTS		7,715	2,000	15,431	157	1,211
Total		551,080		644,948		159,920

155

TABLE 16-4 Publicity Plan First Roll-Out Year, December 22 Mailing, Mayflower Gift Company

LIST SEGMENT	MAIL DATE	MAIL QUANTITY	SALES/M		SALES/$	PUBLICITY COST/M	PUBLICITY COST/$
Sept. Buyers	Dec. 22	3,391	$(.75)^2$	(6,250)	11,921	236	800
Oct. Buyers	Dec. 22	7,483	$(.75)^2$	(6,250)	35,077	236	1,766
Test Year Buyers		2,892	$(.75)^2$	(6,250)	10,167	236	683
Test Year Requests		1,967	$(.75)^2$	2,000	2,213	236	464
First Year Requests		2,053	(.75)	2,000	3,080	236	484
Total House File		17,789			62,458	236	4,197
LIST RENTAL							
Duplicates		69,316	(.75)	(2,000)	103,974	291	20,171
Triplicates		8,664	(.75)	(2,500)	16,245	291	2,521
List E		20,000	(.75)	(2,004)	30,060	291	5,820
List I		30,000	(.75)	(1,340)	30,150	307	9,210
List M		30,000	(.75)	(1,302)	29,295	302	9,060
List V		30,000	(.75)	(1,422)	31,995	291	8,730
List S		30,000	(.75)	(1,165)	26,212	301	9,030
List Z		20,000	(.75)	(1,420)	21,300	340	6,800
List AD		30,000	(.75)	(1,237)	27,832	282	8,460
List A		10,000	(.75)	(946)	7,095	300	3,000
List D		10,000	(.75)	(957)	7,178	306	3,060
List AA		10,000	(.75)	(920)	6,900	300	3,000
List AN		16,148	(.75)	(945)	11,445	292	4,715
Subtotal		280,517		1,237	349,681		93,577
PACKAGE INSERTS		5,119	(.75)	2,000	7,679	157	804
Total		303,425			419,818		98,578

TABLE 16-5 Publicity Plan First Roll-Out Year, Media Program, Mayflower Gift Company

MEDIUM	ISSUE	AD DESCRIPTION	EXPECTED NET SALES/$	PUBLICITY COST/$
Smithsonian	Sept.	Request	4,819	1,265
New Yorker	Sept. 8	Request	1,250	520
Colonial Homes	Sept.	Request	1,068	533
House Beautiful	Sept.	Request	421	700
House Beautiful	Oct.	Request	793	709
Yankee	Sept.	Request	739	314
House & Garden	Sept.	Request	1,076	382
Total			10,166	4,423

TABLE 16-6 DMA* Probability Tables 2A-2F: Sample Sizes
for Various Percentages of Expected Response—
Comparing Mailing to Fixed Point

CONFIDENCE LEVEL = 90.0%			ACCEPTABLE % DIFFERENCES							TABLE (2A)
Expected Response %	0.01	0.02	0.03	0.04	0.05	0.06	0.07	0.08	0.09	0.10
0.10	164188	41047	18243	10262	6568	4561	3351	2565	2027	1642
0.20	328047	82012	36450	20503	13122	9112	6695	5126	4050	3280
0.30	491578	122894	54620	30724	19663	13655	10032	7681	6069	4916
0.40	654780	163695	72753	40924	26191	18188	13363	10231	8084	6548
0.50	817653	204413	90850	51103	32706	22713	16687	12776	10094	8177
0.60	980197	245049	108911	61262	39208	27228	20004	15316	12101	9802
0.70	1142413	285603	126935	71401	45697	31734	23315	17850	14104	11424
0.80	1304300	326075	144922	81519	52172	36231	26618	20380	16102	13043
0.90	1465858	366465	162873	91616	58634	40718	29915	22904	18097	14659
1.00	1627088	406772	180788	101693	65084	45197	33206	25423	20088	16271

CONFIDENCE LEVEL = 90%										TABLE (2B)
Expected Response %	0.05	0.10	0.15	0.20	0.25	0.30	0.35	0.40	0.45	0.50
1.10	71520	17880	7947	4470	2861	1987	1460	1117	883	715
1.20	77942	19486	8660	4871	3118	2165	1591	1218	962	779
1.30	84352	21088	9372	5272	3374	2343	1721	1318	1041	844
1.40	90749	22687	10083	5672	3630	2521	1852	1418	1120	907
1.50	97132	24283	10792	6071	3885	2698	1982	1518	1199	971
1.60	103503	25876	11500	6469	4140	2875	2112	1617	1278	1035
1.70	109860	27465	12207	6866	4394	3052	2242	1717	1356	1099
1.80	116204	29051	12912	7263	4648	3228	2372	1816	1435	1162
1.90	122535	30634	13615	7658	4901	3404	2501	1915	1513	1225
2.00	128854	32213	14317	8053	5154	3579	2630	2013	1591	1289
2.10	135157	33789	15017	8447	5406	3754	2758	2112	1669	1352
2.20	141448	35362	15716	8841	5658	3929	2887	2210	1746	1414
2.30	147726	36932	16414	9233	5909	4104	3015	2308	1824	1477
2.40	153992	38498	17110	9624	6160	4278	3143	2406	1901	1540
2.50	160244	40061	17805	10015	6410	4451	3270	2504	1978	1602
2.60	166482	41621	18498	10405	6659	4625	3398	2601	2055	1665
2.70	172708	43177	19190	10794	6908	4797	3525	2699	2132	1727
2.80	178921	44730	19880	11183	7157	4970	3651	2796	2209	1789
2.90	185120	46280	20569	11570	7405	5142	3778	2892	2285	1851
3.00	191306	47827	21256	11957	7652	5314	3904	2989	2362	1913
3.10	197479	49370	21942	12342	7899	5486	4030	3086	2438	1975
3.20	203639	50910	22627	12727	8146	5657	4156	3182	2514	2036
3.30	209786	52446	23310	13112	8391	5827	4281	3278	2590	2098
3.40	215920	53980	23991	13495	8637	5998	4407	3374	2666	2159
3.50	222040	55510	24671	13877	8882	6168	4531	3469	2741	2220
3.60	228147	57037	25350	14259	9126	6337	4656	3565	2817	2281
3.70	234241	58560	26027	14640	9370	6507	4780	3660	2892	2342
3.80	240323	60081	26703	15020	9613	6676	4905	3755	2967	2403
3.90	246390	61598	27377	15399	9856	6841	5028	3850	3042	2464
4.00	252445	63111	28049	15778	10098	7012	5152	3944	3117	2524

TABLE 16-6 (cont.)

CONFIDENCE LEVEL = 95.%   TABLE (2C)

Expected Response %	0.01	0.02	0.03	0.04	0.05	0.06	0.07	0.08	0.09	0.10
0.10	270332	67583	30037	16896	10813	7509	5517	4224	3337	2703
0.20	540123	135031	60014	33758	21605	15003	11023	8439	6668	5401
0.30	809372	202343	89930	50586	32375	22483	16518	12646	9992	8094
0.40	1078080	269520	119787	67380	43123	29947	22002	16845	13310	10781
0.50	1346247	336562	149583	84140	53850	37396	27474	21035	16620	13462
0.60	1613873	403468	179319	100867	64555	44830	32936	25217	19924	16139
0.70	1880958	470239	208995	117560	75238	52249	38387	29390	23222	18810
0.80	2147501	536875	238611	134219	85900	59653	43827	33555	26512	21475
0.90	2413503	603376	268167	150844	96540	67042	49255	37711	29796	24135
1.00	2678964	669741	297663	167435	107159	74416	54673	41859	33074	26790

CONFIDENCE LEVEL = 95%   TABLE (2D)

Expected Response %	0.05	0.10	0.15	0.20	0.25	0.30	0.35	0.40	0.45	0.50
1.10	117755	29439	13084	7360	4710	3271	2403	1840	1454	1178
1.20	128331	32083	14259	8021	5133	3565	2619	2005	1584	1283
1.30	138884	34721	15432	8680	5555	3858	2834	2170	1715	1389
1.40	149416	37354	16602	9338	5977	4150	3049	2335	1845	1494
1.50	159926	39982	17770	9995	6397	4442	3264	2499	1974	1599
1.60	170415	42604	18935	10651	6817	4734	3478	2663	2104	1704
1.70	180882	45220	20098	11305	7235	5024	3691	2826	2233	1809
1.80	191327	47832	21259	11958	7653	5315	3905	2989	2362	1913
1.90	201750	50438	22417	12609	8070	5604	4117	3152	2491	2018
2.00	212152	53038	23572	13260	8486	5893	4330	3315	2619	2122
2.10	222533	55633	24726	13908	8901	6181	4541	3477	2747	2225
2.20	232891	58223	25877	14556	9316	6469	4753	3639	2875	2329
2.30	243228	60807	27025	15202	9729	6756	4964	3800	3003	2432
2.40	253544	63386	28172	15846	10142	7043	5174	3962	3130	2535
2.50	263837	65959	29315	16490	10553	7329	5384	4122	3257	2638
2.60	274109	68527	30457	17132	10964	7614	5594	4283	3384	2741
2.70	284360	71090	31596	17772	11374	7899	5803	4443	3511	2844
2.80	294589	73647	32732	18412	11784	8183	6012	4603	3637	2946
2.90	304796	76199	33866	19050	12192	8467	6220	4762	3763	3048
3.00	314981	78745	34998	19686	12599	8749	6428	4922	3889	3150
3.10	325145	81286	36127	20322	13006	9032	6636	5080	4014	3251
3.20	335287	83822	37254	20955	13411	9314	6843	5239	4139	3353
3.30	345406	86352	38379	21588	13816	9595	7049	5397	4264	3454
3.40	355507	88877	39501	22219	14220	9875	7255	5555	4389	3555
3.50	365584	91396	40620	22849	14623	10155	7461	5712	4513	3656
3.60	375639	93910	41738	23477	15026	10434	7666	5869	4638	3756
3.70	385673	96418	42853	24105	15427	10713	7871	6026	4761	3857
3.80	395686	98921	43965	24730	15827	10991	8075	6183	4885	3957
3.90	405676	101419	45075	25355	16227	11269	8279	6339	5008	4057
4.00	415645	103911	46183	25978	16626	11546	8483	6494	5131	4156

TABLE 16-6 (cont.)

TABLE (2E)

Expected Response %	0.50	0.60	0.70	0.80	0.90	1.00	1.10	1.20	1.30	1.40
4.20	4355	3024	2222	1701	1344	1089	900	756	644	556
4.40	4553	3162	2323	1779	1405	1138	941	790	674	581
4.60	4750	3299	2423	1855	1466	1188	981	825	703	606
4.80	4946	3435	2524	1932	1527	1237	1022	859	732	631
5.00	5141	3570	2623	2008	1587	1285	1062	893	761	656
5.20	5336	3705	2722	2084	1647	1334	1102	926	789	681
5.40	5529	3840	2821	2160	1707	1382	1142	960	818	705
5.60	5722	3974	2919	2235	1766	1431	1182	993	846	730
5.80	5914	4107	3017	2310	1825	1478	1222	1027	875	754
6.00	6105	4239	3115	2385	1884	1526	1261	1060	903	779
6.20	6295	4371	3212	2459	1943	1574	1301	1093	931	803
6.40	6484	4503	3308	2533	2001	1621	1340	1126	959	827
6.60	6672	4634	3404	2606	2059	1668	1379	1158	987	
6.80	6860	4764	3500	2680	2117	1715	1417	1191	1015	875
7.00	7046	4893	3595	2753	2175	1762	1456	1223	1042	899
7.20	7232	5022	3690	2825	2232	1808	1494	1256	1070	922
7.40	7417	5151	3784	2897	2289	1854	1532	1288	1097	946
7.60	7601	5279	3878	2969	2346	1900	1570	1320	1124	970
7.80	7784	5406	3972	3041	2403	1946	1608	1351	1152	993
8.00	7967	5532	4065	3112	2459	1992	1646	1383	1178	1016
8.20	8148	5658	4157	3183	2515	2037	1683	1415	1205	1039
8.40	8328	5784	4249	3253	2571	2082	1721	1446	1232	1062
8.60	8508	5908	4341	3324	2626	2127	1758	1477	1259	1085
8.80	8687	6033	4432	3393	2681	2172	1795	1508	1285	1108
9.00	8865	6156	4523	3463	2736	2216	1832	1539	1311	1131
9.20	9042	6279	4613	3532	2791	2261	1868	1570	1338	1153
9.40	9218	6402	4703	3601	2845	2305	1905	1600	1364	1176
9.60	9394	6523	4793	3669	2899	2348	1941	1631	1390	1198
9.80	9568	6644	4882	3738	2953	2392	1977	1661	1415	1220
10.00	9742	6765	4970	3805	3007	2435	2013	1691	1441	1243

TABLE (2F)

Expected Response %	0.50	1.00	1.50	2.00	2.50	3.00	3.50	4.00	4.5	5.00
11.00	10597	2649	1177	662	424	294	216	166	133	106
12.00	11430	2858	1270	714	457	318	233	179	141	114
13.00	12242	3061	1360	765	490	340	250	191	151	122
14.00	13032	3258	1448	815	521	362	266	204	161	130
15.00	13801	3450	1533	863	552	383	282	216	170	138
16.00	14548	3637	1616	909	582	404	297	227	180	145
17.00	15273	3818	1697	955	611	424	312	239	189	153
18.00	15976	3994	1775	999	639	444	326	250	197	160
19.00	16658	4165	1851	1041	666	463	340	260	206	167
20.00	17319	4330	1924	1082	692	481	353	271	214	173

*Published through the courtesy of the Direct Marketing Association, Inc.

TABLE 16-7   Orderline for the Mayflower Gift Company Mailings Made in September

WEEK	PERCENT COMPLETE
1	1.1
2	12.8
3	26.8
4	38.2
5	47.7
6	56.2
7	63.2
8	71.1
9	76.4
10	81.5
11	84.7
12	87.7
13	90.5
14	92.2
15	93.0
16	94.6
17	95.7
18	96.7
19	97.2
20	97.9
21	98.2
22	98.6
23	99.2
24	99.5
25	99.8
26	100.0

TABLE 16-8 Monthly Budgets September 1 to August 31, Mayflower Gift Company

	BUDGET FOR YEAR	SEPT.	OCT.	NOV.	DEC.	JAN.	FEB.	MAR.	APR.	MAY	JUN.	JUL.	AUG.
SALES	1,349,600	85,450	142,417	250,451	596,878	232,422	41,982						
COST OF GOODS													
Purchases	674,800	42,725	71,209	125,224	298,439	116,211	20,992						
Freight	4,080	258	430	757	1,804	703	128						
Markdowns	27,030	1,712	2,852	5,018	11,955	4,655	838						
Total	705,910	44,695	74,491	130,999	312,198	121,569	21,958						
GROSS PROFIT	643,690	40,755	67,926	119,452	284,680	110,853	20,024						
PUBLICITY EXPENSE	399,689	25,306	42,117	74,172	176,768	68,832	12,434						
OPERATING EXPENSE													
Gen. and Administrative Personnel	28,900	2,408	2,408	2,408	2,412	2,408	2,408	2,408	2,408	2,408	2,408	2,408	2,408
Operating Personnel	57,200	3,765	5,880	9,899	22,785	9,228	2,145	583	583	583	583	583	583
Payroll Taxes	11,700	838	1,126	1,672	3,423	1,581	618	407	407	407	407	407	407
Outside Labor	1,300	82	137	242	575	224	40						
Legal	2,000	167	167	167	167	167	167	167	167	166	166	166	166
Accounting	6,500	542	542	542	542	542	542	542	542	541	541	541	541
Rent	12,000	1,000	1,000	1,000	1,000	1,000	1,000	1,000	1,000	1,000	1,000	1,000	1,000
Electricity	1,700	142	142	142	142	142	142	142	142	141	141	141	141
Heat	3,000		200	500	700	700	600	300					
Maintenance & Supplies	2,000	167	167	167	167	167	167	167	167	166	166	166	166
Telephone	9,600	550	918	1,614	3,848	1,498	322	250	200	100	100	100	100
Insurance	1,700	142	142	142	142	142	142	142	142	141	141	141	141
Shipping Supplies	16,000	1,013	1,688	2,970	7,076	2,755	498						
List Maintenance	5,000	316	528	928	2,212	861	155	250					
Travel	3,000	250	250	250	250	250	250	250	250	250	250	250	250
Samples	4,000					1,000	1,000	2,000					
Credit Card Fees	18,273	1,157	1,928	3,393	8,081	3,146	568						
Other Bank Charges	400	25	42	74	177	70	12						
Office Postage	2,500	158	264	464	1,106	430	78						
Office Supplies	9,300	589	981	1,726	4,113	1,602	289						
Depreciation	2,200	184	184	184	184	183	183	183	183	183	183	183	183
UPS & Parcel Post	-0-												
Miscellaneous	2,000	127	212	371	884	344	62						
Interest Expense	7,000	584	584	584	584	583	583	583	583	583	583	583	583
Total Operating	207,273	14,206	19,490	29,439	60,570	29,023	11,971	9,124	6,774	6,669	6,669	6,669	6,669
PROFIT (LOSS)	36,728	1,243	6,259	15,841	47,342	12,998	(4,381)	(9,124)	(6,774)	(6,669)	(6,669)	(6,669)	(6,669)

TABLE 16-9 Three-Year Plan of Mayflower Gift Company, Publicity Plan for Second and Third Roll-Out Years

LIST SEGMENT	SECOND YEAR AFTER TEST — SALES AND CIRCULATION			PUBLICITY COST		THIRD YEAR AFTER TEST — SALES AND CIRCULATION			PUBLICITY COST	
	Circ.	Sales/M	Sales	Cost/M	Cost	Circ.	Sales/M	Sales	Cost/M	Cost
SEPTEMBER 1 MAILING										
One-year-old buyers	15,172	6,250	94,825	236	3,580	22,052	6,250	137,825	236	5,204
Two-year-old buyers	2,768	(.8)(6,250)	13,840	236	653	12,468	(.8)(6,250)	77,925	236	2,942
Three-year-old buyers						2,395	$(.8)^2$(6,250)	9,580	236	565
One-year-old requests	2,015	2,000	4,030	236	476	2,015	2,000	4,030	236	476
Two-year-old requests	1,940	(.8)(2,000)	3,056	236	458	1,910	(.8)(2,000)	3,056	236	450
Three-year-old requests						1,859	$(.8)^2$(2,000)	2,380	236	439
Tests	150,000	600	90,000	291	43,650	150,000	600	90,000	291	43,650
List rental	400,000	956	382,400	291	116,400	400,000	956	382,400	291	116,400
Package inserts	7,173	2,000	14,346	157	1,126	8,624	2,000	17,228	157	1,354
Total September	579,068		602,497		166,343	601,323		724,444		174,179
OCTOBER 25 MAILING										
September buyers	7,173	6,250	44,831	236	1,693	8,624	6,250	53,900	236	2,035
One-year-old buyers	14,016	(.75)(6,250)	65,700	236	3,308	20,821	(.75)(6,250)	97,598	236	4,914
Two-year-old buyers	2,599	(.8)(.75)(6,250)	9,746	236	613	11,518	(.8)(.75)(6,250)	43,193	236	2,718
Three-year-old buyers						2,278	$(.8)^2$(.75)(6,250)	6,834	236	538
One-year-old requests	1,966	(.75)(2,000)	2,949	236	464	1,966	(.75)(2,000)	2,949	236	464
Two-year-old requests	1,902	(.8)(.75)(2,000)	2,282	236	449	1,873	(.8)(.75)(2,000)	2,248	236	442
Three-year-old requests						1,830	$(.8)^2$(.75)(2,000)	1,757	236	432
Tests	50,000	600	30,000	291	14,550	50,000	600	30,000	291	14,550
List rental	600,000	1,193	715,800	291	174,600	600,000	1,193	715,800	291	174,600
Package inserts	10,489	2,000	20,978	157	1,646	11,638	2,000	23,276	157	1,827
Total October	688,145		892,286		197,323	710,548		977,555		202,520
DECEMBER 22 MAILING										
September buyers	7,173	$(.75)^2$(6,250)	25,218	236	1,693	8,624	$(.75)^2$(6,250)	30,319	236	2,035
November buyers	10,079	(.75)(6,250)	47,714	236	2,379	10,980	(.75)(6,250)	51,469	236	2,591
One-year-old buyers	13,215	$(.75)^3$(6,250)	34,808	236	3,118	19,631	$(.75)^2$(6,250)	69,015	236	4,633
Two-year-old buyers	2,480	(.8)$(.75)^3$(6,250)	5,231	236	585	10,991	(.8)$(.75)^2$(6,250)	30,912	236	2,594
Three-year-old buyers						2,195	$(.8)^2(.75)^2$(6,250)	4,939	236	518
Current season requests	2,053	(.75)(2,000)	3,079	236	485	2,053	(.75)(2,000)	3,079	236	485
One-year-old requests	1,930	$(.75)^3$(2,000)	1,628	236	455	1,930	$(.75)^3$(2,000)	1,628	236	455
Two-year-old requests	1,874	(.8)$(.75)^3$(2,000)	1,265	236	442	1,846	(.8)$(.75)^3$(2,000)	1,246	236	436
Three-year-old requests						1,809	$(.8)^2(.75)^3$(2,000)	Don't Mail		
List rental	300,000	1,237	371,100	291	87,300	300,000	1,237	371,100	291	87,300
Package inserts	6,139	(.75)(2,000)	9,209	157	963	6,874	(.75)(2,000)	10,312	157	1,079
Total December	344,943		499,252		97,420	366,933		574,019		102,126
Media	2,228		10,166		4,423	2,228		10,166		4,423
Fixed Publicity Cost					42,612					42,612
	1,614,384		2,004,201		508,121	1,681,032		2,286,184		525,860

TABLE 16-10 Three-Year Plan of Mayflower Gift Company, Forecast of Buyers and Requests Counts

MAILING	LIST SEGMENT	FIRST ROLL-OUT YEAR				SECOND ROLL-OUT YEAR				THIRD ROLL-OUT YEAR			
		Start	Upgraded to current year	Acquired	End	Start	Upgraded to current year	Acquired	End	Start	Upgraded to current year	Acquired	End
BUYERS													
Sept.	Buyers acquired test year	3,320	253		3,067	2,768	169		2,599	2,395	117		2,278
Oct.		3,067	175		2,892	2,599	119		2,480	2,278	83		2,195
Dec.		2,892	124		2,768	2,480	85		2,395	2,195			
Sept.	Buyers acquired first year after test	3,391			3,391	15,172	1,156		14,016	12,468	950		11,518
Oct.				7,483	10,874	14,016	801		13,215	11,518	527		10,991
Dec.		10,874		4,298	15,172	13,215	567		12,468	10,991			
Sept.	Buyers acquired second year after test							7,173	7,173	22,502	1,681		20,821
Oct.						7,173		10,079	17,252	20,821	1,190		19,631
Dec.						17,252		5,250	22,502	19,631			
Sept.	Buyers acquired third year after test											8,624	8,624
Oct.										8,624		10,980	19,304
Dec.										19,304			
REQUESTS													
Sept.	Requests acquired test year	2,053	50		2,003	1,940	38		1,902	1,859	29		1,830
Oct.		2,003	36		1,967	1,902	28		1,874	1,830	21		1,809
Dec.		1,967	27		1,940	1,874	15		1,859	1,809			
Sept.	Requests acquired first year after test			2,053	2,053	2,015	49		1,966	1,910	37		1,873
Oct.						1,966	36		1,930	1,873	27		1,846
Dec.		2,053			2,015	1,930	20		1,910	1,846			
Sept.	Requests acquired second year after test								2,053	2,015	49		1,966
Oct.										1,966	36		1,930
Dec.			38			2,053		2,053	2,015	1,930			
Sept.	Requests acquired third year after test											2,053	2,053
Oct.													
Dec.										2,053			

TABLE 16-11 Three-Year Plan of Mayflower Gift Company, Forecasted Profit and Loss

ACCOUNT	%	FIRST ROLL-OUT YEAR	%	SECOND ROLL-OUT YEAR	%	THIRD ROLL-OUT YEAR
NET SALES	100	1,349,600	100	2,004,201	100	2,286,184
COST OF GOOD	52.3	705,910	52.3	1,048,197	52.3	1,195,674
GROSS PROFIT		643,690		956,004		1,090,510
PUBLICITY						
Fixed		42,612		42,612		42,612
Variable		357,077		465,509		483,248
Total	29.6	399,689	25.4	508,121	22.3	525,860
OPERATING EXPENSES						
Fixed		90,878		90,878		90,878
Variable		116,395		172,361		196,612
Total	15.3	207,273	13.1	263,239	12.3	287,490
PROFIT	2.7	36,728	9.2	184,644	12.1	277,160
CIRCULATION		1,175,497		1,614,384		1,681,032

TABLE 16-12   Three-Year Revenue Forecast, Mayflower Gift Company

	ORDERLINE % COMPLETE			TOTAL FOR PERIOD	FIRST ROLL-OUT YEAR			SECOND ROLL-OUT YEAR			THIRD ROLL-OUT YEAR		
	Sep.	Oct.	Dec.		Sept. Mailing	Oct. Mailing	Dec. Mailing	Sept. Mailing	Oct. Mailing	Dec. Mailing	Sept. Mailing	Oct. Mailing	Dec. Mailing
FIRST YEAR													
Sep.	30			85,450	85,450								
Oct.	50	30		142,417	142,417								
Nov.	20	60		250,451	56,967	193,484							
Dec.		10	50	596,878		386,969	209,909						
Jan.			40	232,422		64,495	167,927						
Feb.			10	41,982			41,982						
Mar.													
Apr.													
May													
Total				1,349,600	284,834	644,948	419,818						
SECOND YEAR													
Sep.	30			183,799				183,799					
Oct.	50	30		306,331				306,331					
Nov.	20	60		390,219				122,533	267,686				
Dec.		10	50	784,998					535,372	249,626			
Jan.			40	288,929					89,228	199,701			
Feb.			10	49,925						49,925			
Mar.													
Apr.													
May													
Total				2,004,201				612,663	892,286	499,252			
THIRD YEAR													
Sep.	30			220,383							220,383		
Oct.	50	60		367,305							367,305		
Nov.	20	10		440,189							146,922	293,267	
Dec.			50	873,543								586,533	287,010
Jan.			40	327,362								97,755	229,607
Feb.			10	57,402									57,402
Mar.													
Apr.													
May													
Total				2,286,184							734,610	977,555	574,019

TABLE 16-13 Three-Year Plan of Mayflower Gift Company, Forecasted Cash Requirements

PAID BY	CASH BALANCE	REVENUE	TOTAL OUTLAY	MERCHANDISE PURCHASES FOR SALES	MERCHANDISE PURCHASES FOR STOCK	POSTAGE	OTHER PUBLICITY	FIXED EXPENSE	VARIABLE EXPENSE	FIXED ASSETS
FIRST ROLL-OUT YEAR										
Aug. 31	(26,475)		26,475							26,475
Sep. 30	14,178	85,450	44,797							
Oct. 31	(70,522)	142,417	227,117	44,690		29,852	111,339	7,575	7,370	
Nov. 30	(32,358)	250,451	212,287	74,484		51,250	108,670	7,573	12,265	
Dec. 31	346,240	596,878	218,280	130,985		28,218		7,573	21,560	
Jan. 31	168,415	232,422	410,247	312,239			70,360	7,573	51,504	
Feb. 28	43,084	41,982	167,313	121,556	34,563			7,573	20,075	
Mar. 31	(86,045)		129,129	21,956	99,600			7,573	3,621	
Apr. 30	(115,574)		29,529		21,956			7,573		
May 31	(123,147)		7,573					7,573		
Jun. 30	(130,720)		7,573					7,573		
Jul. 31	(138,293)		7,573					7,573		
Aug. 31	(145,866)		7,573					7,573		
		1,349,600	1,495,416	705,910	156,119	109,320	290,369	90,878	116,395	26,475
SECOND ROLL-OUT YEAR										
Sep. 30	39,301	183,799	77,234					7,575	15,806	
Oct. 31	(86,535)	306,331	353,565	96,126		53,853	159,525	7,573	26,344	
Nov. 30	(30,984)	390,219	334,668	160,211		63,997	133,326	7,573	33,558	
Dec. 31	442,769	784,998	311,245	204,083		32,080		7,573	67,509	
Jan. 31	223,384	288,929	508,314	410,551			65,340	7,573	24,850	
Feb. 28	61,171	49,925	212,132	151,109	49,156			7,573	4,294	
Mar. 31	27,487		33,690	26,117				7,573		
Apr. 30	19,914		7,573					7,573		
May 31	12,341		7,573					7,573		
Jun. 30	4,768		7,573					7,573		
Jul. 31	(2,805)		7,573					7,573		
Aug. 31	(10,378)		7,573					7,573		
		2,004,201	1,868,713	1,048,197	49,156	149,930	358,191	90,878	172,361	
THIRD ROLL-OUT YEAR										
Sep. 30	127,554	220,383	82,451					7,575	18,953	
Oct. 31	109,067	367,305	385,792	115,260		55,923	165,291	7,573	31,588	
Nov. 30	175,287	440,189	373,969	192,100		66,080	136,440	7,573	37,856	
Dec. 31	701,788	873,543	347,042	230,219		34,125		7,573	75,125	
Jan. 31	468,561	327,362	560,589	456,862			68,001	7,573	28,153	
Feb. 28	319,085	57,402	206,876	171,212	23,156			7,573	4,937	
Mar. 31	281,491		37,594	30,021				7,573		
Apr. 30	273,918		7,573					7,573		
May 31	266,345		7,573					7,573		
Jun. 30	258,772		7,573					7,573		
Jul. 31	251,199		7,573					7,573		
Aug. 31	243,626		7,573					7,573		
		2,286,184	2,032,180	1,195,674	23,156	156,128	369,732	90,878	196,612	

TABLE 16-14   Fixed Assets, Mayflower Gift Company

EQUIPMENT	
Cash Register	$ 800
Sign	2,000
Desks	1,000
Shipping Bench	300
Postage Scale	400
Mailing Machine	2,200
Shelving	10,000
Copy Machine	2,000
Label-Gluing Machines (2)	500
Tape Dispensers (2)	800
Calculators	375
Mail Opening Machine	300
Telephone Answering Machine	300
	20,975
LEASEHOLD	
Leasehold Improvements	3,000
Lease Deposit	2,000
Utility Deposits	500
	5,500
	$26,475

TABLE 16-15   Three-Year Plan of Mayflower Gift Company, Fiscal Year Ending August 31

	FORECASTED BALANCE SHEETS			
	Beginning First Roll-Out Year Sept. 1	First Roll-Out Year Aug. 31	Second Roll-Out Year Aug. 31	Third Roll-Out Year Aug. 31
Cash	173,525	54,134	89,622	343,626
Inventory		156,119	205,275	228,431
Prepaid Publicity	111,339	159,525	165,921	
Fixed Assets	26,475	26,475	26,475	26,475
	311,339	396,253	487,293	598,532
Accounts Payable	111,339	159,525	165,921	
Note Payable	100,000	100,000		
Prepaid Mail Orders, Deferred Taxes, Equity	100,000	136,728	321,372	598,532
	311,339	396,253	487,293	598,532

mailing more effectively

High response to one's catalog and a large buyers file almost guarantees a profit. This was covered in the previous chapter. It is the dynamics that makes response high. A well-thought-out concept and theme of the business supported by merchandise, institutional copy, individual product copy, photography, company name and logotype, symbols, and mood are the dynamics that can cause a high catalog response.

But poor mailing and list maintenance practices will weaken the catalog response that the dynamics have built up and can cost the mail marketer profit. The post office can fail to deliver catalogs because of bad addresses, wrong ZIP codes, and a host of other reasons. Names can be duplicated or lost in the file, the changes of addresses can remain unchanged, and the mail marketer can pass by information on the order that he could profitably use at a later time. These are some of the dangers that the mail marketer must guard against as he mails his catalog and maintains his house file.

Maintaining the House File

Protecting the house file from danger

The mail marketer's house file is his most precious asset. Loss of the file will put him out of business. The very first thing the mail marketer must do, therefore, is to make sure that his list of names is protected against fire, theft, computer foul-up, and improper entry of the customer record.

To protect against the danger of fire, the mail marketer should keep a copy of the list in a building separate from where the original is kept, perhaps in the mail marketer's home. Copies of additions and changes to the list should be accumulated and be put with the copy periodically, perhaps once a week or daily in the case of a large company.

The mail marketer protects against the danger of theft, which is usually unauthorized use, by putting decoys in his list. Decoys are names and addresses that are unique to his list and to each mailing and inform him when his list has been used.

The decoy name list is developed with names of the mail marketer's friends and associates throughout the country or is supplied by a service[1] which has the names coded to identify a mailing, usually by an intentional misspelling[2] of the last name. When the decoy persons receive mailings with misspellings of their names, they tear off the covers and send them to the mail marketer. The mail marketer then checks them off in his record to assure that a rented list has not been used an unauthorized second time. Since the spelling of the name is unique with each renting, he can determine who used the list. The fact that decoys so easily identify the unauthorized use of one's list has pretty much kept unscrupulous people from misusing lists. There are few instances of this occurring. In addition to salting decoys in with each list rental, one should keep decoys permanently in his list to protect against internal theft and to check on catalog delivery by the U.S. Postal Service.

There is the danger that a list can be destroyed by a computer foul-up, such as the names being inadvertently erased. The protection against this occurrence is the same as for fire: maintain an extra copy of the list.

An insidious danger is that names might not get added to the list as orders are received. The way this can happen depends upon the operating system. In a manual system, someone may simply overlook sending copies of orders to the computer service bureau that maintains the list. In a computer system, something may occur within the computer that prevents the name from being added. The protection against this is a control, the essence of which is that the number of customers to start plus the number of added new customers should equal the number of customers at the end.

Another danger is that information about the customer that is meant to be captured is not saved. There are many pieces of information about a customer which ought to be saved. It is very possible that some or much of this information is not being keyed into the computer. The mail marketer should devise checks to make sure that this information is being saved.

Composition of the house file record

The most common error made in mail order is failing to gather all the useful information about a customer. The second most common error is failing to fully use the information that is gathered. The information that is usually gathered ranges from a minimal name and address to information necessary for filling orders and supplying answers to customer queries.

What frequently is missing is information useful for marketing. This marketing information comes in two categories: (1) information to select customers for future mailings, and (2) information with which computer letters can be written to customers.

To select customers for future mailings, one might ask: What products did the customer buy? A customer that bought sporting goods would be the target for a catalog of sporting goods. How often did the customer buy? A customer that has bought frequently is likely to buy again. Did the customer order by phone or did he or she mail the order in? Customers that order by phone are more impulsive and spend more. When a group of customers

---

[1] See Appendix A for the name of a decoy service.

[2] The misspelling should occur within the first four characters to prevent the matchcoding system from eliminating it as a duplicate.

have not ordered and have aged to the point that collectively they should be sent fewer mailings, knowing qualities such as these enables the mail marketer to distinguish those customers in the group that are more likely to buy and, therefore, worthy of more mailings.

Information in the customer's record also makes computer letters more effective. The more information one has, the more specific one can be in computer letters to customers. Specificity makes a computer letter effective. Computer letters are the great unexploited opportunity in mail order; for this reason Chapter 21 is devoted to it.

The information about each customer and what they have ordered that should be stored for future marketing use include:

Title of Respect. (Mr., Mrs., Miss, Ms., Rev., Dr., Prof.) Computer letters are least effective when they are impersonal. When a computer letter is addressed to *A. Smith* instead of *Mr. Albert Smith*, it invites being tossed into the wastebasket. Knowing the title of respect can also be used to improve response. For example, mailings to *doctors* are more responsive than to *misters*. More important is that it enables you to distinguish sex so that mailings on masculine or feminine products will be appropriately directed. To make sure you capture this information, put boxes in the name and address section of your order form so that the customer can check it off.

Name. Where possible, the full name should be captured. A letter or catalog addressed to *Mr. Robert C. Bailey, Jr.,* is much better than *Mr. R. Bailey.* Again, *Mr. R. Bailey* is impersonal and there is also the danger that the catalog will go to Mr. Bailey's father, who may not be interested in the products in the catalog.

Street Address, City, State, and Nine-Digit ZIP Code

Original Source Code and Date Customer First Became Active. This identifies the original source of the customer—for example, from which list rental or advertisement the customer was originally acquired.

Buyer, Catalog Request, Retail Store Customer, or Retail Store Catalog Request. The name should be identifiable as being in one of these categories. Perhaps this can be achieved through the original source code. Mailing the catalog to the list of store customers and requests is the most cost-effective way to generate store business. The store clerks should systematically capture the names of people who buy in the store and who request that catalogs be sent to them. These names should be treated the same way as mail-order names; that is, when the customer buys again or the catalog request buys, either in the store or through the mails, the record of the sale is recorded and the customer or request is upgraded to the category of most recent store customers. In this way, mailings to store customers can be controlled and kept cost-effective just as mail-order mailings can be.

Code and Date of the Last Mailing from Which the Customer Bought. This tells how old the customer is, which is the most important criterion in evaluating the responsiveness of a customer.

Method of Payment on Last Order: Check, C.O.D., or Credit Card and Which Credit Card. This is another important criterion in evaluating the responsiveness of a customer. People who have previously bought using a credit card will produce more sales than those who have paid by check. People who buy C.O.D. are the least responsive and create the most problems. Credit cards such as American Express and Diner's Club are carried by more affluent people. Customers identified by these cards are more valuable than those who pay with Visa or MasterCard.

Bad Debt Experience (Stolen Credit Cards, Bad Checks). Names or addresses with a record of a stolen credit card or bad check should be kept on file so as to suppress mailings and shipments of future orders to those names or addresses. In instances of simple cases of insufficient funds where the check is eventually covered, the mail marketer may want to continue to mail a catalog but hold up shipping orders to the customer until the check has cleared. This hold should be put in the customer's record.

Telephone Number. If you have a problem filling the order of a customer, your customer service people can often get the order filled with an alternative product and please the customer with your personal service by calling him. When the customer has spent a lot of money, either on the order in question or in the past, this is money well-spent. The order form should have a line to capture the customer's telephone number.

Size of Clothing or Footwear. This information serves at least two purposes. Computer letters which mention the customer's previous purchase are more specific and, therefore, more effective if they mention the size of the clothing or footwear previously bought. (Mail marketers of other product lines might have some other product characteristic that they might want to retain on the record.) The other use of this information is for inventory liquidation. For example, if you have close-out inventory on certain sizes in certain styles and if you retained the customer's size, your computer can seek out all the customers with that size and write a customized letter selling that product to those customers in the specific size without needlessly mailing to those whose order you cannot possibly fill.

Number and Accumulated Amount of Refunds. Refunds reflect two possible characteristics of the customer's profile: It could reflect that the customer is the type that habitually buys and returns, or it could reflect that the customer, having returned merchandise, is a dissatisfied customer. If it is the former, the customer still could have considerable value if net sales to him are high, or the customer could represent a net loss. If it is the latter, the customer may not respond well to future mailings and, therefore, should be sent fewer mailing as time goes on.

Total Sales to Date and the Number of Times Ordered. The more times a customer orders and the more he buys, the better a customer he is. This information tells you to keep mailing often and longer to the customer who has bought frequently in great quantity.

Value of Last Order. This information tells a little bit about the customer's financial capacity. Customers who spend a high amount at one time usually can spend more money at a later time. If one separates customers who have not bought for some time into two groups, those whose last order was above a certain amount and those whose last order was below a certain amount, the group that spent more originally will spend more per thousand in later mailings. Again, it pays to mail the high average order group longer and more often.

Date Last Matched to an Outside List. As time goes on, customers die, move, become impecunious, or for other reasons stop buying by mail order, but their names remain on your mailing list. If they show up in a merge-purge in someone else's list, you know that they are still alive, still at the address on your file, and still buy by mail order. It is just that they may not have bought from you recently. Customers that match to an outside list are more responsive than those who do not. By keeping a record of when a name last matched with an outside list, you can, again, determine how much and how long you wish to mail to the customer.

Back Orders. Were you slow in shipping the customer's last order? If so, he may not respond well in the future. Keeping a record of how an order was filled and comparing it with later response will suggest how often to mail that customer and permit evaluation of inventory policies.

Phone Orders. Did the customer order by phone? If he did, then he is a more impulsive buyer and spends more. Everything else being equal, he is most likely a more valuable buyer than one who mails in orders. Incidentally, except where C.O.D. is permitted, phone buyers are always credit card buyers.

Products Purchased. Knowing what products were purchased gives specificity to computer letters. If you want to write to customers to promote something new, you most certainly will want to refer to the specific products purchased previously. The product purchased also reflects the customer's interest. This makes possible the development of sub-product lines and promotions. For example, if Norm Thompson sells canned salmon to someone, they have identified a buyer of gourmet foods. Should they come out with a catalog of gourmet foods, that customer should receive more mailings of the food catalog than those who bought only ready-to-wear. This knowledge can be used to aid the rental of one's list. Continuing with the Norm Thompson food example, Maple Grove of St. Johnsbury, Vermont, which sells delicious maple products, needs food lists. While Maple Grove might not be able to mail their catalog profitably to the whole Norm Thompson list, they most likely could mail it profitably to their salmon buyers.

Lifetime Value (LTV). This, as discussed in Chapter 15, is the accumulated sales for the customer less the cost of goods, variable operating expenses, and expense of additional catalog mailings not including the initial publicity expense with which the customer was acquired. The net contribution to lifetime value of each sale (that is, the sale less the cost of its goods sold, variable operating expense, and variable cost of the mailing) should be adjusted for the cost of money so that the value of the customer at the time of the mailing can be calculated. When the lifetime values of the customers have been totaled for an original source code, one can compare it with other source codes and the break-even point and determine if it was the best investment of publicity money.

Decide the composition of the house file record early

I have shown here the types of information about your customer that you should consider retaining. You should review this list plus the other information needed for your particular business. Then you should decide which information you will retain. This decision should be made early so that little information will be lost. Remember, the most valuable asset you have is your customers. The more you know about them and the more you use the information, the more valuable they become.

The information that you gather depends upon your means of storage. If you are storing information manually, what you can keep and use is limited. But even if your present means of using the information is limited, you should consider storing the information for the day that you have a computer and can write computer letters and select customers. A small company that is on a manual operating system should, early on, consider having their list maintained at a computer service bureau. (A word of caution: Do not have your list maintained by someone who is not experienced in mail order and hasn't the ability to store most of the types of information listed earlier in this chapter.[3])

Ways to Reclaim Your List and Mail More Effectively

The Boston Globe newspaper once quoted a spokesman at L. L. Bean as saying that L. L. Bean mails catalogs to 90 percent of the households in the town of Weston, Massachusetts, where I once lived. I believe it. I personally get four copies of their catalog every time they make a mailing.

This anecdote illustrates one of many reasons why mailing lists lose their responsiveness as time passes. Duplicates creep into the list, addresses and ZIP codes are keyed incorrectly, customers die or move, and, of course, some customers buy and are upgraded to a more recent list segment, leaving those with less tendency to buy in the older segment. To offset the effects of aging, the mail marketer should reclaim his list by various methods. Here are some.

Eliminating Duplicate Names. Duplicate names are difficult to remove from a list completely. If the list is maintained on a computer, then the computer will eliminate many duplicates and upgrade customers through its match code. A match code is a set of characters extracted from a name and address. When the set of characters matches another set, duplicate names and addresses are thought to have been found. A typical match code consists of the first four characters of the last name, the first four meaningful characters of the street address, and the ZIP code. Thus Mrs. John Smith and Mrs. Anne Smith at 12 Monument Street, Concord, Massachusetts 01742 would both have the same match code, that is, SMIT12MO01742. This match code would eliminate one of the Mrs. Smiths. This system works fairly well, but duplicates will remain. Because no duplicate elimination method will catch all duplicate names, the list should be printed out periodically in ZIP code sequence, alphabetically within ZIP codes, and visually reviewed to find duplicates.

Correcting ZIP Codes. Most mail-order lists contain about 2 percent keying errors where the city in an address does not go with the ZIP code that is recorded with it. These, of course, will not be delivered by the post office. This means that 2 percent of a mailing will be wasted unless the ZIP codes are corrected. Some service bureaus that do merge-purges are able to make this correction by comparing each name with a master list of cities, street addresses, and ZIP codes.

---

[3] See Appendix A "Mail Marketer's Resources" for names of service bureaus qualified to maintain mail-order lists.

Correcting Addresses. It goes without saying that every mailing that goes out to the house list, except when the mailings are close together, should request address corrections. This is most conveniently done by having the computer print "Address Correction Requested" directly on the address label. By printing it onto the label instead of the catalog, both buyers and rented lists (which, of course, do not have their addresses corrected) can be merged into one ZIP string. More names in a ZIP string means that a higher percentage will be sorted and sacked for direct routing to the postal carrier or ZIP-coded office, thus saving postage.

Matching the House File to Outside Lists. We have already discussed that customers that show up during a merge-purge in other lists will respond better than those that do not. When a merge-purge is done, names on the house file that match an outside list should be identified and marked with the season they matched with an outside list.

Carrier Coding to Identify Mailable Names. When a merge-purge is done and the mailing is large enough to make it economically worthwhile, the names should be coded with the identification numbers of the postal carriers that will deliver the catalogs. At the same time, the computer should code names where there are fewer names than the U.S. Post Office minimum (ten) that can be sent directly to a carrier or a ZIP code but which can go directly to a city with several ZIP codes, known as multiple-ZIP city. The coding makes it possible for labels to be printed so that the mailer can bundle, sort, and sack by post carrier and multiple-ZIP city as well as by ZIP code, sectional center, or state. The coding is done with a tape supplied by the post office.

Only 85 percent of the names, however, have addresses that can be coded. The remaining names cannot be coded because, among other reasons, the address is wrong. The ones with wrong addresses are usually undeliverable. Therefore, if one separates the names to which carrier codes could not be assigned from the ones to which codes could be assigned, the latter will have a higher response. This method is useful for upgrading older, less productive names. Recent names, of course, should be mailed in their entirety.

Writing to the House File. Sometimes when part of the house file ceases to be profitable, it pays to write to the buyer or request and ask if they wish to continue to receive the catalog. Those that reply affirmatively can continue to be mailed, while the others can usually be safely dropped.

Qualifying the House File. If you mail to a list segment, you will always get some orders back. The problem in making the mailing is to separate the customers that are likely to buy from the ones that are not. This can be done by applying the information one has about a customer. Was his last order a large one? Then maybe it is profitable to mail to him. Was he refunded or did he have to wait a long time for his last order? Then maybe it would not pay to mail to him.

To select customers, one, two, or more of these qualifications might be applied. For example, we might say that we will mail only to those people who spent over $50 on their last order, who ordered by phone, and who did not receive a refund. These criteria will winnow out the less productive names and improve response of the remaining ones that are mailed. The problem with applying many criteria, however, is that there are few names left to be mailed. But if one applies only one criterion, the result is crude because most of the knowledge about the customer is ignored. For example, one might establish that if the customer bought over $50 on the last order, he or she would receive a catalog. This overlooks whether or not the customer matched to an outside list, paid by credit card, ordered by phone, or was refunded.

An approach that overcomes these weaknesses is a point system that takes into account all the qualifying factors and makes sure that names with several qualifying factors are included in the mailing. The point value of each qualifying factor would be made by analyzing previous mailings. The sales per thousand where the qualifying factor existed would be compared with where it did not exist. The greater the difference between the sales per thousand of the two groups of names, the more point value that would be assigned to the existence of that qualifying factor. This analysis would be done for every qualifying factor. Points would then be assigned to each name in the segment of the list under consideration for each qualifying factor it has. The total point value for the name would determine whether or not a customer would receive a mailing.

For example, Bill Smith received 71 points and Ann Baxter received 13 points. If the cut-off for a particular mailing were 25 points, Bill Smith would be mailed to and Ann Baxter would not. (See Table 17-1.)

TABLE 17-1

QUALIFYING FACTOR		POSSIBLE POINTS	POINTS FOR	
			Ann Baxter	Bill Smith
Matched to outside list within 6 mos.		25		25
Name could be carrier-coded		10	10	
Paid by Credit Card:	American Express	16		16
	Diner's Club	16		
	Visa	8	8	
	MasterCard	8		
	C.O.D.	−8		
Last order refunded		−10	−10	−10
Times ordered		5 per time	5	15
Value of last order		½ point per dollar over $25		15
Ordered by phone		10		10
Back-ordered on last order for more than three weeks		−10		
			13	71

A different way to select customers for a mailing would be for the computer to calculate for previous mailings the sales per thousand for all the possible combinations of qualifying factors, rank them by their sales per thousand, and then print them out in their ranked order. The mail marketer then would determine what the cut-off point should be and send a catalog to names in every combination for which the sales per thousand were above the cut-off point, which might be the break-even point.

The Merge-Purge and Mailing More Effectively

The merge-purge operation assembles all the lists to be mailed, merges all the names together, codes the names for carrier routing, identifies duplicate names, and then turns out labels grouped according to how the catalog is to travel through the mails. How this merge-purge is done will have significant impact upon the effectiveness of a mailing.

Carrier Coding. If there are sufficient names to warrant the expense, the first step in the merge-purge process after entering the individual lists into the computer is to encode the names with the postal carrier routing using a tape that the U.S. Postal Service supplies for the purpose. About 85 percent of the names will be coded. The remaining 15 percent will be uncodeable because of incorrect addresses or ZIP codes, because the post office's tape is not up to date or complete, or because of other reasons.

Correcting ZIP Codes. The next step should be to have the computer review all names that are uncodeable to correct ZIP code errors (not all service bureaus perform this step). About 2 or 3 percentage points of the 15 that were uncodeable will be found to have ZIP code errors. Correcting them will improve sales, therefore, by 2 percent to 3 percent.

Purging. The next step is purging. In this process, any DMA pandering names that are not to be mailed are suppressed[4] and duplicate names are identified. Pandering names are the names of people who have written to the Direct Mail Marketing Association (DMMA) requesting that their names be dropped from mailings.

The choice of the match code or dupe elimination method significantly affects mailing effectiveness. A match code can overkill; that is, it identifies more duplicates than actually exist. It can also underkill and fail to find duplicates.[5] Recently, one of the service bureaus has replaced the match code with a sophisticated sequence of logic that has increased the finding of duplicate names by as much as 10 percent to 15 percent of the duplicates without overkilling.[6] Finding more duplicates greatly increases the profitability of a mailing because, instead of mailing two catalogs to someone at the same time, only one catalog is mailed at the time and the other is mailed later at a much better than average response.

Duplicate names, in fact, are usually the most profitable rented names to mail. The reason for this is that the person who buys from many mail-order houses is a confirmed mail-order buyer. He or she likes to shop by mail. The appearance of a person's name on several lists is evidence that he or she is such a mail-order buyer. This fact makes it doubly important that duplicate names are correctly identified.

Method of Distribution Within the Postal System. Once the list has been purged, the computer prints the list in four groups according to how the catalogs are to be distributed within the postal system. The four groups are:

1. Names for catalogs to be carrier-routed
2. Names for catalogs to be sacked to go directly to the ZIP code office
3. Names of catalogs to go to multiple-ZIP cities
4. All other names (known in the trade as the basic tier)

---

[4] Pandering names in one's own file, however, should not be dropped because they have demonstrated a desire to receive one's catalog.

[5] If one has the opportunity to choose between a match code system that overkills and one that underkills, it is better to underkill one's own list and to overkill list rental. The logic is that underkilling one's own list means that one does not miss an opportunity to mail one's most productive list, and overkilling list rental names does not mean that an opportunity is lost to mail some names. Overkilling list rental means that more duplicate names will be mailed at separate times, thus improving mailing effectiveness, and that the ones that are overkilled will still be mailed, although at separate times.

[6] See Appendix A.

Analysis of the response to catalogs by their method of distribution within the postal system points to mailing efficiencies. Catalogs sacked to go directly to the carrier produce more sales per thousand than catalogs that go directly to individual ZIP code offices and multiple-ZIP cities. These in turn produce more response than the basic tier. What this suggests is that catalogs not be mailed to the basic tier of lists on which the sales per thousand are anticipated to be below a certain point. This not only eliminates the least productive names, but it also reduces the postage cost per catalog because the basic tier is more expensive per catalog to mail than the other groups. This is, in fact, what some mail marketers are now doing. To avoid the list rental expense of names that they do not use, they make arrangements with the list owners not to pay for the names supplied but not mailed in the basic tier.

Allocation of Duplicate Names. When one measures the results of publicity efforts, one should always measure them in such a manner that one can make the best decisions. We saw this in Chapter 15 when we removed the fixed publicity costs from the consideration of renting a list because fixed publicity costs, by definition, do not increase with the decision to mail an additional list. The need to make the right decision also caused us to allocate unknown orders back to the publicity efforts rather than to treat them as a separate entity. The publicity efforts produced the orders. Failure to give the efforts credit for unknown orders, therefore, would result in decisions not to repeat many worthy publicity efforts.

The same thinking governs the handling of the duplicate names produced by a merge-purge. The mail marketer should handle them so that he or she will make the best decisions. Some mail marketers measure the results of mailing duplicate names separately from the original list from which they came. This, I think, is incorrect.

The decision to be made is not whether one should mail to the duplicate names. This decision is foregone because duplicate names are paid for and in most instances produce sales per thousand better than any list that a mail marketer might rent. The decision is, rather, "Which original list will one rent?" Since the duplicates occur because of a decision to rent a list, their sales and mailing expense should be assigned to the original list.

The right procedure during the merge-purge should be that for the first mailing, one of a pair of duplicates should be coded to the first list and one of the next pair of duplicates should be coded to the second list. For the remailing of the duplicates, the remaining duplicate in the first pair of duplicates should be identified with the second list and the remaining duplicate in the second pair of duplicates should be identified with the first list.

For example, a merge-purge of lists 101 and 102 find these names in both lists:

Wilmot Whitney
Dixon B. White

For the first mailing they should be coded:

101A Wilmot Whitney
102A Dixon B. White

For the remailing of the duplicate names, maybe six weeks later, the names should be coded:

> 101B Dixon B. White
> 102B Wilmot Whitney

Notice that each name is assigned to each list in either the first mailing or in the remailing.

Other Methods of Increasing Mailing Effectiveness

There are so many emerging techniques for improving mailing effectiveness that the mail marketer should make an effort to be aware of all the opportunities to mail more effectively as they develop. An improvement of just a few percentage points in overall response means big dollars added to the bottom line. Two sources of information on new techniques for mailing more effectively are the service bureaus that do merge-purges and list brokers. The mail marketer should keep in touch with several in each category so that when something new comes along he quickly becomes aware of it.

The following are some ways of improving mailing effectiveness that can be considered now.

Pooling of Changes of Address. Some service bureaus that do merge-purging maintain a pool of names with address changes that they obtain from their customers. This pool of names with changed addresses is overlaid the names being merged-purged to correct the addresses of people who have moved.

Maintaining a Suppress File of Changed Addresses. Although you may have changed the address records in your file for your customers who have moved, their names may still appear at the old addresses in the lists that you rent, which means that you will mail catalogs to them at both their old and new addresses. The catalog mailed to the old address, of course, will be wasted. The solution to this problem is to maintain the customer's old name and address, but maintain it as a suppress. That is, it is used not to be mailed to but to identify the name when it shows up in other lists during a merge-purge. The computer then suppresses it so that it will not be mailed.

Printing Carrier Coding on Labels to Obtain Better Delivery. A problem that the mail marketer faces is that, although a customer may not have moved and the catalog mailed to him is correctly addressed, it still might not be delivered. There are a number of reasons for this. The mailer might put the catalog in the wrong bundle so that it is sent off to the wrong post office where it is discarded as undeliverable. If a catalog ends up in the wrong local post office, the post office will not forward it to the post office to which it should have gone. Similarly, the bundle might be put in the wrong sack or the whole sack can be mislabeled; either way, the catalog or catalogs will not be delivered.

These catalogs are undeliverable because of errors made by the mailer. But, even if the bundle or sack with the catalog in it safely arrives in the correct post office, it still may not be delivered. Once in the local post office, the bundle, if directed to the carrier, will be given directly to the carrier for delivery but, if it is directed just to the local post office, then it must be broken down and its contents sorted by carrier. In the process of sorting, there is an opportunity for a careless post office clerk to sort a catalog to the wrong carrier. The carrier, instead of returning it for sorting to the right carrier, may discard it as undeliverable. This may explain why catalogs that are bundled and sacked directly to carriers have more responses than catalogs that are bundled and sacked merely by the ZIP code.

A partial solution to this latter problem of nondelivery after a bundle has reached the local post office is to mark the catalog with the carrier coding even though it is bundled for the post office and not for the carrier. By indicating the carrier sorting as the catalog, the odds are improved that the catalog will be sorted to the right carrier.

Optical Sorting. In the mailing process, labels in the four groups mentioned earlier in this chapter (labels for catalogs to be carrier-routed, to go directly to a ZIP code, to go to multiple-ZIP cities, and all others) are run through a mailing machine that applies the labels and delivers the labeled catalogs down a conveyor to a person who separates the catalogs by carrier, ZIP codes, multiple-ZIP city, or other designation, and who then bundles and sacks them for their destination. It is in this separation of catalogs and sacking where the human errors that result in the nondelivery of catalogs can occur. If the bundler misses a change in ZIP codes or includes a catalog or some catalogs in the wrong bundle, then the misbundled catalogs will not be delivered. At least one mailer (the mailing arm of a printer) has sought to overcome this source of human error by having the labels marked by codes that are optically read by a computer so that the catalogs can be mechanically separated and sorted.

ZIP Code Analysis. Birds of a feather flock together. This is the idea behind ZIP code analysis. The theory is that if one has a high percent response in a certain ZIP code, one should rent more names in that ZIP code because those names will be more responsive as well.

The problem is to determine the responsive ZIP codes. By the time a mailing is distributed over the thousands of ZIP codes in this country, the number of catalogs going into any one ZIP code can become so few as to make a percent response statistically unreliable. A ZIP code that appears to be particularly responsive might only appear to be so because of a random clustering of orders in that ZIP code. Only the analysis of very large mailings or an accumulation of mailings will tell for certain whether one ZIP code is more responsive than another, and even then there will still be many ZIP codes for which the results will remain inconclusive.

A further problem is that within a ZIP code are areas of affluent people, areas of people of lesser means, and areas of people of differing psychographics. In other words, the ZIP code is a coarse subdivision of the mailing to analyze. A more likely subdivision to analyze is the carrier routing, but there is little hope of obtaining a statistically reliable percent response analysis of mail sent to carrier routings.

What this all means is that ZIP code analysis and carrier routing analysis should not be applied to one's workhorse lists or lists that have similar psychographics. The nature of the rented list and the selections requested largely determine the demographics and psychographics of a name no matter where the person lives. For example, the fact that a Horchow customer has spent $100 on his or her last purchase strongly suggests that he or she is affluent. There is no need to differentiate similar Horchow customers by ZIP code in order to determine affluence. Similarly, if the

Eddie Bauer list works for someone who markets outdoor sporting goods and clothing, the existence of a name in the Eddie Bauer list marks it as being the name of a person as having the renter's desired psychographics no matter where that person lives. If one were to apply ZIP code analysis to these situations, one would winnow out good customer prospects.

The ZIP code or carrier routing analysis is best applied, therefore, to large lists with unrelated psychographics that are marginal or submarginal that one wishes to rent and make work. How does one do this?

One company offers to profile the demographics of your list by analyzing the ZIP codes in which your customers reside. It then identifies the ZIP codes with similar demographics and supply a ZIP code overlay of them to the list owner. The list owner then rents just the identified ZIP codes in the marginal and submarginal lists. This seems to work for some mail marketers but not for others.

Another approach is to keep a record of the number of rented catalogs mailed into a ZIP code over a period of time and the number of orders received from those rented catalogs. Then, disregarding the statistical unreliability of the percent response occurring in many of the ZIP codes, one rents from marginal lists names in those ZIP codes with higher percent responses. Although the percent response for any one ZIP code will usually be unreliable, it is accurate to say that the better ZIP codes collectively will perform better than the poorer ones.

This approach is crude, however, because, as was mentioned earlier, many types of people live in one ZIP code. One would target one's mailing with more accuracy if one mailed to selected carrier routes. A carrier route goes to fewer neighborhoods and those neighborhoods tend to be similar; thus, one is more likely to find a higher percent of similar prospects in one carrier route than one ZIP code.

How does one select the carrier routes from which to rent names from marginal lists? One way is to rent names from those carrier routes in which one already has many customers. The logic of this is that carrier routes tend to have the same number of postal patrons because, unlike a ZIP code, a postal carrier is limited by the number of residences he has time to visit during one day. One can assume, therefore, that the more customers one has in a carrier route, the higher the percent customers will be of the postal patrons in that route.

This approach seems to work for those who have tried it. The problem is that list owners generally do not have their names marked with carrier routes. Therefore, it is necessary to take in all the names and then select the ones residing in the carrier route with a high number of customers. If one must pay for all the names, costs may sometimes become so high that this approach is unprofitable. If, however, a deal can be made with the list owners to pay only for names used or to exchange names, then this problem is overcome.

The Two-Stage Mailing

Sometimes when a catalog appeals to a narrow market but has a strong appeal within that market, a two-stage mailing, also known as a catalog subscription offer, pays. The problem for the mail marketer having such a catalog is that prospects for the product are so few and far between that it is difficult to find mailing lists with enough prospects to make renting the list pay. If, instead of mailing catalogs to rented lists, one sends a letter with a reply card suggesting that the recipient send for the catalog, then, because the recipient spends no money, one will receive many responses. If it is profitable to mail the catalog to these respondees repeatedly, then the two-stage approach will pay off. The first stage (the letter) identifies the market. The second stage (the catalog) sells the market. The secret of success in a two-stage mailing is that the catalog have strong appeal to the respondees.

a manual operating system

The Objectives of an Operating System

I shall never forget the very first mail order that came into the British Isles Collection. At about two in the afternoon on the fifth day after we had mailed our catalog, a woman phoned to order a velvet blazer for her husband. We were so thrilled to have our first order that we packed and shipped it that afternoon. She received it just two days later and was so delighted with our prompt service that she then phoned and ordered a shooting jacket.

This story illustrates my belief that the main object of an operating system should be to fill orders fast. Fast service preserves and even enhances the most valuable asset a mail marketer has—his mailing list. Fast service means not merely no negative feelings about the company but also the positive feelings that this story illustrates.

Poor service, on the other hand, means cancellation of orders, fewer reorders, and more returns. The damage to one's customer list that poor service causes is often hard to measure. How much did later business fall off because of poor service? How much did returns increase because the customers no longer wanted the products? The answers to these questions cannot always be easily determined. But the cost of labor in shipping an order is always known. Many mail marketers, when they balance an imponderable cost against a known one, will opt for trying to save on the known cost. For this reason, they tend to skimp on labor at the crucial moment when orders build up. They fall behind and every customer's order is delayed, inevitably causing customer dissatisfaction and worry if the delay puts the shipping date close to a holiday, such as Christmas.

The mail marketer, therefore, should make his plans so that he does not fall behind. The first thing he should do is to determine when the order load will be coming. This he can do easily with the orderline which was described in Chapter 16. Then he should estimate how much labor is required to fill an order. Knowing these two things, he should then calculate how much help he needs week-by-week and even day-by-day. The second thing a mail marketer should do to prevent falling behind in shipping orders is to design his operating system to be efficient and to have as little labor as possible between the receipt of an order and shipment.

Filling orders as completely as possible is just as important as shipping without delay. This, of course, cannot be done if one does not have the merchandise. The mail marketer, therefore, must carefully plan the supply of his inventory, a subject that is covered in Chapter 20. Orders, however, are sometimes not filled even when one has the items in stock because the items are out of place. To avoid this problem, the mail marketer must have his stock well-organized. Bins and aisles should be clearly labeled so that a lazy employee does not have to spend too much time deciding where something belongs. And the inventory control system should be such that a misplaced item can be detected. In other words, personnel should send an order out to the warehouse knowing that it can be filled; then, if it cannot, someone should investigate.

Low order processing cost should, of course, be an objective. This is not necessarily incompatible with fast service. In fact, fast service reduces customer queries about their orders and thus reduces customer service expense.

Another objective of an operating system is an ability to answer quickly customer questions about their orders. This cuts customer service and telephone expense and, of course, makes more satisfied customers.

Finally, the operating system should provide the mail marketer with good control over his cash, the customer's orders, and his inventory.

A Manual Operating System

The balance of this chapter presumes that the reader has not arrived at the point where he is ready for a computer operating system. Certainly, anyone who is just starting out (unless that person is starting on a grand scale), does not need one. And, although good mail-order computer systems are becoming available at low cost (see next chapter), chances are that one can get by without a computer system until one is doing over a million dollars in sales.

The manual operating system that I describe here is very similar to the one we used during the first year of British Isles Collection. It is tested and not theoretical. It gave us control, and at no time did order fulfillment fall behind more than two days.

Envelope control

Unless a mail-order business is so small that the orders are all processed by the mail marketer and his family, any operating system, computer or manual, should have order and cash control to guard against internal theft and the misplacement of orders and mail. This means that the mail must be controlled as soon as it comes in. When the mail arrives, obvious corporate mail should be pulled out and the remainder should be counted into batches of 25 envelopes for which a Batch Control Slip is made out (see Figure 18-1). Recorded on the batch control slip at this point are the date, the number of envelopes, the batcher's initials, the batch number, and the total number of batches.

With each day's mail, a Daily Mail Control Sheet is made out in triplicate (see Figure 18-2). On it is recorded the batch numbers and the

FIGURE 18-1 Batch Control Slip

Date _____	Batch No. _____ of _____
Total Envelopes _____	Counted By _____
Mail Sliced By _____	Deposit Made _____
Mail Opener _____	No. of Env.'s Rec'd. _____
Total Cash $ _____ Stamps $ _____	Credit $ _____ No. of Checks _____
No. of Orders: Reg. _____ Credit _____	Customer Service _____
Catalog Requests _____	Corp. Mail _____
Note: Totals on above line must equal envelope count.	

number of envelopes in each batch. One copy goes to the bookkeeper, one to the Batch Deposit Department, and one to the Order Sort Department.

As the reader can see, control is gained over the mail as soon as the batches are made up. No envelopes or batches can be lost without one knowing about it.

Mail opening

The batches of mail are run through the letter-slicing machine and forwarded to the mail-openers. The mail-openers verify the total number of pieces of mail and initial the Batch Control Slip. If there is an error in the count, then the supervisor must recount and correct the Batch Control Slip.

FIGURE 18-2 Daily Mail Control Sheet

Date _____

DAILY MAIL CONTROL SHEET

Batch Number	Total Pieces
Total	
Prepared By:	

The mail-openers then remove the orders or letters and staple them to their envelopes. The mail-openers record on the order in red ink the type of payment, cash or check, and the total amount received. If the customer has entered the amount, it should be circled instead of being written out again. Credit card orders should be rubber-stamped in large block type with "CREDIT CARD." Checks should be verified for date and signature. The mail should be grouped within the batch by cash orders, check orders, credit card orders, C.O.D. orders, catalog requests, and customer service. A Deposit Control Sheet is made out, one for each day (Figure 18-3). The total number of orders, the number of credit card orders, the total value of checks, and the total cash received are recorded for each batch. The checks and cash are put into a paper wallet, which, in turn, is put with the orders and letters into a portfolio. The portfolio then goes to the Batch Deposit Department.

FIGURE 18-3 Deposit Control Sheet

Mail Date _____   Page No. _____ of _____

Total Batches _____   Date Completed _____

Batch No.	Total Orders	Total Credits	Check Value	Cash Value	Value Credit Card Batches	Total Value

Deposit Date: _____   Prepared By: _____

Depositing and check verification

The Batch Deposit Department (which could be the bookkeeper) makes out the deposit slip and checks it against the Batch Control Slip and the Deposit Control Sheet. At this point any checks that exceed a set amount are verified by calling the banks upon which they are drawn (at British Isles Collection we called on checks of $150 and more). A copy of the deposit slip is attached to the Deposit Control Sheet, and the deposit is put in the bank. In other words, for each batch there is a deposit slip, a copy of which is attached to the Deposit Control Sheet. The Deposit Control Sheet is filed by date when the deposits for all batches have been made.

Order sort department

The Order Sort Department verifies that all the batches have been accounted for and that all Batch Control Slips have been cleared by the Batch Deposit Department by checking against the Daily Mail Control Sheet.

The Order Sort Department then edits the orders for accuracy, checking stock number, size, color, and so on against the master product list. They also check media code, ZIP code, total paid against what should have been paid, that the credit card orders have been stamped as such, and that the address as recorded on the order is complete (checking against the envelope). The envelopes can then be removed and discarded. The orders are stamped with the batch date.

The contents of the batch portfolios are then sorted by cash and check orders together, credit card orders, catalog requestss, customer service mail, and corporate mail.

Catalog requests are sent off to have labels typed, upon which the advertising source code is also typed. A carbon or photo copy is made of the labels, which goes to the computer service bureau to add the names with their source codes to the request file.

Customer service mail and corporate mail get sent off to the appropriate departments.

The two groups of orders, the cash and check orders and the credit card orders, are each batched in groups of 25 orders. The batches should have an Order Batch Slip attached which should be numbered with a number that indicates the order date plus a batch serial number (Figure 18-4). For example, the second batch of orders that came in on April 10 would have the number 0410-2. These batches are listed on the Order Batch Control Sheet, one copy of which goes to the label typist who verifies that all batches are received at that position (Figure 18-5).

FIGURE 18-4   Order Batch Slip

```
                    ORDER BATCH SLIP
  _____

  Date of Orders _____

  Batch No._____

  Total Orders _____

  Orders ☐        Orders ☐

  Prepared By _____    Date _____
```

Inventory control and credit card authorization

Cash orders go to inventory control to have the items ordered deducted from the running inventory. If the inventory record indicates no inventory on an item, then the initials *B.O.* (for *back order*) are written to the left of the item. Even though the record shows no inventory, the clerk should deduct the unfillable item from the inventory record to indicate a back order. In deducting the item from inventory, the mail marketer is also recording the sale of the item. If the mail marketer totals these unit sales each week and records the total for the week in a summary kept for each

FIGURE 18-5   Order Batch Control Sheet

ORDER BATCH CONTROL SHEET	Order Date:
Batch Number	Total Orders

stock number, he has the means for forecasting sales, as will be discussed in Chapter 20.

Credit card orders must first be authorized by the bank-card company. The reason for this step being done before the order is deducted from inventory is to prevent any orders that are not authorized from being deducted from inventory. Once the orders have been authorized, then they can go through inventory control as did the cash and check orders.

The credit card orders then go to the Batch Deposit Department where the credit card charge slips are made out for the amount that can be shipped and a tissue copy is attached to the order. A deposit slip for the charge cards is made out. The deposit is recorded on the Deposit Control Sheet and a tissue copy of the deposit is attached. The charge slips are deposited at the bank. The Deposit Control Sheet should have control numbers to be sure all deposits for credit card batches are accounted for.

Labels and data control

The orders then go to the copying machine and two copies of each order are made. One copy goes to the computer service bureau so that the customer's order information and source code will be captured. The orders with one copy attached go to the typist who types the shipping label. Then the order with the label and copy attached go either to the warehouse for shipping or to the back-order department.

Shipping

When the orders with their extra copies and labels attached are received in the warehouse, the orders are sorted in warehouse sequence by the first item on the order. The orders are then picked and delivered to Inspection.

Inspection checks to make sure that charge card orders have charge slips made out for what is being shipped. The merchandise is checked against the order to make sure that the order was filled correctly by the stock-picker. Inspection stamps each shipped item with the date and the word *Shipped* on both the order and its copy. On the order copy only, each item which is unfilled is rubber-stamped "back-ordered."

The order then goes to the packer who initials and dates order at top and packs it, putting the shipping label on the outside and the order copy on the inside. The order copy shows the customer in his own handwriting exactly what he ordered and how it was filled. There are several reasons for putting a copy in the package. Since it is a photocopy, there is no dispute that the order was filled incorrectly when, in fact, it was correctly filled. Many customers appreciate receiving a copy of their order with their merchandise, as we found at British Isles Collection. Most important is that, if an item was back ordered, the customer was immediately informed and not left to wonder if its lack was a shipping error.

Some mail marketers might feel that a separate inspection step is unnecessary and that it can be handled by the packer. Prior to our making it a separate step at British Isles Collection, we had an unacceptably high number of shipping errors, and we had a number of instances in which merchandise was shipped, mostly back orders, without credit card charge slips being made out. With the introduction of someone specializing in inspection, shipping errors and charge errors dropped close to zero.

The reason why inspection is not done well by the packer is that it gives the packer too much to think about. When one does nothing except inspect, there is little chance one will overlook the only thing one must do, that is, to inspect. It goes without saying that the picker does not inspect his own work.

Completed orders

Completed orders are filed alphabetically in the Customer Service Department. Since filing slows down as a file thickens, a new file should be set up every three to six months to keep the file manageable. As time goes on, the need to go into the file for a given period diminishes. After a year, the file for the period can be put in storage and ultimately discarded.

Back orders

Unfilled and incomplete orders go to the back-order department. Customers are then notified that there is a delay, and the orders are filed by stock number. If there is more than one item on back order, then a photocopy is made of the order. The original order is filed under the first unfilled item, and the photocopy is filed under the second item. To make sure that the photocopy is filed in its correct place, the second item is circled in red, and a red cross is placed next to the first back-ordered item to show where the original is filed. Needless to say, shipments should be made only against the original order, not a copy; otherwise, duplicate shipments will be made.

When a shipment of merchandise is received from a manufacturer, all back orders for the stock numbers concerned are pulled, any necessary charge card slips are made out, and the merchandise is shipped.

If a customer inquires about an unfilled order, the customer service representative must ask him for the stock number and then look for the order under the stock number in the back-order file. This system works well enough when the number of back orders is not enormous or if it usually is easy to identify which stock numbers a customer is inquiring about. If there usually is a considerable problem in finding orders, however, then a photocopy of the back order with the item back-ordered circled in red should be crossfiled with the completed orders.

I never trust inventory records, particularly when the inventory is thinly spread over many stockkeeping units. Too often there is inventory on hand to fill orders that the inventory records say is not there. For this reason, I periodically compare the back orders against what is actually on the shelves to see if some can be filled. Even if only a few are found, it is worth doing. Each item found represents a customer satisfied, an item shipped, and maybe a sale saved.

Some general comments

This manual operating system with its many controls and forms seems like much work, but it is not. The forms are either one per day or one per batch. Entries in the forms are only once per batch. When I refer to departments, such as Batch Deposit Department and Order Sort Department, this suggests a ponderous organization. Actually, these departments are merely labels for functions, and often one person will handle many functions.

The purpose of the batching and forms is to gain control of cash and the orders. It is a sad truth that most mail marketers are subject to internal theft. By gaining control of the mail *before* opening, an employee cannot take cash from an order without it showing up as missing from an envelope or as a missing envelope. The batch and batch control also ensure that no mail is mislaid or hidden away in the desk drawer of an absent or overloaded employee. Batches also organize the mail and make sure one day's work is completed before another is started. Batches also provide convenient work units for moving the mail through the office and warehouse.

Another feature of the system is that the shipping is done from the original order. By not retyping the order, work is saved and mistakes that would creep in because of the retyping are eliminated.

In this manual operating system, I have recommended a computer service bureau to maintain one's list. This ensures that the data necessary for operating the business is captured, most particularly the information about each customer. The service bureaus should also be able to supply a source code report, showing sales by source code.

Customer Service

If operations get out of control at a mail-order company, customer service, both directly and indirectly in the form of customer dissatisfaction, can become expensive indeed. The best way to keep customer service costs down is by eliminating the reasons for customer inquiries. Most customer service inquiries result from unfilled orders, delays in the making of exchanges and refunds, and failure to notify customers that their orders will be delayed. To a lesser extent, mistakes, poor product quality, and technical queries contribute to the customer service load.

You can eliminate unfilled orders and the customer service problems they cause by having enough inventory on hand so that you don't have back orders. However, this is easier said than done. Inventory costs money to maintain, and interest costs and markdowns can mount as inventory balloons. But want of inventory can be even costlier: Orders can be cancelled, losing the entire mark-up; orders are handled and rehandled; telephone expenses go up as customers call collect and are called back; customer service load mounts; merchandise is returned for refund because it arrived too late; and, worst of all, customers never buy again because they have been disappointed. The solution to this problem, beyond committing enough capital to inventory, lies in riding herd upon suppliers and in sound practices for ordering merchandise.

Process your exchanges and refunds within a day or two. They represent customers who already are dissatisfied and who already have waited while the U.S. mails returned their package; any delay in handling their exchange will trigger phone calls and letters.

Always notify your customers if there is going to be a delay of more than a few days in filling their order. The Federal Trade Commission requires that paid orders be notified within 30 days if there is going to be a delay, but I would not wait that long. Customers don't like being left in the dark. Notification of the delay stops them from wondering if their order was lost in the mail and prevents them from writing or calling.

But if they do phone or write, and even though you have shipped the merchandise that has crossed the inquiry in the mails, be sure to answer the inquiry. It is a sign of your efficiency and concern. I always had a rule that all mail had to be answered.

Furthermore, you should answer all mail within a few days. Unanswered letters produce even more letters and collect phone calls. Ultimately, dissatisfied customers write to the attorney general, the Better Business Bureau, and the Federal Trade Commission. A quick response, on the other hand, means less complaint and more customer satisfaction.

A few suggestions

Make a forecast of the workload in your customer service and returns department and plan for help to accommodate the load. You can be guided by the fact that returns and customer inquiries will increase following a period of many orders, which in turn follows an increase in mailings.

Set up some controls on customer service. Don't just go out and ask the customer service representatives how things are going. You are sure to get a noncommittal answer. Often a customer service representative who gets behind will hide unresolved customer problems and mail in a desk drawer rather than admit problems.

Require your customer service manager to submit a report of how much mail is in the house, how old the oldest piece of customer service mail is, and the productivity of each customer service representative. This report should be weekly if customer service is under control, daily if out of control.

The 30-Day Rule

On Wednesday, October 22, 1975, the Federal Trade Commission promulgated what is known in the trade as the 30-Day Rule in some of the most turbid prose ever issued by a federal agency. By comparison, the Internal Revenue Service's instructions for filling out Form 1040 read like a first-grade reader. So impenetrable is the rule that I fear many mail-order firms unwittingly violate it.[1]

The 30-Day Rule tells the mail marketer what he must do when he is unable to promptly fill orders. Since the Federal Trade Commission threatens a heavy penalty for each infraction of the rule, the mail marketer, despite the rule's opacity, must read it carefully and then make sure that his procedures and customer notification letters are in compliance. Indeed, it may well be wise for the mail marketer to engage a lawyer to help in this task. To aid the reader, I have included the Direct Marketing Association's interpretation of the rule in Appendix B.

[1] For those who feel I treat the authors of the rule too harshly, I quote the following sentence (?), which is meaningless because it contains no verb: "Where a seller is unable to ship merchandise on or before the definite revised shipping date provided under paragraph (b)(1)(i) and consented to by the buyer pursuant to paragraph (b)(1)(ii), clearly and conspicuously and without prior demand, a renewed option either to consent to a further delay or to cancel the order and receive a prompt refund."

19
what the computer should do for you

It used to be that everyone with a computer had a horror story in which a program or computer malfunction paralyzed a company's operations. I had mine during the 1970s at Lawson Hill Leather and Shoe Co.

In those days, writing a program for one's operations was expensive and uncertain. Hardware was even more costly, and, unless one went into very large equipment, it lacked the power needed to do the job. It was always a major and traumatic decision to install a computer.

We had been computerized to the extent that all orders were keyed into the computer of a service bureau, and we received picking tickets daily with shipping labels in warehouse sequence. We also had our shipments keyed into the computer so that we could belatedly have microfiche[1] produced that would supply our customer service department with the status of each customer's order. But there was much that the computer system could not do or did poorly. Inventory was not on the system, to say nothing of it being interactive with our customer order file, so we produced picking tickets regardless of whether the merchandise was available. We could produce back-order picking tickets but elaborate precautions had to be taken to avoid shipping twice. The system did not maintain our list; this was done elsewhere. Information about customers' orders was rarely up-to-the-minute; so wrong information and no information were sometimes given to customers who inquired about their orders.

We decided, therefore, that we had to have our own computer system that would integrate all our operations. But we were appalled at the estimated cost of $75,000 to $100,000 for a program, which would be in addition to the computer itself. Someone we knew and who knew our operation said that he could write our programs at a fraction of the cost during evenings and weekends when he was not working at his regular job. We were naive enough to think he could and engaged him. After over six months elapsed

---

[1] Microfiche is microfilm in card form which contains many computer printout pages. It is read with a special viewer that enlarges the required page.

and it had become obvious that we were far away from a program, we engaged him full-time. Many more months passed and finally it appeared as though our program was nearly ready.

As a precaution, I had enjoined both the programmer and the head of our mail-order operations to operate the new system in parallel with the old system and not to discontinue the old system until we were sure of the new. But while I was away on a buying trip in Europe, they switched our operations to the new system without operating in parallel with the old. The new system was so fraught with difficulties that only the programmer could operate it, and it could perform only part of the functions we previously were able to do. But because the programmer then had to operate the machines in order to do the daily work, he no longer had the time needed to correct the program. It was after many costly computer consultants and much time that Lawson Hill Leather and Shoe Co. had a good computer operating system.

The problem was not just that our computer operating system worked so badly; it was that we had long before outgrown our previous operating system and desperately needed a computer to integrate and coordinate our order-processing operations. Paperwork goes up not linearly, but geometrically. As we received more and more orders, it became more and more difficult to process them efficiently and to do the many things we needed to do.

Fortunately, horror stories like this no longer need be the case for the mail marketer. Excellent turn-key programs for mail order exist at a modest cost that run on powerful yet relatively inexpensive equipment. They are on-line to offer instant access and immediate update. They coordinate and control all the mail-order operations. They are so inexpensive now that mail-order companies with annual sales as little as $1,000,000 and maybe less can afford them. I offer one such computer system and program through my consulting practice.

How a Computer System Should Operate and What It Should Do for You

The most important characteristic of a computer system is that it be on-line and offer immediate access and update. As orders are keyed into the system, all the affected files should be changed at once—inventory should be reduced, sales increased, source codes credited, customer records updated, and so on. This immediate adjustment of all files permits order-takers to answer customer inquiries as to the availability of merchandise and customer service representatives to give on-the-spot answers to customer inquiries as to the status of their orders. It greatly decreases the workload in the customer service department.

Normally, an on-line system operates something like this: The operator will key the first two or three letters of the customer's last name and the ZIP code from an order. All customers in the ZIP code with the same first letters in their last name are then flashed onto the screen of the CRT.[2] If the customer on the order appears on the screen, then the existing customer identification number is used for entering the order; if the customer's name does not appear, then the customer is assigned a new number. At the time it projects onto the screen all customers within the ZIP code with the same first letters in the last name, the computer also projects the names of customers within the ZIP code who have defrauded the company and

---

[2] The abbreviation for cathode ray tube or the television-like tube used with computers.

addresses where fraud has occurred. Thus, in this first step, the operator identifies previous customers and screens orders from customers and addresses with bad history.

The computer then projects the order format onto the screen and the operator fills in the order information. The computer verifies stock numbers and price. When the operator is satisfied that the order is correct on the screen, he enters it into the computer. At that moment, the computer adjusts all the affected files: the inventory is reduced, sales are credited, demand for the sold items is increased, the source code is credited with the sale, and so on.

This instantaneous updating of all the files means that a moment later, when another customer phones in to order one of the same items in the previous order, the order-taker can tell the customer whether or not the item is still available. If the item is available, the order-taker enters the order immediately so that the item will be allocated to the customer and not sold to another. Similar to orders, returns, exchanges, retail store sales, and other transactions are entered into the computer with the relevant files being updated immediately.

At the end of the day or whenever management determines, the computer prints picking tickets with shipping labels attached for the available merchandise in the same sequence as the merchandise is arranged in the warehouse. The computer also prints the expected shipping date of unavailable merchandise onto the picking ticket. In a separate run, the computer prints a letter or card to notify the customer of the expected shipping date of the unavailable merchandise. In other runs, the computer prints the 30-day notices required by the Federal Trade Commission, refund checks, credit card charges and credits, back orders, and a host of other needs.

The computer maintains the inventory and all purchase orders with vendors. When goods are received from vendors, they are added to inventory and deducted from open purchase orders. Of course, as customer orders are entered into the computer, information on the demand[3] for each item in inventory is accumulated. The computer then uses the demand history to forecast future demand for the items in inventory. The computer should analyze sales distributions over sizes stocked in an item and over a period of time relative to total demand. In short, the computer should maintain all information and do everything needed to buy merchandise.

Bells and Whistles

For many mail-order companies, the ability of a computer to print computer letters customized by the specific information known about each customer is a bell and whistle, that is, a frill. But for the mail marketer who wishes to take advantage of every opportunity to develop his business, it is a necessity. The opportunities offered by computer letters to build sales and customer goodwill are described in Chapter 21 and to some extent in Chapter 4. My recommendation is that the mail marketer put in a system with this capability.

Similarly, the capability of the computer to gather the information needed to calculate lifetime values of customers, as described in Chapter 15, is no frill for the sophisticated mail marketer. However, few mail marketers have access to this information about their customers. My recom-

---

[3] The word *demand* is used instead of *sales* because it indicates customer orders for a product regardless of whether or not the company was able to ship them. A sale, on the other hand, occurs only when an order is shipped.

mendation is for the mail marketer to insist upon this capability being a
part of any computer operating system that he installs.

195
what the computer should
do for you

A third feature not commonly found in mail-order operating systems
is the ability to calculate three-year plans. Given the net sales per thousand
catalogs experienced on various rented lists, the sales per thousand in the
various segments of the house file, the decay in the sales per thousand in
the house file as time goes on, the rented lists available, the variable
operating costs of the business, the variable publicity costs, and a mail/
don't mail publicity percent criterion, what will be the sales and profits for
a company in one, two, and three years? What will they be if the mail/
don't mail publicity percent criterion is relaxed or tightened? What will
happen if the sales per thousand on rented lists falls off or improves 10
percent? What happens if customer response falls off? What happens if the
cost of the catalog in the mail increases without a corresponding increase
in the sales per thousand catalogs? These questions can be answered by a
three-year plan.

These speculations are not merely questions of academic interest. They
are vital to every mail-order company. A good example is a consulting client
of mine who experienced a drop in the sales per thousand to both buyers
and rented lists. While the client remained profitable, he forecasted that,
because lower response reduced his ability to rent names, this inability to
rent as many names as before would result in fewer new customers to
replace the ones lost by attrition and that within a few years, as active
customers dwindled, the company would become unprofitable. This advance
warning enabled him to take corrective action before it was too late.

The problem with three-year plans, however, is that they take a long
time to develop. (It took me the best part of a week to do the three-year
plan for the Mayflower Gift Company described in Chapter 16.) If one
modifies the variables several times to see what the results are in different
circumstances, one multiplies the work many fold. For this reason, three-
year forecasts, as necessary as they are, are rarely done in the mail-order
business.

With the right program, a computer can quickly calculate the forecasts
for a variety of circumstances. The ability to calculate three-year plans is
a bell and whistle that will serve well those mail marketers who use it.

Computer Output

Management reports

What reports should the mail marketer expect from the computer to help
him guide his business? Here are some of the important ones:

1. *A publicity cost analysis of the mailing program.* This report either is or
   supplies the information for the publicity cost analyses for each mailing effort.
   This is the same report as in Tables 15-3 and 15-4.

2. *A publicity cost analysis of the media program.* This is the same as the previous
   report except it is for media. It corresponds to Table 15-5.

3. *A combined publicity cost analysis.* This is a summary of all publicity efforts
   and corresponds to Table 15-2.

4. *Publicity cost and profit contribution analysis of the catalog.* This corresponds
   to Table 7-1 and is an analysis of catalog space cost, profit margins, and sales
   of the merchandise in the catalog.

5. *History and forecast of product demand.* This report gives the demand history
   of each product and forecasts future demand for the buying period ahead. This
   report is discussed in the next chapter. It usually contains other product
   information, such as returns and exchanges.

6. *Stock status report.* This report gives for each item in stock the inventory on hand, back orders, and open vendor purchase orders. Frequently, this report shows demand.

Operating output

The output of the computer for daily operations usually includes most of the following:

1. *Picking tickets with shipping labels attached.* These should come out in the same sequence as the merchandise is arranged in the warehouse.
2. *Credit card charges.* Instead of making out credit card charges by hand, the computer can make them out on a standard form which can be used for all credit cards.
3. *Credit card credits.* Similar to credit card charges, the computer makes out credit card credits on standard forms.
4. *Listing of credit card charges and credits.* Some banks accept listings of credit card charges and credits in place of individual tickets.
5. *Refund checks.* The computer prints customer refund checks.
6. *Register of open refund checks.* Refund checks, because of their enormous volume, make the checkbook difficult to balance. By maintaining a register, the computer greatly eases this task. Returned checks are keyed in so that the register reflects the outstanding amounts. I always kept a separate bank account for refund checks to avoid confusion in the general disbursements account.
7. *Batch control reports.* Just as in a manual operating system, orders should be controlled by batching. These reports provide the control.
8. *Drop ship purchase orders.* Where the goods are shipped by the vendor directly to the customer, the computer creates a drop ship purchase order.
9. *Work orders for monogram or assembly.* If something needs to be sent out of the warehouse to be worked on, the computer creates a work order.
10. *Summary reports for drop shipments and work orders.* These reports supply control of operations performed outside the warehouse.
11. *Warehouse inventory list.* A listing of stock numbers in warehouse sequence.
12. *List of unavailable inventory.* This is a listing of items being discontinued for which no more inventory will become available.
13. *Back-order report.* A listing of all back orders by stock number.
14. *Customer notifications.* The computer should print all the notifications required by the Federal Trade Commission's 30-Day Rule.
15. *Vendor listing.* A listing of vendors within contact persons, discount terms, and other vendor information.
16. *Purchase orders.* These are the purchase orders which one sends to vendors. If the purchase orders that one sends to one's vendors are printed by the computer rather than written by hand, one can be sure that what is on order and what is entered into the computer are the same.
17. *Open purchase orders.* This is a listing of unfilled purchase orders with vendors. It is convenient for this to be available in both stock number and vendor sequences.
18. *Purchase order receiving.* This is a listing of merchandise received. Like the preceding, it is convenient for this report to be available in both stock number and vendor sequences.
19. *Possible duplicates listing.* The computer prints a listing of all customer names it thinks might possibly be duplicates. It can then be reviewed manually and corrections can be made.
20. *Due bills.* Sometimes customers have paid too little. The computer automatically prints out needed bills to recover the amount owed.

Files Maintained in an On-Line Computer System

Some of the files maintained in the computer would include these:

1. *House file.* This file is the mailing list of buyers and catalog requests with their identification numbers. This file would contain for each customer all the information suggested in Chapter 17.

2. *Order file.* This file maintains the records on all open orders and all recently closed orders. How long the closed orders are kept on the active file depends upon one's situation, but usually keeping the orders on-line six months is long enough. Afterwards, the orders are kept in off-line storage for customer research and computer letters. Among other things, the order file shows for each order the items shipped and still open, the expected shipping date of back-ordered items, and items returned with the dates of their returns.

3. *Inventory file.* This is the file of all inventory on hand and unfilled customer orders. It maintains sales and returns records for each stock number.

4. *Purchase order file.* This is the file of purchase orders with vendors. This file usually can be accessed by keying in the purchase order number, the vendor, or the stockkeeping unit.

5. *Source code file.* This contains the information by source code needed to produce the publicity cost analyses of mailing and media efforts.

6. *Work order file.* This file contains the necessary information to process work orders for monograms and the like.

7. *File of open refund checks.*

8. *Control file.* This file is for the control of each day's operations. It contains the current date, the last identification number assigned to a customer or catalog request, the last refund check number used, the last purchase order number used, and the current catalog year or season.

Selecting a Computer Operating System

The purpose of this chapter is to guide the mail marketer in the installation of a computer operating system. A common error of the mail marketer is to fail to give adequate thought to what should be expected from the computer. The preceding part of this chapter should give some guidance as to what the computer should do and what reports should be received. Beyond this, there are some other considerations in selecting a computer operating system.

My strongest recommendation is to avoid purchasing an untried computer operating system. One should consider only computer operating systems being used successfully by half a dozen mail-order concerns of which one can make inquiries. The system should be one that is designed expressly for mail order; it should never be a packaged off-the-shelf system adapted for mail order. There is, of course, little point in trying to design a mail-order computer operating system oneself when there are a number of good ones available at fairly low cost. Any computerized mail-order operating system should not only have been designed for mail order, but it also should have been designed by someone in or closely associated with mail order. Only by being in mail order oneself can one appreciate all the nuances of mail-order operation and design accordingly.

Needless to say, any system that one adopts should be nearly turnkey; that is, it should be ready to be used. The only program modifications to the system should be the ones that are necessary because of the peculiarities of one's business.

The system should be one that has the ability to grow. That is, as one's business grows, one should be able to add more CRTs, more memory, and more core.

Similarly, as new programs and outputs are developed for the system by the vendor, the mail marketer should have the opportunity to add the new programs to his system. The system should also be flexible so that it is possible to make modifications to meet one's special needs.

It goes without saying that the vendor should be in a position to give considerable support during and after installation. Similarly, the manufacturer of the equipment should have a nearby office so that service calls can be handled promptly.

forecasting sales
and inventory requirements

No mail-order function is more critical than inventory control. Many mail-order companies, otherwise well-conceived, founder on this rock. If there is too much inventory, there is interest expense, high markdowns, and, worst of all, the danger of running out of cash.

But too little inventory can be even more disastrous. Too little inventory results in the extra expense of double shipping multiple orders, correspondence, 30-Day Rule notifications, customer service labor, and telephone. As serious as these expenses are, they are minor when compared to the damage done to sales and that most precious of the mail marketer's assets, the mailing list.

Having made the decision to buy and place his order, the customer then wants instant gratification. Swift delivery makes him happy and speaks well for the company. But slow delivery disappoints a customer, leaves a bad impression, and may even brand a company as fly-by-night. Shipping delays of as little as five days were reported to significantly reduce catalog response by Bill Knowles, owner of the Stitchery in Wellesley Hills in Massachusetts. He said that cash flow was actually better through improved sales six months after he changed to higher inventory levels and to a policy of shipping at once, regardless of how complete the orders are, and away from a policy of holding incomplete orders five days for more stock to come in. Customer disillusionment and loss of interest cause higher returns, more cancelled orders, and fewer repeat sales. This is the costly price of inadequate inventory.

How then does one solve the dilemma? Too little inventory loses sales and customer goodwill. Too much inventory means high interest expense, heavy markdowns, and sometimes the disaster of running out of cash. There rarely is a simple solution, but good inventory control is always a major part of it. Good inventory control greatly mitigates the mail marketer's difficulties. It behooves him to set up sophisticated methods for forecasting his requirements and to maintain close supervision. Much is at stake.

The Reorder Lead Time

Elements of the reorder lead time

The source of the mail marketer's inventory control difficulties is the reorder lead time, that is, the time that elapses between the day inventory requirements are reviewed and when the resulting merchandise ordered is available to fill orders. When the reorder lead time is short, the mail marketer's problems are few and small. But as the reorder lead time lengthens, the difficulty of maintaining the inventory mounts. The further out one must forecast, the more likely it is that actual sales will drift away from forecast. And when the sales density on a stockkeeping unit is low, random orders keep the inventory constantly out of balance. The mail marketer's first task, therefore, is to learn what constitutes his reorder lead time and what steps he can take to reduce it. To do this, he needs to know its elements.

Mail marketers often think of their reorder lead times as the time required for a vendor to make the product; it is this and much more. It consists of the following:

1. The reorder cycle—the time between inventory reviews. Thus, if a buyer reviews his inventory once every two weeks, then two weeks should be included in the reorder lead time. One can see in Figure 20-1 how shortening the reorder cycle reduces the maximum commitment needed for inventory on hand and on order.
2. The time required to transmit an order to the vendor.
3. The time required for the vendor to manufacture the product.
4. The time required for the product to be delivered to the mail marketer's warehouse and put on the shelves.

FIGURE 20-1 How a Shortened Reorder Cycle Decreases Inventory Commitment

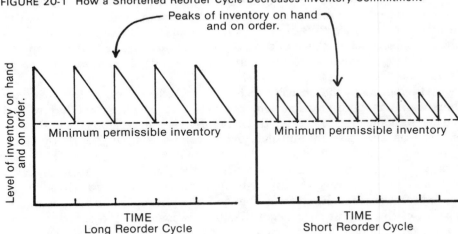

Shortening the reorder lead time

Inventory Reviews. The reorder lead time is often needlessly long because a buyer is indolent and does not reorder frequently or is unaware of how infrequent ordering contributes to back orders and overstock. The more frequently one reorders, the shorter the lead time becomes. It is far better for the buyer to order many times in small quantities than few times in large quantities.

Sometimes it is not a question of indolence or ignorance; the buyer may be so loaded with work and the task of reviewing inventory be so great

200

that he simply cannot get to reordering as often as he should. The problem may well be that the format in which the inventory and forecasting information is presented and the method of review are so cumbersome that they effectively prevent the buyer from doing his job. It always pays to have the inventory report and the sales forecast for the reorder period formatted so that they are easy to use. One never wants to delay reordering because it is time-consuming.

Transmitting the Order. The reorder lead time is often also needlessly lengthened by casual treatment of the purchase order once it is written. Many times the buyer merely drops it in the mail, trusting the regularity of the mail service. But phoning in an order almost always saves two or three days. Two or three days gained means at the other end of the reorder lead time that some customers' orders will be shipped promptly and completely, that some customers will not cancel their orders, and that some customers will not return what they bought. I always phoned or telexed my orders to Britain and Ireland while I operated the British Isles Collection. Phoning my orders to Britain created a sense of urgency that speeded the manufacturing of the order. The cost of the phone calls, expensive as it was, was repaid many times.

Vendor's Manufacturing Time. How to shorten the vendor's manufacturing time depends greatly upon the product, but maintaining pressure on him almost always works. At British Isles Collection, we stressed at the very outset with each new vendor the importance of speedy delivery. In addition, we sent him or her a letter explaining the peculiar problems of mail order—how in mail order when a customer orders one thing it is pretty difficult to switch him to another, how the FTC 30-Day Rule requires us to make refunds after a certain period of time, and how we would much rather ship goods than refund money. We stated in the letter that poor delivery might well cause us to drop them as a supplier regardless of how much we liked their products. Conversely, good delivery would result in our looking favorably upon them.

As I explained above, I always phoned in my orders myself. I phoned them myself rather than have a clerk do it because I carried more authority and it gave me opportunities to pressure the vendors and extract delivery promises. At the same time, if there were manufacturing holdups, I could sometimes suggest ways to speed things up.

Illigitimi Carborundum. This famous fractured Latin expression means "wear the bastards down." And that is just what we did by frequent phone calls to follow up on our orders. After many wearing phone calls, the vendors would in desperation make extraordinary efforts and ship our orders. We never let a casual attitude about delivery develop with our vendors.

Getting the Merchandise to the Shelves. The mail marketer should study transportation methods and test the speed of available trucking lines. Over a year, the consistent gain of even as little as one day will mean many sales saved and much customer goodwill retained. Often there is as much as several days difference between one trucking line and another. At British Isles Collection, I switched trucking lines because one was half a day faster than another; the faster trucking line delivered in the morning rather than late afternoon, which permitted us to ship back orders and get our goods on the shelves one day sooner.

Finally, the mail marketer should make sure that once the merchandise is in-house that it be rapidly received and put on the shelf and onto the on-hand inventory record so that orders can be filled completely.

The Commitment for On Hand and On Order

Safety stock

If one were able to forecast a product's sales with perfect precision, then the amount of inventory one would need to carry on hand to fill orders without delay would range from one unit to no more than the amount sold during the period between reviews (the reorder cycle). But such vision is never possible. New trends develop, external events intervene, orders randomly cluster, business is better or worse than forecast, and the product forecast itself is faulty. For these reasons, the commitment must include not only the merchandise sold during reorder lead time but also a safety stock to protect against these vicissitudes.

The size of the safety stock is best measured in weeks' worth of sales. Thus one's total commitment for on hand and on order would be the sales that occur during the reorder lead time plus the sales that occur for a determined number of weeks after that. The period of time to sell the merchandise for which one commits is called the *reorder period*.

The reason for measuring safety stock in weeks rather than using some other standard is that going into a period of rising sales one can afford to maintain more stock and going into a period of declining sales one can afford less. Furthermore, measuring safety stock in weeks of sales keeps it in proportion to the sales of the product.

How big the safety stock should be depends upon the length of the reorder lead time, the certainty of the vendor's manufacturing time, the sales density on each stockkeeping unit, and how fully the mail marketer, considering all factors, wishes to fill his orders. The mail marketer, in turn, will be influenced by the percent of mark-up in the item, the cost of money, the danger of markdowns, whether the item is to be continued the following season, and the constraints imposed by his cash flow and capital.

The longer the reorder lead time, the more opportunity there is for sales to drift away from forecast. The size of the safety stock, therefore, must go up if the reorder lead times goes up. If the vendor's manufacturing time is uncertain, then the safety stock must again be increased. The percent mark-up should influence the size of the safety stock because if the mark-up is high, the risk and amount of money tied up is low relative to the sales.

If the product is something like shoes where its sales can be distributed over many sizes (at British Isles Collection we offered over 40 sizes and at Lawson Hill Leather and Shoe Co. we offered over 80 and in some styles as many as 140), then sales density on individual stock-keeping units can become very low. Instead of following the distribution of sizes in the universe of customers, orders will randomly cluster, causing stock-outs unless higher inventory levels are maintained.

Having evaluated all the factors, the mail marketer then decides how big his safety stock, measured in weeks, should be. He then adds the weeks of safety stock to the weeks of reorder lead time to get the reorder period. The sales for the reorder period is what he must forecast for each product.

Forecasting a Product's Sales for the Season

Before one can forecast the sales of a product for the reorder period, one must first forecast its sales for the season.

202

The orderline
and the product demand curve

Once into a season, the method of forecasting the sales of the product for the season is to determine the percent of the product's sales that is already in for the season and to calculate the sales for the season by dividing the sales to date for the product by the percent sales are in. To determine this percent, the mail marketer must first construct a composite orderline, which is the sum of all the individual orderlines of all the mailings of a catalog. To refresh the reader's memory, the orderline, which was described in Chapter 16, shows the percent sales are complete, day-by-day or week-by-week, after a mailing has been made. The composite orderline, therefore, shows the percent sales are complete for the season for the entire catalog.[1]

If the sales pattern of a product followed the orderline of the entire catalog, then forecasting the sales of the product would be a simple matter of forecasting the total sales of the product for the season by dividing the sales to date of the product by the percent sales are complete for the season and then multiplying the sales thus forecasted for the season by the percent of the season covered by the reorder period. But most products do not follow the average; they merely contribute to the average. For example, in the women's shoe business, sales of sandals in the fall are concentrated in the early part of the season. But the sales of boots occur largely in the latter part of the fall. When the fall season is 25 percent complete, sandal sales might be 40 percent complete and boots only 10 percent complete.

Product demand curves based upon experience[2] must be set up, therefore, to give the percents the sales of a product are expected to be complete for the various percents complete on the orderline. Table 20-1 shows the percents complete for several product categories for a company that sells clothing and footwear. For example, when the season is 14.7% complete, men's sports jackets are 20.2% complete and women's sheepskin boots are only 12.4%. At first glance, these differences look like only a few percentage points, but 20.2% is 37.4% greater than 14.7%. In other words, if one forecasted sales for men's sports jackets for the season using the percent complete for the season instead of the product demand curve, one would forecast 37.4% more sales than one should.

Here is an example of how to forecast sales. Let us suppose that a company forecasts sales of $1,000,000 for the fall season and that by October 15 it has taken in $147,000 in sales. It is, therefore, 14.7% complete. Let us assume that the company has sold 30 men's sports jackets. From the product demand curve we see that 20.2% of expected sports jacket sales are in. This means that the 30 sports jackets sold by October 15 represent 20.2% of the total jackets that will be sold. That is:

$$\frac{13.0 - 12.5}{14.7 - 12.5} = \frac{.5}{22} = .227$$

This fraction is then multiplied by the difference in the percents complete for men's sports jackets in the previous and following weeks and adding the result to the percents complete for the previous week. That is $(.227)(20.2 - 18.4) + 18.4 = 18.8$.

---

[1] To avoid complicating the discussion, I have treated each season as essentially having one catalog with the same product line but with a number of mailings of the catalog during the season. Cover changes and minor merchandise additions and deletions will not materially affect forecasts except for those products that have been added or deleted. If a whole new catalog is produced in the middle of the season, then the forecasts should be made as if the catalog were a separate business or occupying a separate season.

[2] In setting up product demand curves, one must be careful to use no data that has been influenced by extraordinary events such as sales.

TABLE 20-1   Product Demand Curves*

DATE BASE YEAR	PERCENT COMPLETE FOR SEASON	MEN'S SHOES	MEN'S DRESS BOOTS	WOMEN'S DRESS SHOES	MEN'S SPORTS JACKETS	MEN'S VESTS	WOMEN'S SHEEPSKIN BOOTS
9/17	.28	0.2	0.3	1.8	1.8	0	0
9/24	3.35	4.0	3.2	6.7	4.2	3.4	.6
10/01	7.00	8.8	7.4	10.3	12.7	7.7	6.2
10/08	10.0	12.3	10.8	14.7	15.7	13.3	8.7
10/15	12.5	14.9	14.3	14.7	18.4	15.0	10.6
10/22	14.7	16.8	17.2	16.5	20.2	18.0	12.4
10/29	16.6	17.3	21.4	17.4	21.4	19.3	12.8
11/05	18.7	19.2	21.7	18.3	23.6	22.3	13.7
11/12	24.6	25.4	26.5	24.1	31.4	27.5	20.5
11/19	35.7	37.3	35.7	30.8	42.9	39.5	29.2
11/26	45.1	46.5	45.5	40.6	49.2	48.9	37.3
12/03	53.3	53.3	51.9	49.1	60.1	63.1	46.6
12/10	59.3	57.7	62.4	51.8	64.6	70.3	54.7
12/17	62.8	60.1	66.7	54.0	68.0	73.6	57.8
12/24	64.5	61.2	68.0	54.5	70.1	74.6	59.6
12/31	66.3	61.2	69.0	53.1	71.9	75.5	59.6
1/07	69.7	63.9	72.8	57.6	76.1	76.8	64.6
1/14	75.2	66.4	79.1	63.4	77.3	79.4	68.9
1/21	80.0	72.8	84.7	69.6	83.1	85.0	81.4
1/28	83.6	75.6	86.8	74.1	87.6	85.8	85.7
2/04	85.7	77.2	89.4	75.9	88.8	87.5	88.8
2/11	87.6	78.9	91.0	78.1	89.1	90.1	93.2
2/18	88.7	78.5	92.3	79.9	90.6	90.5	93.2
2/25	90.4	82.7	92.6	80.8	90.9	90.5	91.9
3/04	91.3	86.0	93.7	82.6	90.6	91.0	92.5
3/11	92.5	87.7	93.7	84.4	91.2	91.4	92.5
3/18	94.4	90.0	94.7	87.9	91.2	92.7	93.8
3/25	100	100	100	100	100	100	100

*The product demand curves show typical percents that sales are complete for various product categories in relationship to the percent sales are complete for the season for the catalog as a whole.

In other words, sports jackets would be 18.8% complete if the season were 13.0% complete.

$$(.202) \text{ (Total jackets that will be sold)} = 30$$

$$\text{Total jackets that will be sold} = \frac{30}{.202} = 148.5 \text{ jackets.}$$

Usually the sales to date do not neatly work out to one of the entry points on the product demand curve. The percent complete might have worked out to 13.0%. In this case, it would have been necessary to interpolate.[3]

Accuracy of product demand curves

Product demand curves are the most accurate when the mailing of the catalog is made on the same date of each year. But it is rare that one always makes one's mailings on precisely the same date. Mailing dates can vary one or two weeks one way or the other. Normally, small changes in mail dates will have a negligible effect upon the product demand curve because one enters the product demands curve by the percent the season is complete, not by date.

[3] The interpolation to find the percent complete of the sports jackets if the season were 13.0% complete would be done by subtracting from 13.0% the percent complete at the end of the previous week and then dividing the difference by the difference of the percents complete of the previous and following weeks.

The product demand curves are also the most accurate in forecasting when they reflect only one mailing of the catalog, say, when there is only one mailing and it is mailed always on September 1. But most mail marketers make many mailings of their catalog during a season. For them, unless the calculation is done by computer, it is too cumbersome to forecast a product sales for each separate mailing and then add them together to get a combined forecast. For practical purposes, unless there is a drastic change in the mailing program from the year on which the curves are based, using the product demand curves based upon the completeness of the season is close enough.

Verifying the orderline

In the early part of the season, one uses the preseason forecast for the season's sales of the whole catalog in determining the percent a catalog is complete at any particular time. After sufficient sales have come in and the orders coming in seem to follow a pattern, one makes an adjustment in the forecasted sales for the season.

If in the previous example the sales forecast for the company had been revised from $1,000,000 to $1,176,000, then the $147,000 in sales received by October 15 would become only 12.5% of the total sales expected:

$$\left(\frac{147,000}{1,176,000} \ (100) = 12.5\% \right)$$

The 30 sports jackets sold would then be only 18.4% of the total number of jackets expected to be sold. It would be necessary to revise the forecast for the jackets:

$$.184 \ (\text{Total jackets that will be sold}) = 30$$
$$\text{Total jackets that will be sold} = \frac{30}{.184} = 163 \text{ jackets.}$$

It is obvious that the mail marketer must adjust his orderline frequently, particularly just after mailings. The precision of his sales forecasts of all his products depends upon it. Precise sales forecasts, in turn, mean that the mail marketer will have the right amount of inventory on hand.

A word of caution: The mail marketer should be very careful when forecasting in the early part of a season. The difference of a few orders will greatly affect the total sales of a product forecasted for the season. A wrong estimate of the percent a catalog is complete will create additional error. In the early part of the season, it is always wise to buy cautiously until the forecast settles down. Sales forecasts are quite reliable after 25 percent of the season is in.

Forecasting a Product's Sales for the Reorder Period

There are three situations for which the mail marketer must forecast sales for the reorder period: (1) new products prior to the opening of the season, (2) repeat products prior to the opening of the season, and (3) all products after the catalog has been mailed and the season has opened. We shall consider the third situation first.

Forecasting sales
after the catalog has been mailed

Forecasting sales for the reorder period is a simple matter of determining the percents the sales of a product are complete at the beginning and at the end of the reorder period, subtracting one from the other, and multiplying the difference times the expected sales for the product for the season.

Let us go back to our example where our company had received $147,000 in sales by October 15, where its management expected $1,000,000 in sales for the season, and we forecasted that 148.5 men's sports jackets would be sold during the season. Let us assume that the reorder period for the sports jackets is eight weeks. The season, as we calculated before, is, therefore, 14.7% complete, which means that men's sports jackets are 20.2% complete. We now move down the product demand curve chart the eight weeks of our reorder period, and we find that men's sports jackets will be 68.0% complete. We subtract 20.2% from 68.0% to find that the company will sell 47.8% of the season's sales during the reorder period:

$$68.0 - 20.2 = 47.8$$

We then multiply 47.8% by the 148.5 jackets the company expects to sell for the season to find that it will sell 71 jackets during the reorder period:

$$\frac{47.8}{100} \times 148.5 = 71$$

This means that the company should have 71 jackets on hand and on order on October 15.

One should notice that, although the date that the $147,000 in sales were in was the 15th, the date that season's sales were 14.7% complete in the base year (the year upon which the demand curves were based) was October 22. The percent the season is complete is controlling, not the date. The difference in the two dates merely reflects the fact that in the most recent year the catalog was mailed a week earlier and that everything has been moved up one week. Therefore, even though the date in the year for which the forecast is being made is October 15, we enter the chart opposite October 22.

Forecasting when the reorder period
overlaps two seasons

For part of each season, the reorder period overlaps the following season. The procedure for forecasting is similar to one season except that one must forecast the product's sales for both the remainder of one season and the beginning of the next. This is done by estimating the product's sales for the following season, multiplying them by the percent complete on the product demand curve by which the reorder period overlaps the following season, and adding it to the percent of sales remaining in the current season multiplied by the forecasted sales for the current season.

For example, let us assume that the forecasted sales for a certain product for the current season is 150 units and that for the following season its estimated sales is 200 units. Let us assume that for its product category the portion of the reorder period that remains in the current season corresponds to 30 percent on the product demand curve, and for the following season it is 25 percent. The forecasted sales for the reorder period would then be 100 units:

$$(.30)(150) + (.25)(200) = 100$$

History and Forecast of Product Demand Report. These computations may seem lengthy to the reader, but they go quickly once one is set up. With a computer, they would be no work at all. The History and Forecast of Product Demand Report shown in Figure 20-2 makes the task easy. The form provides convenient columns in which to log weekly gross demand, returns, and exchanges and to record the calculations for the steps leading to sales in the reorder lead time. This is a manual form; the computer, however, could produce the same thing.

Most of the column headings speak for themselves, but a few require explanation. Demand, for the purpose of forecasting, should be net demand to date; that is, any returns should be deducted, and, if the shipping orders for exchanges counted as demand, then the returns for exchanges must be deducted. For this reason, the form has the headings *Gross Demand, Returns for Refund,* and *Exchanges. Combined Reorder Period Sales,* as its name suggests, combines the sales for the reorder periods in the current and following season. Normally, this will be the level to which the buyer will reorder. But sometimes the buyer will have other reasons for buying to a different level—the product will be promoted, will be discontinued, or will have new competition. For this reason, a column marked *Level* is provided, in which the buyer records his buying decision. The *Level* column prevents the buying decision from being purely a mechanical calculation and requires the buyer to make his decision consciously. Often the calculations to arrive at the combined reorder period sales are done by a clerk, and then the buyer decides upon the level.

Forecasting sales for repeat products prior to opening of the season

Thus far we have discussed projecting during the current season sales for products for which one has current season sales on which to base forecasts. Once 25 percent of the sales are in, these forecasts become very accurate. It is more difficult to forecast a product's sales prior to the season.

If one knows the sales of a product for the corresponding previous season, then one has a starting point. A ratio can be made of the forecasted total sales for the season for the catalog divided by its equivalent for the season a year before. Multiplying this ratio by last year's sales for a product will give us an estimate for the season that takes into account the change in the mailing program. For example, if total catalog sales for last year were $1,000,000, this year they are forecasted to be $1,200,000, then if the sales of a product were 500 units last year, one would have an estimate of 600 units:

$$\frac{\$1,200,000}{1,000,000} (500) = 600$$

But before a calculated forecast like this can be used, one must consider other factors that might affect results. One should ask questions like the following and then modify the forecast accordingly.

1. Was the product new the previous year? If it was, it most likely experienced a surge of orders as customers saw it for the first time and ordered. One should not, therefore, expect it to sell as well the following season. Repeat styles tend to sell proportionately better with list rental than with customers.

2. Has the relationship of the sizes of customer and list rental mailings changed? For the reason given in the previous question, the forecast might have to be adjusted.

FIGURE 20-2 History and Forecast of Product Demand

DESCRIPTION _____ STOCK NUMBER _____

VENDOR _____ PRODUCT CATEGORY _____ REORDER PERIOD _____

WEEK ENDING	CURRENT SEASON								FOLLOWING SEASON			COMBINED SEASONS	
	GROSS DEMAND FOR WEEK	RETURNS FOR REFUND	EX-CHANGES	NET DEMAND TO DATE	PERCENT COMPLETE FOR SEASON	FORE-CASTED SALES FOR SEASON	REORDER PERIOD PERCENT	SALES IN REORDER PERIOD	ESTIMATED SALES FOR SEASON	REORDER PERIOD PERCENT	SALES IN REORDER PERIOD	SALES IN COMBINED REORDER PERIODS	LEVEL

3. Has there been an upward or downward trend in the popularity of the product? Has the product gone out of style? Sales of products that go out of style sometimes go down, but sometimes they go up as the products become unavailable in retail stores.

4. Is there more competition for it from other items in the catalog or from outside sources?

5. Is more or less space being given to it?

6. Is it being moved into a better or worse location or receiving more or less prominence? For example, is it going on the front or back cover, inside covers, center spread, or next to the order forms?

7. Has the photograph been retaken and improved? (Or made worse?)

The buyer must weigh all these factors and maybe more and adjust the forecast.

If the product is a repeat product but there is no experience for it in the corresponding period for the previous year (for example, when a product that was introduced in the spring is being repeated in the fall), different ratios have to be formed to make a forecast. If the relationship in sales between the fall and the spring are known for the product category when there is no change in the overall sales of the catalog, then the spring's sales for the item can be multiplied by the ratio representing this relationship. It would then have to be further adjusted by any change in the relative size of the spring and fall seasons.

This calculation can best be explained by an example. Let us assume that in the base year in which the relationship was established between a product category's sales in the spring and in the fall that the overall sales of the catalog in the spring were $1,000,000 and that for the fall they were $1,250,000. Let us assume that sales in the product category improved 50 percent (a factor of 1.5) going from spring to fall. If overall sales had remained level going from spring to fall in the base year, then the factor for level sales would have been 1.2:

$$\frac{1,000,000}{1,250,000} (1.5) = 1.2.$$

Now let us assume that the sales for a particular product was 400 units during the spring in question and that according to the mailing plan sales will be increased from the $2,000,000 that were experienced during the spring to $3,500,000 in the fall—a factor of 1.75. The forecast of the product's sales, therefore, would be the spring sales of the product (400) multiplied by the relationship of the product category sales between spring and fall (1.2) multiplied by the overall factor of sales increase (1.75). The result is 840 units:

$$(400)(1.2)(1.75) = 840$$

Once again, before using this number, the buyer should ask all the questions raised previously to determine if there are other factors that would influence the results.

Forecasting sales for a new product

Most difficult and unreliable of all is forecasting the sales of a new product prior to the season. In this case, there are no sales to which ratios can be applied. Nevertheless, there are some guidelines. Sometimes the product is similar to something that has been sold before. Perhaps it is a color variation of an old product; if one knows the relationship of the colors, one can make a forecast.

If none of these methods can be applied, then the best thing to do is to calculate the dollars of sales the catalog space devoted to the product should yield and then divide the result by the retail selling price to get the units that should be sold. Then the result should be reduced because new products, being experimental, never sell as well on the average as repeat products. Although this method can be wildly wrong on individual products, it will be nearly correct in total when applied to all new products.

Part
four
Opportunities

computer letters: the great unexploited opportunity

Since the beginning of the Industrial Revolution, when Englishman James Hargreaves invented the spinning jenny in 1764, almost every repeated operation in manufacturing and commerce has become standardized for efficiency. Television sets and widgets have come off the production lines in unending uniformity and monotony, each one looking exactly like the one that preceded it.

Mail order has been no less standardized. Millions of catalogs, all looking exactly alike, are broadcast across the nation. Letters to customers, both to sell and to answer questions, have been constrained by cost to being printed and in being printed they all are identical. The customer is well aware that he is being addressed impersonally and so gives the mail marketer's mailing piece no more attention than what something impersonal warrants.

The computer is changing all this. Standardization is giving way to variation. Signals flashing through a computer's brain at just below the speed of light give complex instructions and accomplish at low cost and in an instant a task that formerly took hours or weeks at great expense. Manufacturing is increasingly able, thanks to the computer and its offspring, the robot, to produce a variety of products at low cost.

In mail order, the great unexploited opportunity offered by the computer's ability to produce variety at low cost is *customized* computer letters—letters that are individually written to each customer using the information that is unique to him or her. Computer letters are not new to mail order. We all are familiar with the letters that mention our name five times, our town three times, our street twice, our neighbor once. My wife, Marcia, regularly receives a mailing addressed to M. Hill, which says, "Yes, M. Hill, you can save $4.00," thus betraying its impersonality by addressing her so unnaturally. These letters to her are written in a font that no typewriter uses and that jumps from ten point to eighteen point and back again to confirm that the message did not come off a typewriter and was not just for her. These are not the kind of computer letters I have in mind.

Making the Computer Letter Personal

The computer letters that I have in mind are customized letters that draw upon specific information known about the customer, information which is of special interest to the customer and which makes any letter personal. These letters inform the customer about an order, refer to what he or she has purchased, and then recommend something new to buy that has been suggested by what he or she has already bought.

The reasons for substituting a computer letter for a printed one are to gain attention and to make the customer feel as though he or she were being treated in a personal manner. The computer letter that looks like a computer letter defeats these objectives. We all react as our letter knife zips open envelopes by deciding for each mailing piece whether or not we shall give it attention. If the mailing piece is personal, it is far more likely that it will be read than if it is impersonal.

The computer letter, therefore, must never look as though it were one. Its very first impression must be that it came off the typewriter. The typeface should be one that typically is used in a typewriter and probably should be printed using a carbon ribbon. To ensure that the customer recognizes the letter as being personal and, therefore, reads it, the paper should be regular letterhead in a quality that is normally used for correspondence.

The next impression the customer gets is from the name, address, and salutation. When one captured the customer's name and address, did one capture it completely or did one economize a few keystrokes by skipping the title of respect and keying only the initial of the first name so that one is compelled to address Rev. John A. Smith with "Dear J. Smith"? Be sure to save the title of respect and the full name. It will increase the readership of your computer letters.

Another first impression is the envelope. The envelope is the first thing a customer sees. It creates an impression that is sustained unless it is contradicted by the letter. The best envelope is one that is individually typed with an affixed stamp. This may not be practical. Then the next best choice is a window envelope. The last choice is an address label affixed to the envelope with the postage applied by a mailing machine.

The signature, even though it is at the end of the letter, also creates a first impression because the reader gives it a quick first glance to determine if the letter is personal and worthy of being read. It should be personally signed, not printed. There are machines for this purpose, which our Congressmen regularly use for signing letters. This raises the question of who should sign the letters. One choice is the personality featured in the front of the catalog; the other is the customer service representative. The advantage of the former is that it is more prestigious, but it is not very believable that he would individually sign a letter. The latter would have less prestige but more credibility.

Its first impressions having conveyed that the letter was personal, the letter must then be as personal as possible. The customer must be able to deduce that the letter was written just for him, that there are no others like it. This means incorporating in the letter information that is unique to him—not information that the customer can recognize as having come from his name and address but rather the specific information relative to the customer that one should have saved from the customer's orders.[1] Spe-

[1] See Chapter 17 for the list of information about a customer that should be saved.

cific information might include the products purchased previously, the size of the garment if appropriate, how the previous order was handled, and any change in the person's relationship with the company, such as a request becoming a buyer.

Computer Letters That Can Be Written to Sell Products

One can find a great many excuses for writing a letter to a customer and make a special offer to sell product in the course of writing to the customer. At Lawson Hill Leather and Shoe Co., for example, there was a place on the order form for the customer to give an alternative shoe selection in the event that we were out of the first choice in her size. We conceived the idea that after we had shipped the first choice to a customer that we write to see if she would like to order her second choice. The letter was like the following. Note that to stimulate immediate response, the offer expired six weeks after we mailed the letter.

November 1

Dear Mrs. Smith:

Thank you for your order for our multicolored pump, the Harlequin, in size 10B. I am delighted to tell you that your shoes were shipped yesterday and are on their way to you. You should be receiving them momentarily.

I am also pleased to tell you that your alternative selection, the Rainbow, a multicolored pump, is also available in your size, size 10B. If you are pleased with the Harlequin, you may like to have the Rainbow too.

If you would like to order the Rainbow, I will give you a $2.00 discount if you mail your order before December 15th. If you prefer, you may select any other style and take your $2.00 discount. We have enclosed an extra catalog in the shipment for your convenience. You will find the Rainbow on page eight.

Please return the enclosed coupon to claim your discount.

Thank you once again, Mrs. Smith, for your interest in our shoes.

Cordially,

Marcia Hill

This letter was so extraordinarily successful that we then thought of writing to the customers whose shoes we were late in shipping. We were concerned about losing their goodwill because of the delay. The letter, we hoped, might save some goodwill and stimulate sales. But the results we received from this letter far exceeded anything we dared to hope.

November 1

Dear Mrs. Smith:

I apologize for the delay in shipping your order for the pair of our black, low-heeled pump style Jeanne in size 10B.

I am happy to tell you, though, that they were shipped yesterday and are on their way to you. You should be receiving them momentarily.

Because we shipped your order late and inconvenienced you, I wish to make amends. It occurred to me that you might also enjoy having the Jeanne pump in brown. If you would like it or any other shoe in our catalog, you may deduct $2 from your order providing you mail it before December 15th. Please return the enclosed coupon to claim your discount.

Thank you again for your patience. I hope you enjoy wearing our Jeanne style.

Cordially,

Marcia Hill

These letters were so successful that we then thought about writing to all the other customers who neither were shipped too late nor specified an alternative style. The following letter was conceived:

November 1

Dear Mrs. Smith:

Thank you for your order for our multicolored pump, the Harlequin, in size 10B. I am delighted to tell you that your shoes were shipped yesterday and are on their way to you. You should be receiving them momentarily. I hope you will enjoy wearing them.

If you like the Harlequin, you might also like our Rainbow style which is a similar multicolored pump in pastel colors and which also comes in size 10B. Since you are one of our better customers who has already bought from us this season, I am giving you, in appreciation, the opportunity to save $2.00 on the Rainbow or any other style of your choice if you mail your order before December 15th. Another catalog was enclosed in your shipment for your convenience. You will find the Rainbow on page eight. Please use the enclosed coupon to claim your discount.

Once again, thank you, Mrs. Smith, for your interest in our shoes. If you wish to take advantage of this special $2.00 discount, do be sure to mail your order before December 15th.

Cordially,

Marcia Hill

Notice that in each of these letters specific information was used. We quoted her size and the style she bought and then told her that this same size was also available in the suggested alternative style. In addition, we gave her information that pertained only to her, which was that her order had been shipped—something she would be sure to be interested in. Finally, the suggested style for her to reorder was not selected at random but was established as being an appropriate complement to the style previously ordered. Computer letters might also be sent at the beginning of the season to call to the customer's attention new merchandise with an appeal similar to merchandise previously ordered. For example, the mail marketer might send a computer letter to all previous purchasers of sports jackets announcing a new jacket style. This would stimulate them to open the catalog. The letter might go like this:

November 1

Dear Mr. Brown:

I thought you might like the opportunity to save ten percent on a new sports jacket. Last year you bought our Harris Tweed shooting jacket with leather trim in size 46L. On the assumption that you were pleased with the fit, quality, and comfort of your jacket, I thought you would like to know about our new sports jackets, all of which come in your size, and on which you can save ten percent.

We recently mailed our catalog to you. On page eight you will see our new velvet blazers in navy and maroon. On page ten you will find our authentic gamekeeper's jacket. And on page eleven is our suede leather blazer. Each of these jackets have been made to our quality and size specifications so you can expect them to be just as good and fit just as well as the jacket you purchased last year.

If you wish to take advantage of this offer to save ten percent, send in the enclosed coupon before December 15th with your order and deduct ten percent. Or, if you prefer, you may deduct ten percent from any other item in the catalog.

Sincerely,

Traphagen Hill

Perhaps the most important letter for someone who has to deal in sizes is the one that sells closeouts. The computer can match remnant sizes in discontinued styles with customers who wear those same sizes. The mailing is selective because it does not go to customers who do not wear those sizes.

Many products have complements, that is, other products that go well with them. These products are particularly suited to computer letters because they identify closely related interests that could easily result in an additional sale. Furthermore, it permits a very individual letter. For example, Williams-Sonoma sells coffee roasting trays. These invite a letter suggesting a coffee grinder. Audubon Workshop sells birdfeeders. Birdfeeders suggest a computer letter selling birdseed.

There are many other possibilities for computer letters. I leave it to the reader's imagination to conceive of those that might be profitably sent to customers. Letters can be written to doctors making them a special offer, or they can go to one sex or the other. Letters might be addressed to American Express or Diner's Club card holders. A letter can be written to introduce a class of merchandise. Letters can be written to people who have been refunded. And letters can be written to welcome new customers, as shown in Chapter 4.

Whatever it is, each known characteristic of a customer is a potential opportunity to write a computer letter. The mail marketer should test computer letters to learn what works for him and then exploit the opportunities that they present.

gaining more sales
through solo mailings

A secret of mail-order success is building the buyers list and mailing to it often. It is rare that a mail marketer makes money in the process of acquiring customers. It is the low cost of mailing to customers plus the high sales per thousand that they bring in that makes a profit. This we learned in Chapter 16. In the three-year plan shown there for the Mayflower Gift Company, we saw their profits grow as their house file increased. We also saw in Chapter 15 that the lifetime value of customers and requests increases if we are able to mail them more frequently. In other words, the more times we are able to mail our customers, the more profit we shall make.

The problem for the catalog mail marketer, therefore, is how to increase mailings to his customers and requests without having one mailing stealing excessively from another. Increasing the number of catalog mailings works to a point. Certainly, mailings to best buyers once every six weeks during the active season is not too frequent for most catalog mail marketers.[1] If the catalogs mailed to the house file during the season contain the same products and have only a cover change and, perhaps, a rearrangement of the products, then the number of mailings that can be made cannot be increased much beyond once every six weeks. On the other hand, a drastic change in the products offered in a catalog to eliminate sameness reduces turnover, increases markdowns, and balloons the stock-keeping units to be inventoried to a point that is unacceptably high for most companies.

How does the catalog mail marketer increase mailings without ballooning inventory and making additional mailings look like dull repetitions? A solution to this dilemma is the solo mailing piece. In the solo mailing piece, the catalog mail marketer selects one product or a small group of

---

[1] If it is too much, it means that the mail marketer is getting low sales per thousand and is in deep trouble.

closely related products and treats it in depth in a single printed piece. The products are regularly cataloged products and so create no additional stock-keeping units. The products, if there are more than one, are so closely related that a single presentation of the story of one product sells them all.

The solo mailing piece gives the customer the opportunity to see the product in many lights through many pictures and to understand it better by a thorough explanation in the copy. Typically, the solo mailing piece is a single sheet that unfolds so that the customer can see the whole story on one side, although there are other configurations as well. In the solo mailing piece, there is a large feature picture of the product, illustrating it in all its handsomeness. In addition, there are other smaller pictures showing the product from different angles. Then there are pictures showing construction and design details with supporting explanations. There is substantial copy explaining every feature, use, and benefit. There are endorsements from customers, the guarantee, and anything else the mail marketer can think of to enhance the presentation of the product. And, of course, there is the telephone number—an invitation for the customer to use his credit card, an order form, and an exhortation to order now.

The consequence of all this selling power concentrated on one product and the lack of other, distracting products is to give the product great impact. And because the customer views the product in new light in a mailing that resembles no others and because it has great impact, the solo mailing piece makes more mailings possible. It does not steal sales from the catalogs being mailed in nearby time periods—this is scarcely possible because the solo mailing contains only one product of the many sold in the catalog. Actually, the contrary effect occurs. The great impact of the solo mailing lingers long after its sales, as recorded under its source code, cease coming in. With each mailing of the catalog, the presentation of the product in the catalog is reinforced by the customer's memory of the solo mailing. Sales from the catalog are thus increased.

The mail marketer, therefore, does not need to be concerned that the profit produced by the solo mailing is really profit taken from other mailings. He need only be concerned with whether the solo mailing itself is sufficiently profitable. The implication of this fact is enormous: One is limited in the number of mailings one can make to one's buyers list only by the number of solo mailings that can directly be made profitable. Some mail marketers have been able to get the number of mailings they make to customers up to 15 times a year and more. One mail marketer told me that he was able to send mailings to his customers every week.

But the mailing of solo pieces to one's house list is not their only use. They also can be inserted with great effect and low cost into one's own packages and sometimes effectively into the packages of other catalogers. Because they don't compete with a catalog but rather reinforce it, solo mailings can be tested with one's best rental lists. Solo mailings are not as productive as a catalog, but each list to which a solo mailing can be sent on a break-even basis is a list to which both a catalog and a solo mailing can be sent during one season.[2]

There are other advantages to the solo mailing. I have said that the solo mailing does not increase stockkeeping units. It also has the advantage of increasing turnover. For a cash-short company, increased turnover can be crucial. Furthermore, by concentrating sales in one product, the solo mailing creates economies of scale. Large sales means large orders for the

---

[2] Usually, it is not profitable to mail a catalog to the same rented names twice in one season.

manufacturer, which, in turn, often means that lower prices can be negotiated.

A strength of the solo mailing is its low cost. The printed piece itself is inexpensive. Usually, its size is the equivalent of eight 8½ × 11 pages. Preparation costs are correspondingly small. One also saves money because, if the piece is in folded rather than in stapled booklet form, it does not go into the printer's bindery but instead goes directly to the mailer, saving overhead and labor. If the order form is part of the printed piece, the costs of the order form and the envelope into which it and the solo mailing piece would have to be inserted would also be eliminated. Finally, the mail marketer would have no list rental expense because he would be mailing to his own list. He would not even have postage when he inserts it in his own packages. In short, his expenses would be only the printed piece, the mailing service, and the postage; the last two would be eliminated if the piece were put in his own packages.

There are some weaknesses to the solo mailing. The most important one is that it does not produce the sales per thousand that a catalog does. For this reason, it is difficult to make it work when mailed to list rental, although this is often done successfully. But, as we discussed earlier, so long as it is profitable, it is very worthwhile sending out and it is a powerful complement to a catalog.

Another weakness that the mail marketer must recognize is that the customer that is upgraded to the most recent season by a solo mailing will not, depending of course on what the product is, respond as well as the customer who bought from the catalog. The point here is not that one should not send out solo mailings because a customer is upgraded that will not respond as well in the future as a customer who rebought from the catalog. We know the solo mailing is worth sending out because it makes a profit. The point is merely that the mail marketer must identify how customers were upgraded—by catalog or solo mailing and which product in the solo mailing—and make the budget accordingly so that he or she will not be disappointed when the season's results are in.

What products work well in a solo mailing? The product should have either an appeal to a broad audience or a very strong appeal to a narrow one. It should also be something that can be sold better through a bigger presentation. It should have features that can be illustrated and explained, a story that can be told, and romance or history. More pictures should tell more about the product. And, of course, the product should be one that has been proven in the catalog.

The single product of the solo mailing narrows its appeal. But it also permits all the selling power to be concentrated on one product and, in so doing, creates great impact. This great impact makes up in large part for the narrowness of appeal and creates a lasting effect that makes later catalog mailings more profitable. That only a single product is offered means that there is no competition with the mail marketer's other mailings. These are the strengths of the solo mailing sent to one's buyers that the catalog mail marketer should not ignore.

23

mail-order synergism

All mail-order businesses eventually peak out; that is, they reach maturity. In the early stages of a mail-order business, the mail marketer rents only lists that are sure to work. Later, when he enlarges his mailings and has exhausted the sure lists, he rents marginal lists. As he goes along, he improves his selection of products and their presentation in the catalog. By so doing, he expands the profitable universe to which catalogs can be mailed. He also refines mailing techniques and finds selections that work within lists that were previously unusable. This expands even more the universe of names that can be mailed to profitably. Each of these improvements permits him to acquire more customers and expand the business. Ultimately he will develop these possibilities to their limits. Then the mail marketer may decide to buy customers, that is, to acquire the customers at a cost that is not break-even in the first season or the first year.

If the buying of customers is done at such a cost that the acquisition breaks even when all the future net income from the customers acquired is discounted to their present value by the desired rate of return, and if the rate of acquisition of customers matches the rate of attrition, then the mail marketer can expand the business no further. The business has peaked out. At this point, if the economy slackens or the dynamics of the company weaken, then the mail marketer must contract the business or suffer even greater reduction in profit.

Where does the mail marketer go once his business has reached this maturity? One answer is synergism.

Synergism is an old word with new favor. It is not one of these pretentious Latin words that serve no more than substitute for common Anglo-Saxon ones. It is a useful word that expresses a complex thought in three syllables. For those who do not attempt to keep up, Webster's defines *synergism* as "the simultaneous action of separate agencies which, together, have greater total effect than the sum of their individual effects." Cabell Brand, chairman of Stuart McGuire and Ortho-vent, expresses it more succinctly: "It's when one plus one equals three."

Reasons for the synergism of retail stores and mail order

Retail stores and mail order make a situation where one plus one equals three. The two operating together create far more profit and sales than the sum of the two if they each were operating separately. The main reason for this is the enormous latent demand built up by circulating catalogs. The more catalogs that are circulated, the more latent demand is built up. While many people buy by mail order, there are far more who do not or who only occasionally buy by mail order. Many people see something in a catalog but are uncertain whether it is just what they want and do not order. They would, if given the opportunity, visit the store to see if the product is what they want. And, of course, once in the store, they will browse throughout and look over all the merchandise. Other customers may just like the general look of the catalog and come to browse without any particular product in mind. Whatever the reason for their shopping, they come from near and far because of the large number of catalogs in circulation.

That the catalog brings in customers I know from firsthand experience. At Lawson Hill Leather and Shoe Co., when we moved from the fourth floor of an old turn-of-the-century industrial building to a modern building in an industrial park and featured our store in our catalog, our sales shot up to almost 8 percent of our combined sales of store and mail order of $9,500,000. Yet our store was in neither a shopping center nor directly on a highway.[1] This 8 percent, however, does not tell the whole story. Since the cost of circulating the catalogs was mostly charged to mail order, almost all the gross profit generated by the store, after paying the sales clerks, contributed to overhead and profit. The impact of the store was enormous.

But the huge untapped sales reserve created by catalogs in circulation is not the only reason for the synergism of retail stores and mail order. Stores are a convenient way to dispose of items discontinued from the catalog. In fact, stores are the most logical vehicle for selling discontinued merchandise because they already have a clientele conditioned to appreciate the type of merchandise offered by the catalog. Jobbing the merchandise to stores that deal in closeouts will not be as profitable because the closeout stores do not have a similar clientele. For this reason, it should be more profitable to sell discontinued merchandise through the store than through a jobber.

The flow of merchandise, however, can be reversed. Stores can supply merchandise to the catalog to fill back orders. They can act as a reserve to prevent mail-order stock-outs.

Stores also can be a vehicle for product development. Although it is generally conceded that what sells in a retail store does not necessarily sell well through mail order and products featured in the catalog will sell in the store far better than products that are not, offering products in the retail store prior to putting them in the catalog provides an opportunity to gain customer reaction and learn if there are design defects. Stores provide an opportunity for buyers to meet and talk with customers. Because my wife and I bought the merchandise for both British Isles Collection and

---

[1] We were located, however, within ten miles of the intersection of the Massachusetts Turnpike and Route 128 (a circumferential highway around Boston) which meant that many people were within easy driving distance.

Lawson Hill Leather and Shoe Co., I spent much time talking to customers in the retail store (and also over the telephone) and gained many inspirations from them. Marcia spent every Wednesday afternoon in the retail store at Lawson Hill Leather and Shoe Co. warehouse talking to customers.

Increasing store sales by selling the store better in the catalog

Marcia's presence in the retail store every Wednesday afternoon was, in fact, a key element in promoting our store sales and mail-order sales as well. Most mail-order companies recognize the value of having a retail store in their warehouse. What they fail to do is to promote it sufficiently. I see few mail-order catalogs that sufficiently promote their store in their catalog. As I said in Chapter 3, if mail marketers were to divide the cost of the space in their catalog allocated to the store by the store sales, they would find that it would have the lowest publicity cost in the whole catalog and should conclude that they are giving the stores too little catalog space. Marcia's presence in the retail store every Wednesday gave us an opportunity to productively devote more space to the store.

Marcia was the personality lionized in the front of the catalog. She had a shoe size that was very hard to find (11AAAA), which gave her a problem with which her many customers who had a similar difficulty could sympathize. We pictured her in the retail store talking to customers. This created the image of a friendly atmosphere at the store and made the customer feel welcome and as though she would receive a good fit. There was another advantage to featuring that Marcia was in the store Wednesday afternoons to help customers with their shoe needs: It demonstrated to customers far across the country, who had no hope of ever coming to our store, that there really was a Marcia Hill who was concerned with the problem women have in getting shoes that fit well.

There are other ways for the catalog to increase store traffic. If there is only one store, then describing the setting, if it is attractive, gives the feeling that it is a pleasant place to visit. That is what we did for British Isles Collection. We described our mountain setting and showed a picture of snow-capped Mount Washington, the highest mountain in the northeast. L. L. Bean, of course, has the unusual policy of keeping their store open 24 hours 365 days a year, a policy that attracts considerable national attention to the company and store. However, in some catalogs, they fail even to mention the store, to say nothing of their policy of keeping their store continually open. Considering the staggering volume that they do in their store in Freeport, Maine, this has to be an oversight of monumental proportions.

Perhaps the best way to increase store sales through the catalog is to give good directions on how to find the store and to give store hours. Would-be customers often hesitate to invest time and gasoline looking for a store in an unfamiliar locale. Making it sound easy to find the store will surely increase store traffic. We used a map in the Lawson Hill Leather and Shoe Co. catalog to give our location. A map greatly helps the customer visualize where the store is located. It may be one reason why our store did so much volume—it made it easy for our customers to find us and emphatically said "Come visit."

Giving store hours will also increase store sales. Uncertainty about the store hours might prevent the customer from visiting even though the store is open. This is particularly important if the store is open at unusual times.

The warehouse store

Opening a chain of retail stores is a remote consideration for one who is just entering the mail-order business. But opening one in the warehouse is a different matter. Because inventory is already in place and catalogs are already in circulation, the retail store in the front of the main warehouse is virtually a free ride. Only the sales clerks create extra cost and even they may be used for mail-order work when the store is not busy. Putting a retail store in the front of the main warehouse is one thing that should be included in the original business plan of anyone entering the mail-order business.

A chain of retail stores

The sales impact of the catalog that is felt in the warehouse store can, of course, be multiplied throughout the country. This is the sales growth development plan of such well-known mail-order companies as Lee Ward, Talbots, Eddie Bauer, and Yield House.

The usual strategy for opening of a chain of mail-order stores is to select areas into which the company is already mailing many catalogs and then increase the density of catalogs going into the area by renting more names of mail-order buyers in the area. At the same time the company opens the store, they announce it to their mail-order clientele and rented names in the area. By establishing a preexisting market, the company eliminates the slow process of building a loyal clientele that the ordinary store usually encounters and thus virtually guarantees a profitable store. Stores supported by mail-order are usually extraordinarily successful and grow at a compounded rate that surpasses most others.

A synergistic proposal
for the mail-order industry

The secret of the great success of a catalog store is the familiarity that the customers have with the company and its catalog long before the store is established. Typically, customers come long as well as short distances to obtain what they see displayed in the catalog. Customers have been known to come a day's drive and spend the night in a motel in order to visit a catalog store. How much more effective it would be and how many more customers would come if they had many catalog stores to visit instead of just one!

Mail-order customers for one catalog are built by renting and mailing catalogs to the customers in the lists of other catalogs. Thus one catalog's customers are familiar with other catalogs. People who buy regularly through mail order receive hundreds of catalogs a year. They know many companies beyond the ones from which they have purchased and, no doubt, have a curiosity about them. These people who receive catalogs from companies from which they have purchased and who are familiar with so many more could be attracted well beyond their normal trading area if they thought they could find these catalog companies conveniently clustered together in a shopping center restricted to catalog stores.

There is a phenomenon occurring in many parts of the country, particularly in Mount Washington Valley of New Hampshire where I live, of factory outlet stores springing up in clusters. Sometimes these factory stores are in shopping centers devoted exclusively to them. People drive long distances in order to visit the factory outlets, and the stores do staggering sales volumes. The same result would occur, I predict, if the mail-order industry would do the same. By clustering many catalog stores together, each, because of its recognition by the customers of the other catalog stores, would do better than if it stood alone.

It will take a leader in the mail-order industry to lead other mail marketers to this opportunity. If this opportunity is taken, I predict that mail order and even retailing will be transformed.

Chicken or the egg?

There is one final question that naturally stems from this discussion of the synergism of mail-order and retail stores. Which comes first? Do the retail stores start a mail-order business, or does a mail-order business start retail stores?

It has gone both ways, but stores more successfully result from mail order than the reverse. Most often, the stores that successfully go to mail order are small specialty shops with unusual products or ideas. In these shops, the owner already has or acquires the mail-order mentality. Because the shop is small, it can adapt to mail order. In fact, mail order soon dominates the store and merchandising for the mail order soon becomes the store's merchandising.

It is different, however, for large stores. Their large existing operation does not permit the modification of merchandising to suit mail order. The store buyer cannot put merchandise in the stores because it is right for mail order; he must, instead, put in merchandise that is right for the stores. If, however, the catalog is merchandised separately from the stores, then the synergism that is created by the catalog preselling for the stores is lost. Too, store buyers do not seem oriented towards buying for mail order. Roger Horchow, in his book *Elephants in Your Mailbox,* confirmed that store buyers with the specific interests and sales demands of the store cannot be responsible for catalog buying. Thus, few large department stores and retail chains have true mail-order catalogs. It is true that many department stores have catalogs, but the purpose of these catalogs is to bring customers to the stores. Without the stores, these catalogs would not support themselves. Bloomingdale's is one of the few noteworthy exceptions.

When synergism exists, that is, when one plus one equals three, the risks of a business are greatly reduced. The decision of the retailer to go into mail order or the mail marketer to go into retailing should be based on whether synergism will be created with the new venture. The central fact of any synergism that exists between retail stores and a mail-order business is the driving force of hundreds of thousands and maybe millions of catalogs in circulation. If these catalogs can bring sales to the stores as well as to mail order, which means the stores must carry the catalog merchandise, then one plus one will equal three.

The Synergism of Multiple Catalogs

The mail marketer just starting out is in no position to consider having two separate product lines and catalogs, but we all like to dream. Those mail marketers who have established successful mail-order businesses that are approaching maturity and have delegated much of the day-to-day responsibility for operations can turn their sights to another catalog.

Once again, one plus one can equal three. Synergism will occur by adding another catalog to an existing business because many of the things required for a successful mail-order business are already in place and do not need to be duplicated. The most important of these is the knowledge of how to run a mail-order business. Although particular product knowledge is required for the new catalog, mail-order knowledge, the lack of which condemns many good ideas to failure, is not wanting.

Operating expenses, which ordinarily are very heavy for a new mail-order company, are very low for an add-on catalog. They certainly are no more than for the existing mature catalog and perhaps are even less if the mature catalog picks up all the fixed operating costs. Later, as the volume of the add-on catalog grows, even greater efficiencies might occur as the operation is streamlined.

An add-on catalog can save on list rental. A new mail-order company must rent every name to which it mails. It does not have a list of its own that can be exchanged with other list owners to reduce this very substantial cost (without exchanges it is almost 25 percent of the cost of the catalog in the mail). But if there exists a list that can be used without list rental charges and that has a customer file that would supply a suitable customer, then money is saved to the extent that the list is used by the new catalog.

If there is only one list and it is small, the synergism resulting from the use of the list by the new catalog is limited. But as the company acquires more and more catalogs, the cost of launching a new catalog becomes less and less as more internally-owned names are used at no charge. This is a secret of the success of Hanover House Industries. At last count, they had over 25 different catalogs. They have so many catalogs that they can launch a new one without having to rent a single outside name. Furthermore, each of the catalogs can use the names of the others without paying rental charges so they all have access to lower-cost names.

The synergism of multiple catalogs is a great opportunity, but the mail marketer should be cautioned that the synergism should not be allowed to cover a conceptual weakness. That is, the new catalog should be strong enough to stand by itself. If each additional catalog is marginal and dependent upon the efficiencies of its association with the other catalogs for its existence, then a house of cards will be built that will come fluttering down when an ill economic wind blows.

Brand synergism

As filled with potential as this synergism of multiple catalogs is, if each catalog has a different brand, the add-on catalog does not benefit from the greatest of all the mail marketer's assets—the goodwill towards the company residing in its list of customers. A person is far more likely to buy from catalogs of a company from which he has bought before than from one he has never tried. It is true that he rebuys from a catalog because it has the types of things in which he is interested. But it is also true that he buys from the catalog because he has bought from it before and has grown to know and trust it. Because he knows the name and trademark and feels goodwill towards them, he just naturally gives a second look at, and perhaps buys, from any catalog bearing them.

The opportunity for the mail marketer, therefore, is to take advantage of existing brand loyalty by sending to one's customers a catalog of a new product line bearing the same name and trademark.[2] Such a product line for the new catalog should be related. For example, sending a catalog of garden tools, even if it is well-conceived, to one's list of men's shoe customers is a poor choice. Garden tools are far removed from a demonstrated interest.

---

[2] In Chapter 1 we discussed how the logotype must have high visibility, favorable associations, and memorability. These requirements become doubly important when the product line is changed. The mail marketer must make certain that the new catalog is not discarded for lack of recognition.

They will interest few customers and will confuse them as to what the company is. But a catalog of shirts, trousers, neckties, or clothing in general will cater to a demonstrated interest—dressing himself—and is not incongruous. When Cabell Brand, president of Stuart McGuire, which owns Ortho-vent Shoe Division, a consulting client of mine, asked me what additional products they might sell beyond their existing line of men's shoes, I recommended a clothing catalog.

The key to success of the new catalog is doing it well enough so that it could stand on its own if it were sent to list rental. This means a sound, well-presented concept of the business backed up with interesting products in a good selection. Too often the tendency is to send out a very ordinary catalog of ordinary products just to have something to send out. One should apply the test of "Is the catalog good enough to send out to list rental?" If it is not, then it should be made better. If it is made good enough to send to list rental, the catalog will work extraordinarily well for one's own customers who know the brand and trust it from their past experience.

This leads to another synergism. If the new catalog is mailed to list rental to generate customers on its own, then its customers will become a source of sales for the old catalog. Effectively, the customer base will be broadened. For example, Ortho-vent could develop customers by mailing a shirt catalog and then mail their shoe catalog to the shirt customers.

starting a mail-order business

Mail order is an interesting and exciting business. It is a growth business with all the opportunities that growth offers, and it has made substantial sums of money for many people. But it also is competitive. And when businesses are competitive, some succeed and others fail.

I have reviewed many books on mail order. Some of them say or imply that it is easy to make money in mail order, that one can make this money in one's spare time, and that mail order will make one rich. Many people have indeed grown rich in mail order, but others have lost their money. Only those who have done what they do exceedingly well have succeeded. It is nonsense to say mail order is anything except a full-time commitment. Competition permits nothing else.

Mail order demands all the energy, determination, and skill that one can muster. The first requirement for starting a mail-order business, therefore, is that one be resolved to give it one's all.

Mail order also imposes its risks. In the early stages of a mail-order business, while one develops and tests one's formula and builds a mailing list, these risks are very great: publicity plans fail to achieve forecast; catalog response is disappointingly low; expenses and returns for refund are greater than expected, and vendors deliver shoddy merchandise or fail to deliver on time. The greatest risks, perhaps, are those that result from one's own mistakes.

But without risk, there rarely is reward. The very word *entrepreneur* is French and means to enter and take. The entrepreneur enters to take a reward, but he also takes risks. The second requirement of the would-be mail-order entrepreneur, therefore, is that he be prepared to risk his capital.

The Plan

Having committed the resources of capital and personal energy to a mail-order venture, the mail-order entrepreneur must then turn his thoughts

229

to the strategy for launching the business, the concept of the business and the products required to support it, and the financial requirements of the business. These considerations are interrelated. The strategy that the entrepreneur employs to launch the business depends upon its concept and products and upon the available financial resources. Yet financial resources might dictate the concept and strategy. And, finally, it is the concept of the business that really should determine the strategy and the required financial resources. They all should be put together in a coherent plan.

Strategies

In this quicksand, there is one firm rock: Almost all mail-order businesses that succeed, no matter how started, end up with a catalog,[1] and the catalog ultimately becomes the main selling vehicle. We must consider, therefore, what the strategies are for starting a mail-order business.

The strategies with which people start or attempt to start mail-order businesses are the following or combinations of the following:

1. They run ads in magazines and newspapers to sell products.
2. They run ads to sell products and then follow up with catalogs.
3. They run ads to sell products and then follow up the customers acquired with solo mailing pieces or flyers.
4. They run ads to solicit catalog requests and then send catalogs to the requests.
5. They mail catalogs to rented lists.
6. They send out solo mailing pieces to rented lists. These are followed up with a catalog or other mailing pieces.
7. They insert package stuffers in the packages of other mail-order companies.

Each of these methods has its advantages and disadvantages. Usually, the less money that is risked, the more likely it is that the money risked will be lost.

Running ads to sell products

Running ads in magazines and newspapers is the popular approach that those who dream of starting a mail-order business try. For a few hundred dollars, they run a small ad in a magazine to see if their product will sell. Since they are advertising only one or a few products, their money in inventory that is at risk is low. And if the ads work, they recover the ad cost quickly.

But associated with low risk exposure are low prospects for success. The chances are that on their first try they will pick the wrong product, and that the medium they select will not be the best for mail order or for the product. This means they must spend more money to try a new product, a new medium, or both.

But even when the product succeeds, it is rare that a business can be built on one product. Products, no matter how well they sell at first, tend to wear out or, if they are very successful, will be copied. The mail-order entrepreneur must, therefore, continue his search for new products to replace the old.

---

[1] Some mail-order firms mail envelopes stuffed with slips of paper featuring different products. For practical purposes these are catalogs because they perform the function of a catalog, which is to offer an assortment. They are, in effect, unbound catalogs.

The biggest drawback to just running ads to sell product is that it offers no way to cash in on the customer list that has been built up, and it is in the customer list, as we learned earlier, that money is made in mail order. Without going back to the customer list, the entrepreneur cannot just break even with the ad; he or she must make a profit with it.

Selecting products for ads

Sooner or later the mail-order entrepreneur who starts with just ads asks himself "Where do I go from here?" The answer almost always is a catalog, or at least a flyer or a solo mailing piece.

But as soon as he comes to this conclusion, the entrepreneur must then ask if the different products that he has advertised are compatible with one another; that is, do they, satisfy common desires and interests, or do they have diverse appeal? If one advertises a garden implement, then one will be able to identify the buyers acquired as being interested in gardening. But if in the next ad one advertises a kitchen utensil, the buyers from that ad will indicate an interest in cooking but no interest in gardening. The two groups of customers, therefore, are heterogeneous, not homogeneous. Gardening tools will not sell well to the buyer of kitchen utensils, and kitchen utensils will not sell well to the gardener. The entrepreneur who sells incompatible products, therefore, does not have a base of customers for building a business, for he or she cannot send a catalog of one product line to the buyers of the other with any great success. If a combined catalog is sent to both groups, it fails to gain the impact of catering to one interest well.

The strategy, therefore, must be to select products that are compatible; that is, they must appeal to common desires and interests and fit the concept of the business as the entrepreneur has conceived it. This is what Sofwear Shoe did. They ran ads selling a variety of inexpensive women's sandals and slippers. The sandals and slippers sold well in the ads, and Sofwear had a homogeneous population of customers to which they could send their catalog and circulars.

There is one other consideration in selecting products for an ad: Does the product lead to a good catalog customer? One case illustrates the significance of the question. One mail-order company obtained many customers from ads by advertising low-priced products; but, when the company mailed catalogs to the customers thus acquired, response was very low. Eventually, the company was sold. The product, because of its low price, did not result in a good mail-order customer.

Following up ad customers

Once the entrepreneur has decided to follow up ad customers, he or she must then ask "With what?" A catalog is usually the most effective means because it generally is more powerful than anything else. And customers should be worthy of the most powerful mailing piece that the mail marketer can muster. But to produce a catalog, one must have color photographs, separations, typography, and inventory for many pages. Producing a catalog is a commitment and expenditure of large proportions. A few thousand customers will not support a catalog, and, of course, much money is at risk. To be successful in following up ad customers with a catalog, one must have many customers or plan to mail the catalog to list rental as well.

An alternative to sending out a catalog is to send out flyers with a limited selection of merchandise. This is often a good interim measure that bridges the yawning crevasse that separates merely running ads from producing a full catalog. The commitment for fixed creative costs and inventory for a flyer is comparatively small. Sending out flyers is, in fact, what Sofwear Shoes did for years before they started sending out a full catalog. But in going to a flyer, the entrepreneur must recognize that he or she is sacrificing effectiveness for lowered risk. A flyer will never produce the business that a catalog will, nor can it be mailed as often.

Sending out solo mailing pieces is another interim tactic that bridges merely running ads to sell products and mailing full catalogs. For example, one might run ads that sell garden implements. One then might follow up the customers by sending them solo mailing pieces on garden tools. A solo mailing piece, as the reader will recall from Chapter 21, takes one product, preferably one with many selling points, and develops it in depth. A solo mailing piece is rarely as effective as a catalog, but its commitment in inventory and creative expenditure is a small fraction of that required for a catalog.

A third bridge to a four-color catalog is a minicatalog in black and white, or black and white and some color. The fixed creative costs of photography, color separations, and press start-up are far less for black and white printing. The importance of color varies from product line to product line. For food and ready-to-wear, it is of utmost importance. For garden tools, it is probably less, but even for garden tools, I am told by Smith-Hawken, sales are greatly improved when they are illustrated in color. If the mail-order entrepreneur should decide upon black and white, he or she should calculate that whatever the results obtained, they will be much better when the catalog later goes to color.

There is a drawback to using ads selling product as a stepping stone to building a catalog mail-order business: The ad might fail, yet the concept of the catalog business might be sound. The failure of the ad might discourage the entrepreneur from proceeding with a catalog. A former consulting client of mine, Montgomery Schoolhouse in Montgomery, Vermont, faced this choice of either starting with a catalog or going with a less costly ad program. My advice to them was that, if they dabbled with the ads instead of testing a catalog, they would never know if the catalog would work. And, since only a catalog would give them the kind of volume they wanted to keep their wooden toy plant busy, I advised that they save the cost of the ads and proceed directly with a catalog.

Running ads to get catalog requests and sending out a catalog

The problem with placing ads to sell merchandise is that it usually builds a mailing list slowly and much time is required before the mailing list reaches a size that makes it economical to print a catalog. Running ads to get catalog requests usually results in many more names and thus builds the house list faster.

This is the way I started Lawson Hill Leather and Shoe Co. I ran small ads headlining "We have your size" and offered a free catalog featuring women's shoes in hard-to-find sizes. The ad apparently had great appeal, for we received many catalog requests at low cost, and when the persons requesting the catalog received it, they responded well, building our customer list rapidly. The catalog we sent out, incidentally, had color only on the cover—the balance was black and white.

A variant of the catalog request approach is to sell extremely low-priced items through an ad, such as a packet of seeds for twenty-five cents, and then follow up with a catalog. Ads like these produce myriads of small orders. The customers who send in these orders act more like catalog requests in that, with repeated mailings, they wear out much faster than customers who have sent in a substantial order.

Running ads to get catalog requests and sending out a solo mailing piece

When the product is very high-priced, the strategy sometimes is to make one's profit with the first sale and not be too concerned with making further profit with the customer. This is the strategy of Troy-Bilt Roto Tillers and the people who make powered chairs that will take an infirmed person up a stairway. What they do is solicit many requests and send out repeated mailings of a solo mailing piece to them. The obvious advantage of this method of going into the mail-order business is the relatively low cost and possibly low inventory investment. It is particularly suited to a manufacturer who already has an inventory of a high-priced product and is seeking a way of selling it.

Mailing catalogs to rented lists

Starting a mail-order business by mailing a catalog to rented lists risks the most capital. Expenditures for catalog design, layout, color photography, color separations, platemaking, and inventory must be committed before even one catalog is printed. Then the entrepreneur must print 25,000, or 100,000, or even 250,000 catalogs and put up money for postage and list rental fees.

Yet, while the amount at risk and the capital required are the highest, the chances of success are also the greatest. There is no trifling with intermediate steps that might result in failure. There is no compromising of a product's catalog worthiness to make it suitable for ads—the product can be selected and designed to fit the concept and theme of the business. And, too, the customers are the ones that fit the concept of the business; that is, they have the interests and desires that make them look beyond their first purchase towards the other products offered in the catalog. In short, by proceeding directly to the ultimate mode of the business and risking more, the entrepreneur greatly increases the likelihood of success.

Chances of success are better because even if the results of individual list tests are not break-even and much merchandise fails, enough will be learned to greatly improve the results in a following attempt. And even if only a few lists are break-even or profitable, the effort can be called a success, for in repeat mailings the proven lists can be rolled out to generate profit-making customers. Going directly to mailing a catalog to rented lists suits best the well-financed company that has the capital and can stand the risk exposure.

This is, in fact, the way I launched the British Isles Collection. We started with a concept of the business and developed the merchandise and catalog to go with it. In our first test season, we mailed 300,000 catalogs. If our concept of business, merchandise, and catalog had any merit, this large test virtually assured that we would succeed. Because we mailed so many catalogs, we would be certain of finding good lists and knowing which merchandise was good and which was bad. The result was that the roll-out of this test was a stunning success. By risking more in the beginning, we learned more and could roll out 1,250,000 names with confidence and expect to reach a profitable level sooner.

Solo mailing pieces
to start a mail-order business

Mail-order businesses are sometimes started by mailing solo mailing pieces to rented lists. For a solo mailing piece, a single product with many selling points that can be featured and with broad appeal is selected. The product is featured in a large four-color mailing piece. There usually is a large picture of the product supported by many small pictures and explanations, which illustrate the features and functions of the product. Frequently it is mailed in an envelope with a letter, an order form, occasionally a coupon, and, if appropriate, a swatch.

The advantage of the solo mailing piece is that it requires a far smaller commitment in inventory and in creative and printing expense. It is also particularly suited to selling certain types of products. But, like running ads to sell product, its failure does not mean that the concept of the business, if it is to be a catalog business, is inadequate. Solo mailing pieces are not usually as powerful as catalogs.

Again one must raise the question of how one follows up the customer that has been acquired with a solo mailing piece. One obviously cannot send the same solo mailing piece to the customers acquired by it because the customers already own the product. The product selected, therefore, must be one of a series that can appeal to the customers acquired or be a precursor of a catalog. The Stuart McGuire Company started their Ortho-vent Division with a solo mailing. Originally, they followed up their customers with other solo mailing pieces. Later they began sending catalogs.

Package stuffers
in the packages of others

A low-budget method of starting a mail-order business is to put a small flyer illustrating a few products in the packages of others. The preparation and printing of the product is relatively inexpensive, and there are no postage charges to pay. There is the charge for inserting the stuffer in the package, but little inventory is required. This is how Chuck Roast in North Conway, New Hampshire, is starting its mail-order business.

Here again, one must consider how one is going to follow up the customers acquired. The interim answer is to print another flyer and send it to the customer. This might be enough for the business to break even or make a small profit. But one must recognize that mailing out flyers is far less effective than mailing out catalogs, and, furthermore, flyers are usually not effective enough to permit the repeat mailings to customers that are a big source of the mail marketer's profit. If the flyer shows promise and the mail-order entrepreneur perserveres, a catalog will result.

Summing Up the Product and Product Line

I have said throughout this book much about what the product and product line should be. For the would-be mail-order entrepreneur, it is worthwhile that I summarize those thoughts here.

Is the product that one hopes to market by mail order a part of an overall concept of the business? There is almost no hope for success if the product advertised is randomly selected and is not the precursor of related merchandise that fit one theme. To advertise one product one month and an unrelated product the next produces a heterogeneous customer file. Only if one of the products can be expanded to a product line will there be success. When you advertise a product, think of what your business will become.

If the product is for an ad, the product must be one such that the ad breaks even and the ad should produce many customers as a by-product. Usually, but not always, ads that produce many customers sell low-priced merchandise. This raises the question of whether the customers so produced will be responsive to the catalog that is later mailed to them.

Does your product offer a special reason why someone should buy it from you? Is it unusual and appealing? Is it hard to find? Or do you offer it at a very attractive price?

Does the product line sell in both the spring-summer and the fall-winter seasons? If it sells in just one season, you must accept the fact that it takes twice as long to build a business as when it sells in two seasons. Furthermore, you have the problem of what to do with your staff during the quiet season.

Will the items in your proposed product line result in a low average order, or will they have a very high ticket? If the average order is very low, it will be harder to make the business profitable because a large unit volume is required and because operating costs will eat up the margins and leave little to pay for catalog and overhead. If the product carries a very high ticket, one may have difficulty in building a customer base, although there are successful mail-order companies selling expensive products, such as Troy-Bilt Roto Tillers.

Does the product line have many stockkeeping units, as in shoes? If it does, then higher sales are required in order to maintain turnover. For this reason, many stockkeeping units make it difficult to start up slowly. Many stockkeeping units are both a boon and a bane: a bane because it complicates maintaining inventory and filling orders, a boon because by concentrating all sales into one inventory and thus increasing the sales density and turnover of the stockkeeping units, a mail-order firm is able to offer a selection that retail stores cannot match. Offering many stockkeeping units was the reason why Lawson Hill Leather and Shoe Co. existed.

Is the product consumable? If it is, a repeat business is assured. This is one reason why mail-order shoe businesses have been successful—shoes wear out.

Finally, to quote Harold Schwartz, president of Hanover House Industries and a leader in the mail-order industry, "Innovate, don't imitate." While picking up on a hot item may be sound, aping a competitor condemns one to being a follower, not a leader. Many have copied Roger Horchow; none has achieved his success.

Financial Considerations

Financial planning

The most serious mistake that many would-be mail-order entrepreneurs make, a mistake often made by both novices and those who should know better, is to start a mail-order business without a financial plan. Few mail-order businesses generate sufficient cash to internally finance their launching and growth during the early years. The great danger is that the entrepreneur will launch a business, perhaps well-conceived, for which there are insufficient cash resources.

The entrepreneur should, therefore, sit down with accounting pads[2] and put his three-year strategy for building the mail-order business down in numbers. Will there be enough cash? Do the numbers show that the proposed business has prospects of making a handsome profit? What will

---

[2] I find 13-column accounting pads particularly useful for doing three-year plans.

the profit formula look like? These questions he should answer as best he can. Of course, he is going to be wildly wrong on some of the estimates while others will be quite precise, but at least he will have some sense of where he is headed and will establish checks on the progress and validity of the business.

To make this plan, the entrepreneur should obtain quotations for the publicity costs: preparation and publishing of ads, preparation and printing of the catalog[3] or flyers, postage and mailing expense, and list rental costs. He should estimate operating costs, both fixed and variable, mark-up as well as markdowns, the sales and returns that will result from the business strategy, and, finally, the necessary investment in fixed assets, as leasehold improvements and equipment. All these estimates and quotations should then be assembled into a three-year plan of profit or loss, assets and liabilities, and cash flow. The method for doing this is described in Chapter 16.

Keeping track

A common mistake of novice businesspersons is to keep an inadequate track of financial progress. Keep a sharp eye on profit and loss. Measure the result of each individual publicity effort as shown in Chapter 15. Prepare monthly financial statements in the format given in Chapter 14 and use an orderline, as described in Chapter 16 to estimate what remains of your prepaid publicity expense and thus determine your profit. Financial statements tell you where you stand. If you are in trouble, you want to know about it early, not late, so that you can make corrections.

Taking the Plunge

The thoughts that I have expressed in this chapter are the ones that have resulted from people coming to me to learn how to start a mail-order business. Some have had little more than a notion that they want to go into the mail-order business, others have had a specific product that they wished to sell, and still others had started a business and wanted to know how to continue.

The three broad areas that I explore with them are the concept of their business, their strategy, and their financial planning. Until they decide what their mail-order business should be, my advice to them is that they proceed no further. Second, they should devise a strategy that leads them to their objective, is commensurate with their resources, and offers sufficient prospects of success. Finally, they should reduce their plan to numbers, a financial plan, to learn if they have sufficient resources and will make the profit they seek.

If one has sufficient resources and can afford the amount of risk, starting out with the ultimate mode of business is the surest course because one does not risk the loss and discouragement that follow the failure of intermediate modes. In most cases, the ultimate mode of the business is a catalog. The catalog best presents the concept of the business and is the most profitable vehicle for selling the product. But one does not always have the wherewithal to pursue this course. One must then follow a riskier path that risks less.

---

[3] The beginning mail marketer should obtain printing quotations in both sheet-fed and web offset. In the early years, the press runs may be too short to justify web printing, but if the business is successful and the mail marketer rents lists, it soon will be economical to use web printing. He or she needs to know in advance that there is this opportunity to save money at a later time.

catalog mail order
step by step

This chapter gives the beginner in mail order an overview of what needs to be done, step by step, to set up and operate a catalog mail-order business. It provides a framework for the detail that is fleshed out in the other chapters, a checklist by which the beginner can guide himself. The experienced mail marketer can safely pass this chapter by.

Steps for Getting Started

This section reflects my experience in launching the British Isles Collection. These steps parallel the ones I took.

Decide upon the concept of your mail-order business. Don't let it just evolve. Decide what customer interest or desire the business as a whole intends to satisfy. Then think through the theme, name, logotype, copywriting, and merchandise that will support the concept of the business. This is covered in Chapter 1.

Decide upon your strategy for launching your mail-order business. Will you start with ads in media, a catalog mailed to list rental, or what? This is covered in Chapter 14.

Make your three-year plan. This is putting down your strategy in numbers. Your three-year plan should contain your budget for the first year and, for three years, your mailing plan, forecasted profit and loss, balance sheets, and cash flow. See Chapter 16 for an in-depth explanation.

Plan how you are going to raise money for your venture. How much equity capital is going to be put in? How much bank credit will be required? Will the ratio of debt to equity be satisfactory? Will you have enough equity to continue in case there is a temporary setback or will everything have to

237

work perfectly? Meet with your banker and prospective investors, but before you meet with them, prepare your proposal.

Your proposal should contain all the elements of your three-year plan: mailing plan, profit and loss, balance sheets, and cash flow for three years, all backed up with as much data and sources as you can muster. Where you make assumptions, and there will be many of them, explain the rationale behind them. The proposal should also contain a narrative. The narrative should explain the concept of the business, why you think the concept will occupy a profitable niche in the market, the competition that exists, and how you will fill the niche better than the competition. It should give any problems that you foresee and the ways you will overcome them. It should also give your plans for managing the business, the degree of risk, and your contingency plans in the event sales and expenses are worse than forecast. In short, the proposal should demonstrate that, as much as anyone can under the circumstances, you know what you are doing.

Plan the execution of your publicity program.   This includes the advertising, catalog, any other sales promotion, and their schedules.

You should start your own advertising agency in order to place your ads and save the 15 percent agency commission. Starting an agency consists of picking a name with the word *advertising* in it, printing letterhead and envelopes, and opening a checking account. You don't need to go to the expense of incorporating your agency; a proprietorship will do.

Plan for your merchandise.   Make sure that you place your orders well in advance so the manufacturer has time to produce them. New products often take longer to deliver because it takes time to get the special materials required for them.

Remember that you will not have sufficient information on which to base a reorder until four or five weeks after the mailing is made. Therefore, you must plan enough stock to cover this period plus the reorder period. See Chapter 20. You do not need to take all this merchandise in at once but can spread out deliveries using the orderline as a guide. Don't trust the manufacturer to deliver on time. Phone well enough in advance of when you need the goods so that if you detect a problem, you will have time to do something about it.

Decide upon your fiscal year end.   The best date is after you have incurred the most publicity expense and the least amount of sales have resulted from it. This, as explained in Chapter 16, results in lower tax payments.

Plan for your retail store in the warehouse.   Things to think about include the sign, remodeling for the selling area, cash register, display stands, cabinets, shelves, and so on. Be sure to promote the store in the catalog.

Plan for your operations.   Following are the necessary steps.
Select a building. You should calculate the floor area that you will need based upon the peak inventory or upon a smaller inventory if you can decide what to do with the peak quantities. Allow room for growth. You should consider whether the building is suitable for both warehouse and store. A store requires a convenient, identifiable location with high visibility. These locations, however, are often costly and this cost might be too much for warehousing. If your product line requires much space to store, the site selected might be different than if it does not. Think about shipping, receiving, and materials handling.

One lesson that I have learned well is that it does not pay to crowd stock. When stock is crowded, picking stock and putting it away can take twice the time. Worse is that stock can become misplaced and orders, consequently, are not filled. Therefore, plan for enough space.

Be sure that you label the shelves and aisles where everything is to be kept. Poor labeling will result in lazy receivers putting something anywhere in order to get rid of it. The labeling should be clear and the stock logically arranged so that anyone can find what they are looking for.

Think about security—alarm systems, locks, fire extinguishers, and so on. One lock system that I have used and found convenient is one with a removable core. When an employee who has had a key leaves, you change the core and, hence, the key required to open the door yourself.

Plan for your equipment. Here are some of the things you will need:

- Desks and chairs
- Shipping benches
- Scale for weighing packages
- Mailing machine with postage meter
- Shelving for stock
- Photocopier
- Sealing tape dispenser
- Calculators
- Mail-opening machine
- Telephone answering machine to take night orders

Decide upon your operating system—manual or computer. In most circumstances, I recommend starting with a manual system and using a service bureau to maintain the mailing list. A manual operating system worked well for us at British Isles Collection during the first year. I do not recommend a halfway computer system. You will spend much time and money yet not get what you need. Stick with a manual system, such as the one described in Chapter 18, until you have proven the concept of your business and can afford a well-designed mail-order computer system as described in Chapter 19.

Have your forms ready to go when the first orders come in. Many of the forms needed for operating can be duplicated on your copying machine so that all you need to do is to rule up masters. Labels, however, need to be printed. They can be bought in continuous rolls very cheaply. Have your history and forecast of product demand form (Figure 20-2) ready to go.

Plan for your personnel. Your orderline will tell you how your orders will come in. Order processing and shipping will closely follow it. The customer service burden will lag the orderline by three to six weeks. If you become seriously out of stock, your personnel requirements for customer service will become very substantial indeed.

You will need personnel for the following functions: order processing in the office, stock picking, inspecting, packing and shipping, receiving and putting stock on shelves, customer service, store, and bookkeeping. Many of these functions can be performed by the same person. When the first orders come in, take some time studies with a stop watch to determine how many people you will need at your peak. Be sure you have a competent bookkeeper who can keep up with the load. You don't want to have your time and energy drained by books that are snarled and that don't tie in with one another; and, most of all, you don't want financial reporting of which you are not sure.

Make arrangements with the trucking lines to deliver your merchandise to you and with the United Parcel Service and the United States Postal Service for shipping of your packages. It takes a while to obtain the necessary slugs for the meters, so do not wait until the last minute.

Meet with the postmaster. You will put an extra burden on his office, but you will also generate income for it. His cooperation will smooth matters for you.

Plan for your list maintenance. If you have a manual system, you should have your list maintained at a service bureau that is experienced in mail order and able to maintain most of the information about a customer recommended in Chapter 17. If you decide to put in an interactive computer system as described in Chapter 19, be sure you don't lose information about your customers. Finally, make sure you protect your list from loss by having accurate, up-to-date copies outside the building.

Make arrangements to have decoys salted in your list as described in Chapter 17. You will want to spot misuse of your list and track the delivery of your catalog. Have your decoys mark the date received on the covers of the catalogs and send the covers to you.

Make arrangements for your telephone and telephone answering machine. You will want a machine unless you plan to man the phones twenty-four hours a day—unlikely for a starting company.

Make arrangements with a credit card company. Be sure to shop around at different banks to get the best rate on your credit card processing charges. The rates for processing Visa and MasterCard are negotiable. Even American Express can be bent. Diner's Club will match American Express.

Make arrangements for an accountant. Have him set up your books, probably with a one-write system for making your double entries. Have him make sure your books tie in with one another and have him approve your selection for bookkeeper, or, better still, have him recommend one to you.

Steps in Producing a Catalog

For some people, the production of a catalog is mysterious. This listing of the steps to be taken in the production of a catalog is intended to make it less so.

First, make your catalog analysis. Before you design your new catalog, you must analyze the previous catalog, as described in Chapter 7. This determines not only merchandise decisions but how much space should be allocated to each product as well.

Second, make a dummy. A dummy shows where each product is going in the catalog and approximately how much space is devoted to it. It shows where institutional and other nonselling elements go. Chapters 5 and 7 give some of the principles of where merchandise should be placed.

Third, make your layout. The layout is the dummy in greater detail and in more accurate form. The space and position of each product and other elements is precisely determined. At this point careful consideration must be given to eyeflow, as discussed in Chapter 8. Some artists lay out a catalog in great detail, showing the exact position of the product and even people in the illustration and then turn it over to the photographer who is expected to follow it precisely. I prefer a more flexible approach wherein the space is allocated and the product roughly positioned, and then the final positioning of the product is made on set, preferably, with the layout artist working with the photographer.

At the time the layout is made, thought must be given to how much space will be devoted to the copy. A decision must be made by someone who understands what is being sold and how it is best sold to determine how much space copy should have.

241
catalog mail order
step by step

Layouts are usually done in pencil on onionskin paper. Layouts done by an agency are sometimes done in color, which makes it easier for the client to visualize the catalog. For me, this is a needless expense.

Fourth, plan for photography. Think about backgrounds and props before you go on set. Keep in mind some of the principles given in Chapter 8 on eye flow and Chapter 9 on color. In selecting a photographer, be sure to check what lighting he has available. If you are shooting with live models, be sure to plan every item of clothing being worn—not just what is being sold. Every item must coordinate with the others. Everything must be pressed and ready to photograph.

Fifth, write your copy. There are three choices in writing copy to fit the space. Copy can be written to fit the space given to it; the space given to copy can be increased to fit the copy written; or the type size can be made smaller to accommodate the copy. I use an unorthodox method of writing copy that works well for me because, although I spend more for typesetting, I save time. Keeping roughly in mind the amount of space available, I write as much copy as I think needs to be written. If the typesetter cannot get it to fit, then I edit the copy, increase the space, rearrange some of the elements, or, once in a great while, I change the type size. This procedure, while it works well for me, would not work well in a situation where catalog production is departmentalized.

Sixth, arrange for the making of the mechanicals. Mechanicals are the layouts done even more precisely on boards. There is a mechanical for each page or pair of pages. There is an outline of the actual photograph showing precisely how it is to be positioned. This outline can be a pencil outline of the photograph or it can be a black and white photographic print of the photograph pasted down on the board. The set type is pasted down precisely in its intended position. It is then photographed and incorporated in the black separation.

Seventh, arrange for the assembly of the photographs. The photographs are butt-assembled to correspond with the precise position indicated on the mechanical. If the photographs are not in their correct size, then a reproduction in the correct size, called a "dupe," is made before assembly. If the photographs are separated individually, then the dupe does not have to be made. The separation will be made to the size indicated on the mechanical. Sometimes the positions of the photographs are indicated on the mechanical after assembly. The positions must be indicated very accurately to avoid the danger of the type getting onto the product.

Printers like to see that type gets no closer than one-quarter of an inch from the trim lines. I find that this is a good rule to follow. If there is any imprecision in the folding and trimming of the catalog, type could be trimmed off if the rule was not followed.

Eighth, arrange for separating. When the photographs are selected and assembled, they can be sent off to the color separator. If the color separator is to strip in the type, then the mechanicals must be sent to him too. You will receive proofs back from him which you will correct. This is all covered in Chapter 11. When the separations are completed, they will be delivered to the printer in flats. Flats are the separations assembled together in the page arrangement, called an imposition, required by the printer.

Finally, arrange for printing. When the printer receives the flats with the type in place, then he can make his plates and print. When the catelog goes on press, you will be called in for a press okay. This is covered in Chapter 12.

Steps in Producing an Ad

Producing an ad is less involved than a catalog.

The first step in producing an ad, of course, is the conceptual work described in Chapter 14 under the heading "How to Put Together a Mail-Order Ad."

Second, the ad is then laid out to the size upon which you have decided. You should obtain the mechanical requirements either from the magazine or Standard Rate and Data Service. Mechanical requirements include width of column, ad sizes, screen size, and the format in which the ad must be received (usually a negative or a glossy print). Headlines, picture of product, location of copy, and logotype are shown on the layout.

Third, the copy should be written to fit the space available.

The next step is typesetting and paste-up. The type is then set and pasted onto a board. A screened photo is also pasted on. As for catalogs, this board is called a mechanical.

Fifth, assign the source code key. The key can be set at the time the ad is sent out or sometimes the magazine or newspaper will set it for you. When the same ad is repeated in several issues, the magazine or newspaper will change the key for you.

The final step is to send out a negative or a glossy photostat of the ad to the medium, keeping the mechanical with you.

Steps in Planning Publicity

Publicity planning should be well-organized.

The first step is to measure the previous year's results as described in Chapter 15.

Next, decide upon the media program. Decide what ads you will use and into which media and issues you will insert them. Determine the cost of each ad and the sales expected from it as shown in Table 16-5.

Third, meet or talk with list brokers and select tests. At the same time, negotiate exchanges with other list owners to reduce list rental costs.

Fourth, decide which lists and list segments you are going to mail and make your publicity plan as shown in Table 16-2. This plan should show the size of each list or list segment, the time or times mailed, the anticipated sales per thousand, the total sales expected from the list, the publicity cost per thousand, and the total publicity cost expected for the list. This is all described in Chapter 16.

Fifth, place your list rental orders. If you place your list orders through a broker, he will coordinate the delivery of the tapes to the computer service bureau that does the merge-purge.

Finally, arrange for the merge-purge. The computer service bureau will do the merge-purge as discussed in Chapter 17. The service bureau will deliver labels or magnetic tape (needed in case the names are to be ink jetted onto the address block and order form) to the person who mails your catalog. Frequently, that person is also the printer.

Scheduling

Chapter 16 emphasized the importance of sticking to one's scheduled mailing dates. It bears repeating: missed mailing dates are very common, but they are also very costly. Make your schedules and stick to them. There are other things that should be scheduled. Here is a list.

243
catalog mail order
step by step

1. Mailing dates for housefile and list rental.
2. Catalog product dates. Mailing dates determine catalog production schedule. The printer will tell you when he must have the flats from the separator, and the separator will tell you when he must have the photo assemblies. Similarly, you must work backwards in time to determine schedules for photographers, layout artists, and so on. This, in turn, tells you when you should have all your merchandise samples in. All the creative functions should be set up on a schedule. This schedule should be prepared many months in advance so that you do not get caught by surprise and not have enough time.
3. Ad schedules. Similarly, you should schedule the planning and preparation of your ads. Magazine closing dates have a habit of coming up fast. Make your plans well in advance and have your ads ready so that you don't miss running an ad because you were late.
4. Merchandise schedules. Schedule your merchandise arrivals, and, to make sure you have your merchandise on time, schedule your ordering dates.

Setting Up Controls

No business works well without controls. Set up good ones and your life will be a lot easier. The most important ones for a mail-order company are the following:

1. Inventory controls as described in Chapter 20.
2. Catalog and merchandise effectiveness controls as described in Chapter 7.
3. Effectiveness of publicity efforts controls as described in Chapter 15.
4. Financial controls including balance sheet, profit and loss statement, and cash flow statement. In some ways, the cash flow statement is the most important of these because it tells you whether or not you are generating enough cash internally to continue your growth.

organize for success

Much of what I have written in this book would seem obvious. There should be a concept and theme of the business that enforces the concentration and development of merchandise to satisfy well one customer interest. Merchandise, copy, layout, catalog design, and photography must be marshalled and coordinated to meet that interest. Since merchandise is sampled and decided upon with its possibility of selling well in view, the merchandiser must keep in mind how well it will photograph, how it is to be displayed, and what can be said about it.

Why is it then that merchandise and copy are often inconsistent with the theme or fail to support it? Why is copy frequently weak, not developing all the virtues of the product? Why does the photograph often not illustrate the product to best advantage?

The answer is that when mail-order companies become large, they become departmentalized. The merchandiser selects merchandise and does rebuying but does not write copy, make layouts, or supervise the photography. The copywriter was not in on the merchandise selection and does not experience the enthusiasm of the merchandiser that should animate his copywriting. And the merchandiser, knowing that he will not write the copy, will not seek out products that strong copy can be written about. The result is uninspired merchandise and insipid copy.

Furthermore, there is no one to arbitrate the functions of copywriting and layout. Should more space be assigned to the picture or to the copy? Often it is the lowly layout artist who determines how much space the copywriter has available, and the artist, being graphically-oriented, will prefer a large representation of the product and leave little room for the copywriter. Yet, the product might be such that good copy would sell it better than a large picture.

Often the merchandiser has limited say as to how much space should be devoted to a product, where it should be located, or how it should be portrayed. Rarely is he on set to approve the angle, position, and lighting of the product—the photographer or layout artist decides. Yet after the catalog has been mailed, the sales have come in, and the truth has been revealed as to how well each product is to sell, management turns to the merchandiser to ask why this or that product is not selling. If the product should sell but does not, the merchandiser can only make lame excuses, saying that the angle, the position, the photograph, or the copy was not adequate. In addition, with so many people involved, it is easy for one or more of them to lose sight of their obligation to support and develop the theme.

In short, the merchandiser, the copywriter, the layout artist, and the photographer operate each in his own partial vacuum with each doing his job as he sees it but not taking responsibility for the sale of the product. It is a problem of coordination, which can be best solved by having one mind encompass all the responsibilities.

But coordinating and inspiring the merchandiser, copywriter, layout artist, and photographer is only one problem of harmony that must be worked out for a mail-order company. Once the photograph has been taken, the exposure must be selected to balance with the other photographs, color separations must be made, and the catalog must be printed. Each of these affects the others and the failure of one can impair the final representation of the product. Good service to the customer requires speedy processing of orders and intelligent and immediate answering of queries, for which data processing, order processing within the office, customer service, warehousing, and shipping must all be coordinated. Budgeting, accounting, and financial reporting must be coordinated, as must the planning of the mailing and advertising programs.

The solution to these problems of coordination lies in thinking through the organization's structure, the assignment of responsibilities, and the drawing of an organization chart to define the areas of responsibilities. The organization chart is not something to be put behind glass in a gift frame and hung on the wall in the president's office to reassure him that he is indeed at the top. Rather, it is a working sheet of paper to be kept on his desk to be erased and added to as changes within the organizational structure occur.

I have worked out an organization chart in Figure 26-1, the way I see it should be for a mail-order company. Much of it is conventional: the merchandiser, the publicity manager, the retail stores manager, the operations manager, and the controller all report to the president. Each, with the exception of the controller, is responsible for one of the main expense headings of the income statement. What is not conventional is the division of responsibilities between the merchandiser and the publicity manager.

What this chart proposes is that one mind, that of the merchandiser, govern not only the selection of the merchandise but the copywriting, layout, and photography as well. He should write his own copy so that he can be sure what he wants said about the product is, in fact, said. If he understands the principles of eye flow, and he should understand eye flow, then he can do the layout.[1] But, if he does not, or does not have the time, then he should at least plan the organization of the catalog (or the organization of his section of the catalog if there are several merchandisers) and direct the layout artist, giving final approval to the layout.

The merchandiser should also control the photography. He should be on set to make sure the product is photographed in the right position and

---

[1] One myth that needs to be disposed of is that one needs to be an artist in order to do a layout. Anyone can do a layout if he or she understands eye flow.

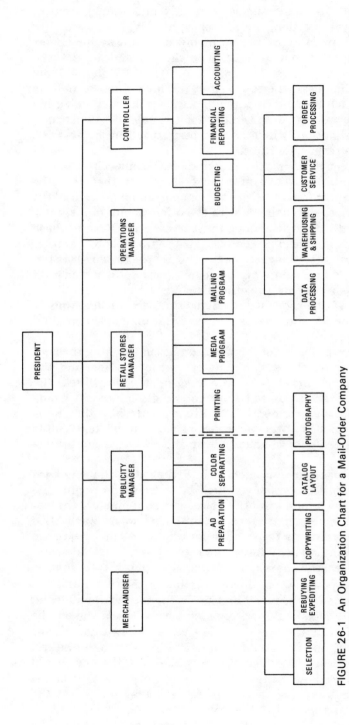

FIGURE 26-1 An Organization Chart for a Mail-Order Company

correct angle and to make sure the lighting highlights the product's features. He should approve or disapprove the photograph, making sure there is no compromise in the quality of the photograph that would impair the sale of the product. What he should not do is to select the exposure, since the densities of the various transparencies must be balanced in order to make the separations.

Here the merchandiser's reponsibilities end. He is responsible for developing merchandise that supports the theme and sells, writing the copy to make the merchandise move, allocating the catalog space and approving the layout, and directing and approving the photography. Beyond that he need go no further. Merchandise, copy, layout, and photography are integrated under his sole control; his responsibility is complete for the success or failure of the merchandise, and he has the opportunity to create the conditions for its success.

Selection and balancing of exposures, making color separations, and supervision of the printing are steps that take the representation of the product from the photograph to the printed page. They do not affect the other responsibilities that we have discussed so far but interact among themselves and require the knowledge of a specialist—someone who understands the making of separations and printing.

I have assigned, therefore, the responsibilities of selection of exposures, color separating, printing, planning of the mailing program and the media program, and ad preparation to the publicity manager.

The responsibilities of the operations manager are quite conventional. He coordinates data processing, warehousing and shipping, customer service, and order processing within the office. I would like to add, however, this further comment. Success in operations management should be measured primarily on how good the service is to the customer. Good service preserves and enhances the most valuable asset of the mail-order company—the mailing list. Cost efficiency gained at the expense of service may damage the productivity of the list more than it saves money.

The other responsibility blocks on the organization chart are quite normally located. The controller is responsible for accounting, budgeting, and financial reporting. The retail stores are shown as reporting to the president; but, if there are just a few, not a large chain, then they might report to the publicity manager. The merchandiser directs rebuying and expediting. There is a good reason for this: because the merchandiser knows the vendors and has the power to redirect business, he can wield a big stick in obtaining better deliveries to replenish unexpected stock outages.

Clearly, the success of the mail-order company depends upon the merchandiser. Of those who report to the president, he is of supreme importance. The merchandise is what the business is all about. It is what the customer is willing to pay for. The merchandise fulfills the particular customer interest, which the business, guided by its concept and theme, is designed to satisfy.

What this organizational structure does is to recognize the importance of the merchandiser and to give him the power to carry out the function of selling the product. Obviously, the merchandiser must be a talented, versatile, and highly-paid person with the ability to select, write about, display, and supervise the photography of the merchandise. He is little short of being the same stature as the president.

As I write this, I can hear my friends who run fairly large mail-order companies complain: "My merchandiser knows the product but cannot write a complete sentence." Or "My merchandiser is not qualified to write copy, do layouts, or approve photographs." And my friends are probably right that the existing persons they have doing merchandising are not qualified to perform these other functions.

But this is the way their organization has grown given the division of responsibilities that has existed. Existing merchandisers can be trained to write copy, do or approve layouts, and supervise photography, or someone can be hired who is equal to the tasks. For, although this organization chart is novel to a large company, it is the way it is in a small company where the president does everything.

The merchandiser is the most important person in a mail-order company. He must be given the responsibility and authority needed to sell the merchandise.

mastery and concentration

How does one build a multi-million dollar catalog mail-order business? What are the secrets of catalog mail-order success? The twenty-six chapters that precede this one unfold what I see to be the answers to these questions. They are the distillations of what I learned from building two of my own multi-million dollar catalog businesses and from my observations of other growing mail-order companies for whom I have consulted.

The very number of chapters says a lot—there is much one must learn, master, and do to be successful in catalog mail order. The beginning mail marketer must think through the concept of the business and then give it substance through the merchandise and its presentation in the catalog. He must learn how to develop merchandise that sells in a catalog and how to achieve leadership in the product line. The mail marketer must learn how to write copy that creates mood, supports the theme, and sells the product. He must decide upon a name and logotype that promote the theme. He must create confidence in his customers. He must learn how to design an effective catalog and provide it with good photography, separations, and printing. He must learn to prepare profitable ads.

The mail marketer must also control the business with the profit formula and measure the results of publicity efforts. He must budget, make publicity plans, and plan for three years in advance. He must develop and rent the workhorse lists that supply the customers with which he builds his own list. He must discover new lists to replace the ones that wither and to build his business even more. The mail marketer needs to learn how to mail all his lists more effectively and how to take advantage of the opportunities offered by computer letters and solo mailings. He has to master the myriad complexities of processing orders efficiently and servicing the customers. He must control his inventory with all the precision that is possible. And if the mail marketer is just starting out, he must decide upon a strategy for launching his business.

Studying and marketing what is contained in these twenty-six chapters give one a perspective of the catalog mail-order business. One can see most of the things one must learn and do to achieve success. The problem is, however, that one cannot do it all. He who concentrates on everything concentrates on nothing. While he must maintain a perspective of his company, that is, keep everything in view, the mail marketer must also concentrate most of his effort on those things that will produce the greatest results.

Where then should the mail marketer concentrate his attention? Placing additional effort in some areas will produce only marginal improvements in profit. If a mail marketer does not have good financial controls, if his accounting is in disarray, or if he fails to budget or fails to forecast where he is headed several years ahead, he can reap disaster. But once the mail marketer sets up these financial controls and places them in competent hands, he gains little if he puts additional effort into them.

Similarly, a malfunctioning operating system can bring disaster to the mail marketer. But if he has a trouble-free computer system that controls mail-order operations and produces management information as described in Chapter 19, if he has streamlined the other aspects of his operations, and if he has placed a capable person in charge of operating, then, once again, additional effort will bring only marginal returns.

The ordering and rebuying of merchandise is surely a critical function. One can have too much or too little inventory and this can have enormous impact on profit and loss. Too much inventory means markdowns, high interest costs, and maybe a shortage of cash. Too little inventory is perhaps worse because sales are lost and, unseen on the statement of assets and liabilities, damage is done to the mailing list. Cash can be just as short with too little inventory as too much because when one refunds for nonfulfillment of orders, one returns not only the cost of merchandise but the mark-up as well. Worst of all is to have at the same time both too little and too much inventory, that is, to have too few of some items and too many of others. These problems demand good inventory controls. But good inventory controls can be set up, and, once set up, they can be delegated. Then the mail marketer need only monitor the buying as additional effort will bring only small additional result.

The same is true of list buying and list testing. In the beginning years, the mail marketer must test many lists to find the workhorse lists with which he will build his business. After that, profitable new lists will come only a few at a time. Deciding which lists to repeat or roll-out is reduced to reading the publicity percent in the publicity cost analysis of mailings. Lists are not an area where additional effort will produce great additional results.

These functions are the basics. They can be learned. Indeed, the mail marketers must master them. A weakness in the basics can be fatal, but, once the mail marketer has gained mastery over them, he can delegate them to others. Additional effort on his part will improve results but will improve them only marginally.

To achieve great results, the mail marketer must concentrate on the effectiveness of each catalog sent out. The effect of improving catalog effectiveness is exponential because if more sales come to each catalog, then more catalogs can be mailed, thus increasing sales even more. A 10 percent improvement in the sales per catalog might make so many more lists profitable to rent that circulation could be doubled, thus more than doubling the ultimate size of the business. It would not be too much of an exaggeration, therefore, to say that the mail marketer cannot spend too much time in improving the effectiveness of his mailings.

Eliminating duplicate names in a mailing and increasing the percent of catalogs delivered within the postal system, as we discussed in Chapter 17, certainly has this exponential effect. But these efforts demand little time.

Where then must the mail marketer concentrate his attention to improve his mailing effectiveness? He must concentrate on what he sends out in the mail to his customers and would-be customers. He must concentrate on the driving forces of his business—the dynamics.

Many times I have seen the mail marketers place most of their attention on operating, finance, and other basics while merchandise and catalog received far too little attention. Important as it is for the basics to be mastered and controlled, it is strong dynamics that result in high sales per catalog. It is effort applied to the dynamics of a mail-order business that improves results exponentially. I know of one company that had a change in management. With this change came confusing layouts, awful photography, and bad separations. When the catalog was printed, the printer failed to run enough ink, and so he made worse what he received from the separator. What was the result? List for list, sales per catalog fell 20 percent to 30 percent.

In another company, new management changed merchandise and pricing policies. The change was so devastating that only the enormous financial resources of the owners of the company saved it from extinction.

The number one element of mail-order dynamics is the concept of the business with its theme. It must be established at the very outset of the business. Although it is rarely changed once established—indeed a change is often disastrous—the concept of the business should be periodically reviewed to see if it should be broadened or contracted or have a new emphasis.

The concept of the business is fulfilled by the merchandise. The merchandise is what the catalog is all about. It is what the customer buys with his money. Make the merchandise selection more attractive, and more sales will come to each catalog, making it possible for more catalogs to be mailed. The mail marketer, therefore, must allocate much of his time and effort to merchandise.

Does his merchandise truly express the concept of his business or is some of it incongruous? Are there many new exciting merchandise ideas that will motivate customers to buy? Has he sufficiently researched merchandise to develop a dazzling array that will arrest customers as they thumb through his catalog and cause them to buy? Are there new product categories that fit the concept of the business and need to be developed? Are there opportunities to hit merchandise home runs? Will the customers be pleased with quality? Are the prices competitive, and do they permit selling opportunities, or do new venders and new products need to be sought? Can the merchandise be displayed well in the catalog and is it conducive to writing good copy? If not, how can the merchandise be changed to make it so? These are questions to which the mail marketer must devote a large share of his time and effort.

But no matter how well the merchandise fulfills the concept of the business, it will be ineffective if it is poorly presented in the catalog. If the catalog fails to convey the merchandise's attractiveness, if the eyeflow is so confused that the merchandise is obscured, if the selling features remain undisclosed, and, if the copy fails to sell the product and create a buying ambience, then what has been achieved in the merchandise will be lost in the catalog. The mail marketer must, therefore, spare no effort to ensure that what he sends out to his customers is superlative. He must be vigilant that the catalog design, layout, and eye flow do not stray from sound mail-order principles. Photography must show the product in clear detail, in depth, and with realism. The product must seem to jump off the page. Little of what is achieved in the photography should be lost in the separations and printing. Finally, both institutional and product-related copy must be written that supports the concept of the business, creates mood and confidence, and sells the product.

The basics and the dynamics of mail order: these are what this book is all about. The mail marketer must gain mastery of the basics and control over the many day-to-day functions of his business. Although he may safely and probably should delegate these functions, he must always monitor them. But having done that, the mail marketer should turn his energy to developing the dynamics of his business. If he masters the basics and develops strong dynamics, the mail marketer will have discovered the secrets of mail-order success. He will be well on his way towards building a multi-million dollar catalog mail-order business.

Appendix A: resources for mail marketers

Listed below are some good resources for the mail marketer.

Color Separating:
    Expercolor, Inc.
    3737 Chase Avenue
    Skokie, IL 60076

Computer Operating System:
    Lawson Traphagen Hill
    Green Hill Road
    Jackson, NH 03846

Consulting:
    Lawson Traphagen Hill
    Green Hill Road
    Jackson, NH 03846

    Concord Mail Marketing
    60 Domino Drive
    Concord, MA 01742

Decoy Service:
    U.S. Monitor Service
    43 Maple Avenue
    New York, NY 10956

Fulfillment Service:
    MarkeTechs, Inc.
    115 Brand Road
    Salem, VA 24156

    Under one roof MarkeTechs maintains your inventory, processes and fills your customers' orders, handles customer service, and maintains your list. Minimum volume required.

List Brokerage:
    Direct Media, Inc.
    90 South Ridge Street
    Port Chester, NY 10573

    For any regular consulting clients, I place list brokerage through Direct Media, Inc.

List Maintenance Computer Service Bureau:

Dominion Data
3333 Littleton Road
Parsippany, NJ 07054

Figi's Data Center, Inc.
Marshfield, WI 54449

Mailing Service:

Brigar, Inc.
25 Sand Creek Road
Albany, NY 12205

Mail-Order Graphics:

Concord Mail Marketing
60 Domino Drive
Concord, MA 01742

Concord Mail Marketing specializes in graphics for mail-order companies.

Merge-Purge:

Direct Marketing Technology
5400 Newport Drive #11
Rolling Meadows, IL 60008

Printers, Order Form:

Alden Press, Inc.
480 Boylston Street
Boston, MA 02116

Spencer Press, Inc.
c/o Industrial Park Road
Hingham, MA 02043

B & W Press, Inc.
41 Popes Lane
Danvers, MA 01933

Webcraft
Rt. 1 Adam's Station
North Brunswick, NJ 08902

Printers, Web Offset, Catalog:

Alden Press, Inc.
480 Boylston Street
Boston, MA 02116

Spencer Press, Inc.
c/o Industrial Park Road
Hingham, MA 02043

Appendix B: the federal trade commission 30-day rule

The Direct Marketing Association published a clarification of the Federal Trade Commission 30-Day Rule, which we reprint here through their courtesy.

Unless there is a reasonable basis to believe goods will be shipped within 30 days of receiving a properly completed order, an advertisement must include a clear and conspicuous notice of the time in which the seller expects to make shipment. If no statement is made, the rule requires that shipment will be made within 30 days.

The rule provides procedures for buyers to be able to cancel for delayed delivery and get a refund.

When to include a statement of expected shipment date in your ads?

Unless there is a reasonable basis (past experience) to believe that shipment can be made within 30 days, direct marketers must clearly and conspicuously state a time in which they expect to make shipment. A statement such as "Please allow eight weeks for delivery," if genuine is an example of a proper notice of expected shipment. The rule does not permit the seller to state, "Shipment will be made as soon as possible."

When does the 30-day period start?

Upon receipt of a properly completed order. With any sale, the 30 days start when an order is received containing all the information needed to process and ship the order.

Cash sales: when the seller gets full or partial payment with an order.

Credit sales: when the seller charges the buyer's account (not defined by the rule).

255

Notice of delayed shipment

If shipment cannot be made within the unstated 30-day period, or the specifically stated period, a notice of revised expected shipment date *must* be sent to the buyer:

— by first class mail before expiration of the original 30-day period.
— with a postage-paid reply form for the buyer.
— notifying him of the revised shipping date and offering the option of consenting to the delay or of cancellation and a refund.
— informing him that unless the seller receives—prior to shipment and expiration of the revised date—a response rejecting this first delay, the buyer will be deemed to have consented to the delayed shipment.

Delay of 30 days or less

No reply by the buyer means acceptance of the new delivery date.

Delay of more than 30 days

No reply within the 30-day period must be treated as a request for cancellation and refund. If the revised shipping date cannot be met, a second notice must be sent offering the buyer the same options. With the second notice, no reply within 30 days requires a cancellation and refund (unless shipment has been made).

Refund

Cash sale: sent within seven working days of receipt of a request for cancellation or the date of implied cancellation, by first class mail. It must be with a check, cash or money order and cannot be a credit slip on other merchandise.

Credit sale: removal of the charge on the buyer's account must be within one billing cycle from receipt of the request for cancellation or the date of implied cancellation.

Systems of compliance

The rule requires records, or other documentary proof, establishing that systems and procedures assure shipment in the ordinary course of business in the time period advertised; or, if none is stated, within the unstated 30-day period.

Lack of documentary proof of an established system may itself be a violation of the rule.

Further information
available upon request

Because of the importance of this regulation to our industry, voluminous articles have appeared in the trade periodicals. DMMA will provide a selected *Packet of "Delayed Delivery" Information* to any member who requests such from Information Central in the New York office. Included in the material are the following:

1. A copy of the full text of the Trade Regulation Rule on Mail Order Merchandise, as it appears in the *Code of Federal Regulations* Title 16, Chapter 1, Part 435.
2. Answers to the Most Commonly Asked Questions About the "Mail Order Merchandise" Rule—compiled by DMMA's Government Affairs Department.
3. Selected articles and memos that appeared in trade industry journals that offer further explanatory notes.

glossary

Basic tier: Basic tier consists of those names in a mailing that do not qualify for a carrier sack or a ZIP code sack.

Bells and whistles: Bells and whistles are frill outputs of a computer.

Bindery: The bindery is the part of a printing plant where the printed signatures of a catalog and the order form are assembled, stapled, and trimmed.

Break-even point: The break-even point is where sales equals all expenses including cost of goods. Variable break-even occurs when an increment of sales is matched by an equal increment of expenses.

"Buy" customers: To acquire customers at a variable cost that exceeds variable sales.

Catalog request: This term refers both to the act of requesting a catalog and to those who have requested a catalog.

Color bars: Color bars are bars of the three printing primary colors plus black at the edge of a printed sheet. These can be read with a densitometer to determine ink density.

Color separations: Color separations are film intermediates that determine the proportion of yellow, magenta, cyan, and black colors in the transparency or reflective color original.

Cyan: A specific printing primary color. The uninitiated would call it a light blue or sky blue.

Demand: The dollar value of an order or a group of orders for a specific time period. Demand does not equate to *sales* because some orders are not filled or are not filled completely. Demand, as sales, can also refer to the units of an item.

Densitometer, ink density: A densitometer is an instrument that measures ink density. Ink density is the ability of ink to absorb light.

257

Digest-sized catalog: A catalog that measures $5\frac{1}{2} \times 8\frac{1}{2}$ inches.

Dupes: Jargon term that means a duplicate of a photograph made to the same scale or to a different scale.

Exposure: The amount of light that is permitted to act on film. It can be controlled by the size of the lens opening or the amount of time the light is permitted to pass through the opening. Exposure also refers to a specific combination of shutter speed and lens opening.

File: The list of customers (customer file), catalog requests (request file), or all names with their related data (house file).

Fit: *See* Register.

Flats: A collection of correctly-imposed negatives or positives from which the printing plate will be exposed.

Form: The group of catalog pages that will be or have been printed together in one pass through the press. Printers might refer to a form of four, eight, or sixteen pages.

Gate fold, gate flap: An extension of the order form in the form of another sheet that results in another fold in the order form.

Halftone: A reproduction of the transparency, or continuous tone reflective art that simulates the original with dots of varying diameters.

Highlight: The whitest portion of the transparency or reflective art. There may be a very fine dot or no dot at all.

Imposition: The arrangement of pages within a form.

Magenta: One of the primary printing colors. The uninitiated would call it pink.

Markdown: The amount the price or cost of an item is reduced on the books. The reduction can be considered to occur at retail (a price reduction) or at wholesale (a cost reduction). Markdown can also refer to the item that has had its price or cost reduced.

Mark-up: The amount the retail price is over the wholesale cost. This can be expressed in dollars or percent. If expressed as a percent, it usually is expressed as a percent of the retail selling price.

Match code: An alphanumeric code created to identify duplicates in a list or lists, composed of characters from the name and address of a customer. A frequently-used match code is a number comprised of the first four characters of the last name, the first four meaningful characters in the street address, and the ZIP code.

Microfiche: Microfiche is microfilm in card form that contains many computer printout pages. It is read with a special viewer that enlarges the required page.

Multiple-ZIP city: A city with several ZIP codes.

nth name selection: A sampling of names from a mailing list in which every nth name is selected. For example, if n is set equal to 10, then every 10th name is selected.

Orderline: An orderline tells for a given day after a mailing has been made, what percent the orders received to date are of the total to be received for the season.

Plugging: A situation where the non-print area between dots fills in with ink so that it is solid ink.

Point size: Type is measured in points. There are twelve points to a pica and six picas to an inch. This would mean that the distance from the top of a capital to the bottom of a descending letter, like a lowercase *g*, for seventy-two points is one inch. In practice, the distance is usually a little less.

Product demand curve: A product demand curve gives the percent sales are complete for a product category for a given percent that the sales of all products are complete.

Publicity cost: Any expense directly related to promoting sales. Catalog publicity costs are broken down into two categories—fixed and variable. *Fixed publicity costs* for a catalog include layout and design, photography and related costs, color separating and stripping, and press start-up. *Variable publicity costs* for a catalog include the cost of printing the catalog and order form (excluding press start-up), postage, merge-purge, mailing expense, and list rental. The *publicity costs of advertising* include the cost of the advertisement and its preparation and catalogs sent out to respondents to the advertisement, less any money received from respondents for the catalog.

Rebuying: The placing of orders with a vendor after the preseason order has been placed and after sales have commenced.

Register, fit: Register is the overall alignment of the images of the four printing colors, one on top of the other. A color is out of register when its image is displaced relative to the others. Fit refers to the register of the individual images within one overall separation. Poor fit exists when the color components of the overall separation are aligned, but one or two colors of a particular image are out of alignment.

Reorder lead time: The time that elapses between the day inventory requirements are reviewed and when the resulting merchandise order arrives and is available to fill orders.

Reorder period: The period of time required to sell one's commitment for merchandise. This would be the sum of the reorder lead time and the time required to sell the safety stock.

Reverse type: Type that is created by printing in the areas surrounding the type, not by printing in the type areas.

Safety stock: Inventory carried in excess of what will be sold during the reorder lead time.

Sales: *See* Demand.

Scanner: A machine that passes a laser beam through or reflects from the original art. It separates the light into its primary components and creates the color separations.

Screen: The dot grid for making halftones. A screen is described by the number of rows of dots to a linear inch, such as a 120-line screen.

Sectional center: A postal distribution center indicated by the first three characters in the ZIP code.

Separations: *See* Color separations.

Sheet-fed press: A sheet-fed press prints one sheet of paper at a time, and for four-color printing, it would print on one side of a sheet at a time, requiring two passes through the press to print both sides. Some sheet-fed presses will "perfect," which means that in one pass two colors can be printed on one side, the paper flopped, and two colors printed on the opposite side. A web press prints four colors on both top and bottom of a web of paper in one pass and then sheets and folds the completed signature.

Signature: The folded and printed result that comes off a press. The signature by itself or in combination with other signatures and the order form constitutes the untrimmed and unbound catalog. Sometimes where a catalog is of the small $5\frac{1}{2} \times 8\frac{1}{2}$ inch "digest" size, a signature contains forms for two catalogs.

Solo mailing: A mailing in which one item or only a few very closely-related items are sold.

Split-run test: Sometimes known as an A/B split test. A test in which an element of a catalog or an ad is tested against a control. Catalogs whose forms are printed two to a signature are ideal for inexpensive A/B split-run tests. Certain magazines which are printed two at a time also permit A/B split-run tests.

Spot-pasting: A spot of paste applied to gate flaps on order forms to prevent the flaps from falling and disrupting the binding operation.

Stockkeeping unit (SKU): An item carried in inventory that is unique in all respects, for example, a shoe of a particular style in a certain size and in a certain color. A shoe style that is stocked in four colors and in fifty sizes for each color would have two hundred stockkeeping units that would have to be maintained.

Stripping: The process wherein two or more sets of color separations are joined together to make one larger separation.

Yellow: A specific yellow color used as a printing primary.

Web: The continuous roll of paper used in a web press.

Web press: *See* Sheet-fed press.

bibliography

The following books have been useful and influenced my thinking.

Cheskin, Louis. *Business without Gambling.* Chicago: Quadrangle Books, 1963.

———. *Cheskin System for Business Success.* New York: Frederick Fell, 1973.

———. *How to Predict What People Will Buy.* New York: Liveright Publishing Corp., 1957.

———. *Secrets of Marketing Success.* New York: Trident Press, 1967. (This book may be out of print.)

———. *Why People Buy.* New York: Liveright Publishing Corp., 1959.

Louis Cheskin's books explain market research methods, the use of color in marketing, and eye flow.

Drucker, Peter F. *Managing for Results.* New York: Harper and Row, 1964.

Hodges John C. and Mary E. Whitten. *Harbrace College Handbook,* 8th ed. New York: Harcourt Brace Jovanovich, 1977.

This is the best handbook on writing that I have found. I have used it for almost 40 years.

Southworth, Miles. *Pocket Guide to Color Reproduction.* Livonia, New York: Graphic Arts Publishing Co., 1979.

This book explains many of the steps in making color separations and in color printing.

SRDS. *Magazine Rates and Data.* Skokie, Illinois: Standard Rates & Data Service, n.d.

———. *Direct Mail List Rates and Data.* Skokie, Illinois: Standard Rates & Data Service, n.d.

Standard Rates & Data Service publishes these useful books which give advertising or list rental rates, mechanical requirements, addresses, and other information on magazines and lists. They also publish one for newspapers.

Strunk, William, and **White, E. B.** *Elements of Style,* 3rd ed., New York: MacMillan Publishing Co., 1979.

Zinsser, William. *On Writing Well,* 2nd ed. New York: Harper & Row, 1980.

index